SCSU

DEC 04 2002

H.C. BULEY LIBRARY

WITHDRAWN

BABYLONIAN INSCRIPTIONS

IN THE COLLECTION OF

JAMES B. NIES

YALE UNIVERSITY

VOLUME X

BABYLONIAN INSCRIPTIONS IN THE COLLECTION OF JAMES B. NIES, YALE UNIVERSITY · VOL. X

SUMERIAN ADMINISTRATIVE DOCUMENTS FROM THE REIGNS OF IŠBI-ERRA AND ŠŪ-ILIŠU

BY

MARC VAN DE MIEROOP

NEW HAVEN AND LONDON, YALE UNIVERSITY PRESS, 1987

b-10314994
$ 52-25

Published with assistance from the James B. Nies Trust Fund.

Copyright © 1987 by Yale University.
All rights reserved.
This book may not be reproduced, in whole or in part, in any form (beyond that copying permitted by Sections 107 and 108 of the U.S. Copyright Law and except by reviewers for the public press), without written permission from the publishers.

Designed by Ulla Kasten and Gary A. Tuttle and set in Scotch No. 2 type by The Publishing Nexus Incorporated, Guilford, Conn.
Printed in the United States of America by The Murray Printing Co., Westford, Mass.

Library of Congress Cataloging-in-Publication Data

Van De Mieroop, Marc.
Sumerian administrative documents from the reigns of Išbi-Erra and Šu-ilišu.

(Babylonian inscriptions in the collection of James B. Nies, Yale University; vol. 10)
Unpublished material used in author's doctoral dissertation; the early Isin craft archive. Yale University, 1983.
Includes index.
1. Sumerian language—Texts. 2. Babylonia—Politics and government—Sources. 3. Išbi-Erra. 4. Šu-ilišu.
I. Title. II. Series.
PJ3719.N5 vol. 10
PJ4075.V35 1987 499'.95 86-28958
ISBN 0-300-03805-4

The paper in this book meets the guidelines for permanence and durability of the Committee on Production Guidelines for Book Longevity of the Council on Library Resources.

10 9 8 7 6 5 4 3 2 1

O
PJ
4075
.V35
1987

CONTENTS

PREFACE

After the completion of my doctoral dissertation "The Early Isin Craft Archive" (Yale University, 1983), William W. Hallo, curator of the Yale Babylonian Collection, suggested that I copy the unpublished material used in that study. He gave me free access to the resources of the Yale Babylonian Collection and advised me during the preparation of this volume. Norman Yoffee brought to my attention the texts of the Ashmolean Museum in Oxford, which are published here with the permission of P. R. S. Moorey and by courtesy of the Visitors of the Ashmolean Museum. Piotr Steinkeller informed me about one text in the Harvard Semitic Museum, published here with the permission of W. L. Moran, and gave me the transliterations of three texts in private collections, published by courtesy of I. J. Gelb.

The seal design of Ash. 1932–259 was drawn by D. Stein, and those of NBC 7568 and 7742 by Z. Bahrani. Ulla Kasten, Museum Editor for the Yale Babylonian Collection, gave me invaluable advice and assistance in the preparation of this volume.

Financial support for the work on this publication was partly provided by a grant from the Alexander Kohut Foundation.

To all these persons and institutions I would like to express my sincere thanks.

New York, 1986

Marc Van De Mieroop

INTRODUCTION

The 317 texts in this volume belong to the Isin craft archive. This archive records the activities of a workshop active in Isin during the reigns of Išbi-Erra (I.E.: 2017–1985 B.C.) and Šū-ilišu (Š.i.: 1984–1975 B.C.), the first two rulers of the First Dynasty of Isin.[1] A major part of the archive was published by V. Crawford in *BIN* IX, and by others elsewhere.[2] The majority of the remaining unpublished material known to me is presented in this volume, which includes 288 texts from the Nies Babylonian Collection at Yale University, twenty-five texts from the Ashmolean Museum in Oxford, one text from the Harvard Semitic Museum (previously at the Zion Research Library), and three texts from private collections in the Chicago area published in transliteration, as I was unable to locate them. Two additional unpublished texts from the Ashmolean Museum will be published by J-P. Grégoire, and twenty texts from the de Liagre-Böhl Collection in Leiden were recently published by G. Th. Ferwerda.

The texts are ordered typologically, and the five main types of transactions documented in the archive[3] are:

Receipt of raw materials (Nos. 1–58)
Receipt of materials by the craftsmen (Nos. 59–71)
Receipt of finished products by workshop officials (Nos. 72–82)
Receipt of finished products and their disbursement (Nos. 83–86)
Issue of finished products (Nos. 87–195)

Finally, there is a group of miscellaneous archival texts, such as labels (Nos. 196–207), and a large group of worker lists, attendance records of the craftsmen (Nos. 208–314). It is not always possible to determine with certainty what type of transaction is documented by a text, since the same terminology is found in several groups, and often the only indication is given by the personal names.

Within each group the texts are ordered chronologically. Since the sequence of Išbi-Erra's year names is still a matter of dispute, the catalogue uses two systems, namely V. Crawford's in *BIN* IX and that of my "The Early Isin Craft Archive." Crawford based his

[1]For a detailed study of the archive see my "The Early Isin Craft Archive," Ph.D. diss., Yale University, 1983.
[2]For a detailed list see "The Early Isin Craft Archive."
[3]For a discussion of these five categories see "The Early Isin Craft Archive," and "The Administration of Crafts in the Early Isin Period," in K.R. Veenhof (ed.) *Cuneiform Archives and Libraries: Papers read at the 30th Rencontre Assyriologique Internationale, Leiden 1983* (Publications de l'Institut historique et archéologique néerlandais de Stamboul, vol. 57), Istanbul, 1986, pp. 87-95.

text dates on the list of year names published by T. Baqir.[4] Since that list was broken at the top, he was aware that his year 1 was to be regarded as x+1. Year names only found in the economic texts were assigned the letters A–L. B. Kienast[5] attempted to place these unassigned year names and to establish an absolute chronology based on a gap of three years at the beginning of the date list. In "The Early Isin Craft Archive," I restudied the entire problem, and suggested a break of six years at the top of the date list. In the catalogue here the texts are ordered according to the latter system, but further study may warrant changing this order.

The following sequence of year names is used:[6]

VC	MVDM	NAME
I.E.		
I	4	mu Kiri$_8$-tab^{ki} ba-hul
J	5	mu-ús-sa Kiri$_8$-tab^{ki} ba-hul
B	6	mu giš-nú ^{d}Inanna ba-dím
1/G	7	mu nin-dingir ^{d}Nin-urta ba-hun/ba-íl
2	8	mu uru^{ki} Mar-tu ba-hul
3	9	mu-ús-sa uru^{ki} Mar-tu ba-hul
4	10	mu a-šà-gibil a-ta im-ta(?)-DU-a
5	11	mu nin-dingir ^{d}Iškur ba-íl
6/A	12	mu ^{d}*Iš-bi-Èr-ra* lugal ma-da-na-ke$_4$ bàd-gal *I-ti-il-pá-šu-nu* mu-dù/mu bàd-gal I-si-in-na^{ki} mu-dù
7	13	mu en-GABA ^{d}Inanna ^{d}*Iš-bi-Èr-ra* máš-e in-pà
8	14	mu bàd *Li-bur-*^{d}*Iš-bi-Èr-ra* ba-dù
9	15	mu-ús-sa bàd *Li-bur-*^{d}*Iš-bi-Èr-ra* ba-dù
10a,b	16	mu-ús-sa bàd *Li-bur-*^{d}*Iš-bi-Èr-ra* ba-dù mu-ús-sa-bi/mu ^{d}*Iš-bi-Èr-ra* lugal-e ugnim lú-SU.A ù Elam bi-in-ra
11a,b	17	mu-ús-sa ^{d}*Iš-bi-Èr-ra* lugal-e ugnim lú-SU.A ù Elam bi-in-ra/mu bàd *Eš$_4$-tár-tá-ra-am-*^{d}*Iš-bi-Èr-ra* ba-dù
12a,b	18	mu-ús-sa bàd *Eš$_4$-tár-tá-ra-am-*^{d}*Iš-bi-Èr-ra* ba-dù/mu ^{d}*Iš-bi-Èr-ra* lugal-e $^{d/giš}$šu-nir-gal ^{d}En-líl ù ^{d}Nin-urta mu-ne-dím
13	19	mu bàd ^{d}*Iš-bi-Èr-ra-ri-im-*^{d}En-líl ba-dù
14a,b	20	mu-ús-sa bàd ^{d}*Iš-bi-Èr-ra-ri-im-*^{d}En-líl ba-dù/mu ^{d}*Iš-bi-Èr-ra* lugal-e ^{d}Nin-me-an-ki ^{giš}šu-nir-gal ^{d}Inanna mu-ne-dím
15	21	mu-ús-sa ^{d}*Iš-bi-Èr-ra* lugal-e ^{giš}šu-nir-gal ^{d}Inanna mu-dím
16	22	mu Nin-zi-an-na dumu-SAL-lugal máš-e in-pà
17a,b	23	mu-ús-sa Nin-zi-an-na dumu-SAL-lugal máš-e in-pà/mu nin-dingir ^{d}Lugal-már-da ba-íl

[4] T. Baqir: *Sumer* 4 (1948): 103-13.
[5] B. Kienast, *JCS* 19 (1965): 45-55.
[6] VC = V. Crawford, MVDM = M. Van De Mieroop. For a detailed list of the variants see V. Crawford, *BIN* IX: 6-24. No new variants are found in the texts published here.

18a,b	24	mu-ús-sa nin-dingir ^{d}Lugal-már-da ba-íl/mu en ^{d}En-líl-lá ba-íl
19	25	mu ^{d}*Iš-bi-Èr-ra* lugal-e ^{giš}gu-za bára ^{d}Nin-urta mu-ne-dím
20a,b/E	26	mu-ús-sa ^{d}*Iš-bi-Èr-ra* lugal-e ^{giš}gu-za bára ^{d}Nin-urta mu-ne-dím/mu Elam šà Urí^{ki}-ma durun-a ba-dab$_5$/im-ta-e$_{11}$
21/F	27	mu-ús-sa Elam šà Urí^{ki}-ma durun-a ba-dab$_5$/im-ta-e$_{11}$
22	28	mu ^{giš}gu-za ^{d}Nin-líl-lá ba-dím
L	29	mu ^{giš}gu-za ^{d}Nanna ^{d}Nin-gal ba-dím
H	30	mu nin-dingir ^{d}Nin-gi$_4$-lí-in ba-íl
K	31	mu Urí^{ki} ki-dúr-ba bi-in$^{!}$⟨-ge⟩-en
C	32	mu nin-dingir ^{d}Lugal-ír-ra ba-íl
D	33	mu-ús-sa nin-dingir ^{d}Lugal-ír-ra ba-íl

Š.i.

1	1	mu ^{d}*Šu-ì-lí-šu* lugal-àm
2	2	mu ^{d}*Šu-ì-lí-šu* lugal-e ^{giš}šu-nir-gal ^{d}Nanna mu-ne-dím
3a,b	3	mu-ús-sa ^{d}*Šu-ì-lí-šu* lugal-e ^{giš}šu-nir-gal ^{d}Nanna mu-ne-dím/mu ^{d}*Šu-ì-lí-šu* lugal-e nin ^{d}Nin-urta mu-un-íl

Drawings of the seal impressions on the tablets are at the end of this volume (scale 2:1). Those also found on the *BIN* IX texts are redrawn and given the same letter as there. The new ones are assigned the letters a–j. Indices are provided for personal names, divine names, geographical names, temple names, and for the terms found in these documents. The latter index records the basic Sumerian terms with an Akkadian translation, when known, for easy reference to the lexical material. The English translations and some of the readings could not be argued in this volume.

CATALOGUE

Register and Description of the Texts

TEXT	MUSEUM NUMBER	MEASUREMENTS IN mm	REIGN	YEAR VC	YEAR MVDM	MONTH	DAY	SUBJECT MATTER
Receipts of Raw Materials								
1	NBC 7599	39×35×12	I.E.	2	8	XI	–	bitumen
2	NBC 7062	30×29×11	I.E.	5	11	III	–	bitumen
3	NBC 7164	40×35×12	I.E.	5	11	V	–	wool
4	NBC 7412	32×30×12	I.E.	6	12	VI	–	wool
5	NBC 7255	33×29×12	I.E.	5	11	VII	–	glue and im-KÙ.GI
6	NBC 7085	35×33×15	I.E.	6	12	X	29	bitumen
7	Ash. 1932-405	36×31×15	I.E.	7	13	X	–	skins
8	NBC 6461	40×34×15	I.E.	7	13	XI	–	reed baskets
9	NBC 8489	45×35×13	I.E.	8	14	XI	–	wool
10	NBC 7572	47×38×12	I.E.	9	15	III	–	wool
11	NBC 7098	38×32×14	I.E.	10a	16	I	21	wool
12	NBC 7522	37×32×14	I.E.	10a	16	I	25	skins
13	NBC 5671	35×30×12	I.E.	10b	16	VI	28	gypsum
14	NBC 7365	36×31×15	I.E.	10b	16	XIII	–	bitumen
15	NBC 7070	32×28×14	I.E.	11b	17	VI	–	bitumen
16	NBC 6473	29×26×11	I.E.	11b	17	IX	8	bitumen
17	NBC 7252	32×30×11	I.E.	11b	17	IX	25	bitumen
18	NBC 5630	32×30×14	I.E.	11b	17	XII	–	bitumen
19	NBC 5629	29×25×13	I.E.	12a	18	I	3	bitumen
20	NBC 6482	33×29×11	I.E.	12a	18	(broken)	16	bitumen
21	NBC 8435	32×28×12	I.E.	14b	20	X	25	wool
22	NBC 7121	38×32×12	I.E.	15	21	VI	6	skins
23	Ash. 1932-252	35×30×12	I.E.	15	21	XII	–	skins
24	NBC 5638	44×32×12	I.E.	16	22	II	–	pomegranate products

Ash. = Ashmolean Museum; HSM = Harvard Semitic Museum; LHS = Lindblom High School; NBC = Nies Babylonian Collection; ZRL = Zion Research Library

TEXT	MUSEUM NUMBER	MEASUREMENTS IN mm	REIGN	YEAR VC	YEAR MVDM	MONTH	DAY	SUBJECT MATTER
25	NBC 8433	41×36×12	I.E.	16	22	II	–	pomegranate products
26	NBC 8439	37×33×12	I.E.	16	22	II	–	skins
27	NBC 7120	36×32×12	I.E.	16	22	IV	–	bitumen
28	NBC 6479	31×31×12	I.E.	16	22	V	–	bitumen
29	NBC 7043	34×29×11	I.E.	16	22	V	–	bitumen
30	NBC 7077	33×31×11	I.E.	16	22	V	–	bitumen
31	NBC 7049	37×33×14	I.E.	16	22	X	–	bitumen
32	NBC 9282	43×35×11	I.E.	16	22	XII	–	oil
33	Ash. 1932-257	41×34×12	I.E.	17b	23	IX	–	*allaḫarum*
35	NBC 5632	39×36×13	I.E.	18b	24	VI	7	wool
36	NBC 7091	37×34×14	I.E.	19	25	II	–	bitumen
37	NBC 7593	38×32×11	I.E.	19	25	IV	23	bitumen
38	NBC 8484	45×38×13	I.E.	19	25	IV	30	sesame oil
39	NBC 6382	45×35×14	I.E.	19	25	VIII	–	skins
40	Ash. 1932-384	57×41×12	I.E.	E	26	VIII	–	skins
41	NBC 8441	37×33×11	I.E.	21	27	VI	–	bitumen
42	NBC 5608	36×34×11	I.E.	19	28	VII	–	wool
43	NBC 5649	28×31×11	I.E.	19	28	XII	–	wool
44	NBC 7118	37×34×14	I.E.	D	33	IV	–	oil
45	NBC 7480	56×44×15	I.E.	D	33	IX	30	reed
46	NBC 7468	49×39×13	I.E.	D	33	IX	–	wood
47	NBC 7187	49×41×16	I.E.	D	33	X	–	reed
48	NBC 7659	60×40×14	I.E.	D	33	X	–	reed
49	NBC 7366	38×31×16	Š.i.	1		IV	–	sesame oil
50	NBC 7535	35×33×13	Š.i.	1		VII	–	sesame oil
51	NBC 7239	31×28×11	Š.i.	1?		X	–	fat, glue and im-KÙ.GI (document cancelled)
52	NBC 8425	37×32×10	Š.i.	1		X	–	bitumen
53	NBC 8952	48×40×12	(broken)			VIII	–	beds
54	NBC 8496	28×27×14	–	–		XIII	30	thread
55	NBC 7784	40×35×11	–	–		XIII	–	skins
56	Ash. 1932-262	35×33×12	–	–		–	14	skin
57	NBC 7400	44×34×14	–	–		–	–	wood
58	NBC 7544	65×43×18	–	–		–	–	reed

Receipt of Materials by the Craftsmen

TEXT	MUSEUM NUMBER	MEASUREMENTS IN mm	REIGN	YEAR VC	YEAR MVDM	MONTH	DAY	SUBJECT MATTER
59	NBC 7673	49×41×12	I.E.	3	9	IV	–	reed objects (seal illegible)

TEXT	MUSEUM NUMBER	MEASUREMENTS IN mm	REIGN	YEAR VC	YEAR MVDM	MONTH	DAY	SUBJECT MATTER
60	NBC 7505	46×39×10	I.E.	5	11	II	–	wool (seal d)
61	Ash. 1932-249	39×34×8	I.E.	5	11	III	–	wool (seal d)
62	Ash. 1932-260	33×28×12	I.E.	6	12	XII	–	bitumen
63	Ash. 1932-240	40×32×10	I.E.	7	13	IX	–	leather scraps (seal illegible)
64	Ash. 1932-250	37×32×10	I.E.	7	13	XI	–	wool (seal c)
65	Ash. 1932-242	47×38×12	I.E.	8	14	IV	–	wool (seal O or c)
66	NBC 8503	31×28×13	I.E.	9	15	II	10	wool
67	NBC 7099	36×34×12	I.E.	9	15	XII	–	*zamirītum*
68	NBC 6417	55×38×13	I.E.	13	19	VIII	–	skins
69	NBC 6372	41×37×12	I.E.	19	25	VII	–	wool (seal c)
70	NBC 8521	32×30×11	–		–	VII	6	glue and flour
71	NBC 7721	34×31×12	–		–	XI	29	thread

Receipt of Finished Products by Workshop Officials

TEXT	MUSEUM NUMBER	MEASUREMENTS IN mm	REIGN	YEAR VC	YEAR MVDM	MONTH	DAY	SUBJECT MATTER
72	NBC 7201	49×40×15	I.E.	2	8	XII	–	wool (seal d)
73	NBC 8497	38×31×14	I.E.	3	9	V	–	cloth
74	NBC 8428	37×31×11	I.E.	3	9	IX	–	cover
75	NBC 7221	39×32×16	I.E.	8	14	II	14	rope
76	NBC 7459	38×34×12	I.E.	13	19	III	8	rope
77	NBC 8079	40×34×13	I.E.	21	27	X	–	context broken
78	ZRL 134 (now HSM)	36×46×10	–		–	VIII	15	date palm fibers
79	NBC 7620	38×33×15	–		–	–	–	wool
80	NBC 8011	48×38×11	–		–	–	–	tables
81	Ash. 1932-403	41×35×16	I.E.	(broken)		IV	(broken)	rope
82	Ash. 1932-401	38×32×16	(broken)			(broken)	22	glue

Receipt of Finished Products and their Disbursement

TEXT	MUSEUM NUMBER	MEASUREMENTS IN mm	REIGN	YEAR VC	YEAR MVDM	MONTH	DAY	SUBJECT MATTER
83	NBC 9995	66×37×11	I.E.	7	13	VI	–	account of oil
84	NBC 7250	34×19×11	I.E.	7	13	XII	6	rope
85	NBC 8414	40×34×12	I.E.	D	33	XIII	–	felt
86	NBC 7732	50×42×18	Š.i.	2?		II	–	yokes (?)

TEXT	MUSEUM NUMBER	MEASUREMENTS IN mm	REIGN	YEAR VC	YEAR MVDM	MONTH	DAY	SUBJECT MATTER
Issue of Finished Products								
87	NBC 8486	46×39×15	I.E.	B	6	I	–	musical instrument and reed objects
88	NBC 5631	41×37×15	I.E.	B	6	III	–	wood
89	NBC 7571	47×40×13	I.E.	B	6	III	–	doors and door parts
90	NBC 6386	49×40×14	I.E.	B	6	VI	–	glue
91	NBC 6436	34×40×13	I.E.	B	6	VIII	–	wood
92	NBC 6422	45×36×12	I.E.	B	6	X	–	bitumen
93	NBC 9177	30×25×11	I.E.	B	6	X	–	leather and bitumen
94	NBC 7078	33×28×12	I.E.	B	6	–	–	door
95	NBC 7463	36×29×11	I.E.	1	7	V	–	wood
96	NBC 7183	60×40×15	I.E.	G	7	?	–	wood (iti kin-^{d}Nanna)
97	NBC 7454	37×31×14	I.E.	G	7	–	–	bitumen
98	NBC 8466	50×39×14	I.E.	2	8	VIII	–	sieves (seal f)
99	NBC 7745	38×40×10	I.E.	2	8	?	–	reed baskets (iti[ ]^{d}Nin-a-zu; seal illegible)
100	NBC 7357	34×33×10	I.E.	4	10	VIII	4	basket
101	NBC 8442	38×35×14	I.E.	5	11	VI	–	wool
102	NBC 7608	35×30×12	I.E.	6	12	X	–	tables
103	NBC 5669	33×29×12	I.E.	6	12	XII	10	flutes and baskets
104	NBC 10075	41×33×10	I.E.	7	13	II	–	musical instruments
105	NBC 7527	27×25×13	I.E.	7	13	V	20	bitumen
106	NBC 6374	35×32×12	I.E.	7	13	VI	17	bitumen and wool
107	NBC 7094	38×31×11	I.E.	7	13	VI	19	bitumen
108	NBC 6358	35×31×13	I.E.	7	13	VII	–	reed tables
109	NBC 6476	33×30×12	I.E.	7	13	VIII	–	bitumen
110	Ash. 1932-259	48×38×17	I.E.	7	13	VIII	–	water bags (seal j)
111	NBC 9227	45×37×11	I.E.	7	13	IX	21	context broken (seal g)
112	NBC 7643	34×29×11	I.E.	7	13	XI	–	basket
113	NBC 8136	41×33×14	I.E.	7	13	XI	–	furniture
114	Ash. 1932-261	31×28×16	I.E.	8	14	IV	–	leather, glue, and thread

TEXT	MUSEUM NUMBER	MEASUREMENTS IN mm	REIGN	YEAR VC	YEAR MVDM	MONTH	DAY	SUBJECT MATTER
115	NBC 7109	39 × 35 × 15	I.E.	8	14	VI	22	tables
116	NBC 6336	42 × 35 × 15	I.E.	8	14	VII	3	cover
117	Ash. 1932-383	50 × 34 × 13	I.E.	8	14	XI	22	boots and sandals
118	NBC 7639	39 × 32 × 15	I.E.	8	14	XI	–	*zamirītum*
119	Ash. 1932-258	40 × 35 × 12	I.E.	9	15	III	–	waterbags (seal i)
120	NBC 7456	42 × 34 × 12	I.E.	9	15	IV	23	beams and baskets
121	NBC 7498	35 × 30 × 10	I.E.	9	15	IV	28	baskets
122	NBC 7368	45 × 34 × 14	I.E.	9	15	VI	28	baskets
123	NBC 9224	41 × 37 × 11	I.E.	9	15	X	–	context broken (seal g)
124	NBC 5617	55 × 46 × 16	I.E.	9	15	–	–	*zamirītum* (seals a and b)
125	NBC 7227	37 × 34 × 12	I.E.	10a	16	I	26	wood
126	NBC 7073	31 × 28 × 12	I.E.	11b	17	III	22	glue?
127	NBC 7473	51 × 36 × 13	I.E.	13	19	I	23	doors
128	NBC 9931	60 × 40 × 11	I.E.	13	19	V	27	bags and sandals (seal M)
129	NBC 5645	50 × 37 × 13	I.E.	13	19	VI	7	bitumen (seal M)
130	NBC 8235	85 × 62 × 12	I.E.	13	19	VII	30	materials
131	NBC 7597	34 × 29 × 13	I.E.	13	19	IX	28	thread
132	NBC 7063	32 × 28 × 13	I.E.	14b	20	VII	–	copper
133	NBC 7396	52 × 39 × 14	I.E.	15	21	XIII	12	flutes and bags (seal B)
134	NBC 6424	45 × 36 × 15	I.E.	16	22	II	10	bitumen
135	Ash. 1932-243	49 × 41 × 11	I.E.	16	22	II	16	bitumen and leather (seal illegible)
136	NBC 6365	42 × 35 × 12	I.E.	16	22	III	11	rope
137	NBC 7205	49 × 39 × 12	I.E.	16	22	IV	14	bitumen (seal M)
138	NBC 6370	39 × 29 × 11	I.E.	16	22	IV	16	bitumen
139	NBC 7190	53 × 37 × 14	I.E.	16	22	IX	26	thread
140	NBC 6454	44 × 33 × 10	I.E.	16	22	X	3	wool
141	NBC 7609	39 × 34 × 12	I.E.	16	22	X	18	thread
142	NBC 7065	32 × 30 × 11	I.E.	16	22	XI	18	thread
143	NBC 7122	36 × 31 × 9	I.E.	16	22	XI	–	chairs
144	NBC 7418	31 × 30 × 12	I.E.	16	22	XII	5	thread
145	NBC 7417	31 × 28 × 11	I.E.	16	22	XII	7	thread
146	NBC 7578	42 × 37 × 14	I.E.	16	22	–	–	Amorite girl

TEXT	MUSEUM NUMBER	MEASUREMENTS IN mm	REIGN	YEAR VC	YEAR MVDM	MONTH	DAY	SUBJECT MATTER
147	NBC 7568	50×40×11	I.E.	16	22	(broken)	–	baskets (seal e)
148	NBC 7598	31×28×12	I.E.	16	22	(broken)	(broken)	skin
149	Ash. 1932-241	46×37×11	I.E.	17a	23	I	23	sandals
150	NBC 7178	57×37×14	I.E.	17b	23	IV	–	im-KÙ.GI and oil
151	NBC 7142	54×38×15	I.E.	17b	23	VII	16	bitumen
152	Ash. 1932-251	37×42×9	I.E.	18	24	XIII	–	skins (seal h)
153	NBC 6447	63×39×13	I.E.	19	25	II	3	products
154	NBC 7218	58×42×13	I.E.	19	25	II	11	baskets
155	NBC 7197	66×44×14	I.E.	19	25	III	7	doors and baskets
156	NBC 7534	37×35×13	I.E.	19	25	V	26	bitumen
157	Ash. 1932-253	40×35×12	I.E.	19	25	VIII	21	bags
158	NBC 7140	47×32×11	I.E.	19	25	IX	19	reed items and vessel
159	NBC 10073	70×45×12	I.E.	19	25	(broken)	6	bags
160	NBC 10069	71×47×11	I.E.	20b	26	IV	11	bags
161	NBC 7244	32×30×11	I.E.	19	28	II	20	ropes
162	Ash. 1932-255	51×37×20	I.E.	19	28	XI	5	materials
163	NBC 7429	35×32×13	I.E.	19	25/28	IX	–	cover
164	NBC 7471	45×39×14	I.E.	D	33	IX	–	bottles
165	NBC 6377	37×31×12	I.E.	D	33	XIII	25	leather bag
166	NBC 10076	40×35×11	Š.i.	1		I	6	mats and baskets
167	NBC 7213	58×40×11	Š.i.	1		VI	–	vessels (tag)
168	NBC 7391	46×40×15	Š.i.	1		VI	–	vessels (tag)
169	NBC 7362	31×34×15	Š.i.	1		VII	17	bitumen
170	NBC 7577	51×39×13	Š.i.	2		VII	–	tables (tag)
171	NBC 7233	43×35×17	Š.i.	2		XI	13	baskets
172	NBC 7404	35×33×13	Š.i.	3b		III	29	context broken
173	NBC 8468	50×36×11	–	–		I	24	bitumen
174	NBC 8016	48×39×13	–	–		V	7	vessels
175	NBC 8504	36×31×14	–	–		IX	–	doors
176	NBC 6487	34×28×11	–	–		X	4/5	glue
177	NBC 7742	30×32×11	–	–		XII	5	skins and glue (seal B/M)
178	NBC 7746	30×26×13	–	–		XII	15	leather
179	NBC 7796	32×30×13	–	–		XII	19	leather
180	NBC 7747	34×32×13	–	–		XII	29	leather
181	NBC 7508	38×30×14	–	–		?	–	bitumen (iti gu_4-zag-a)

TEXT	MUSEUM NUMBER	MEASUREMENTS IN mm	YEAR REIGN	VC	MVDM	MONTH	DAY	SUBJECT MATTER
182	NBC 7752	55×39×14	–		–	–	5	skins, sandals, and baskets
183	NBC 7155	36×23×12	–		–	–	–	wood
184	NBC 7236	41×34×13	–		–	–	–	products
185	NBC 7398	39×31×14	–		–	–	–	baskets and sieves
186	NBC 7442	43×35×13	–		–	–	–	doors
187	NBC 7457	42×37×15	–		–	–	–	products
188	NBC 7640	56×41×14	–		–	–	–	roof beams
189	NBC 7656	58×37×14	–		–	–	–	reed objects
190	NBC 7760	114×58×20	–		–	–	–	vessels
191	Ash. 1932-408	44×35×13	(broken?)			(broken)	1+	leather
192	NBC 8510	36×32×17	(broken)			(broken)	11	leather
193	NBC 7537	76×48×14	(broken)			(broken)	(broken)	products
194	NBC 9932	34×32×13	I.E.	3	9	V?	14	context broken
195	NBC 8462	52×37×17		(broken)		V?	(broken)	bags

Miscellaneous Archival Documents

TEXT	MUSEUM NUMBER	MEASUREMENTS IN mm	YEAR REIGN	VC	MVDM	MONTH	DAY	SUBJECT MATTER
196	NBC 7519	34×37×12	I.E.	16	22	IV	–	label
197	NBC 7452	36×30×12	I.E.	D	33	V	4	no activity (duplicate of 198)
198	NBC 7743	28×25×11	I.E.	D	33	V	4	no activity (duplicate of 197)
199	NBC 7110	34×30×12	I.E.	D	33	V	10	no activity (duplicate of 200)
200	NBC 7629	31×28×11	I.E.	D	33	V	10	no activity (duplicate of 199; seal M)
201	NBC 7624	34×31×13	I.E.	D	33	V	12	no activity
202	NBC 7234	33×30×10	I.E.	D	33	V	22	no activity (seal M)
203	NBC 7621	37×33×11	I.E.	D	33	VI	10	no activity (seal T)
204	NBC 7602	38×41×14	I.E.	D	33	XIII	–	label
205	NBC 7664	46×37×12	Š.i.		3b	I	30	list of tablets
206	NBC 7173	57×36×11	–		–	III	29	list of tablets
207	NBC 7225	43×35×16	–		–	–	–	list

Worker Lists

TEXT	MUSEUM NUMBER	MEASUREMENTS IN mm	YEAR REIGN	VC	MVDM	MONTH	DAY	SUBJECT MATTER
208	NBC 7177	64×41×14	I.E.	1	7	?	15	(iti kin-^{d}Nanna)

TEXT	MUSEUM NUMBER	MEASUREMENTS IN mm	REIGN	YEAR VC	YEAR MVDM	MONTH	DAY	SUBJECT MATTER
209	NBC 7203	56 × 36 × 15	I.E.	1	7	VII	1	
210	NBC 5643	53 × 38 × 12	I.E.	G	7	VII	4	
211	NBC 6442	59 × 39 × 12	I.E.	G	7	VII	6	
212	NBC 7484	58 × 37 × 15	I.E.	G	7	VII	21	
213	NBC 6390	55 × 34 × 13	I.E.	1	7	VII	24	
214	NBC 7217	55 × 35 × 11	I.E.	G	7	VII	26	
215	NBC 7168	60 × 35 × 13	I.E.	1	7	VII	(broken)	
216	NBC 7653	59 × 37 × 16	I.E.	G	7	VIII	14	
217	NBC 7388	51 × 37 × 12	I.E.	1	7	VIII	17	
218	NBC 8478	59 × 40 × 12	I.E.	G	7	VIII	25	
219	NBC 7475	51 × 33 × 12	I.E.	G	7	IX	22	
220	NBC 7483	56 × 35 × 14	I.E.	G	7	X	4	
221	NBC 8946	59 × 34 × 11	I.E.	G	7	X	8	
222	NBC 8492	67 × 44 × 14	I.E.	2	8	IV	3	
223	NBC 6414	52 × 38 × 12	I.E.	2	8	V	9	
224	NBC 6393	53 × 36 × 11	I.E.	2	8	V	10	
225	NBC 8475	54 × 35 × 13	I.E.	2	8	V	15	
226	NBC 7266	69 × 42 × 12	I.E.	2	8	VII	1	
227	NBC 8463	58 × 36 × 11	I.E.	2	8	VII	8	
228	NBC 7136	71 × 40 × 14	I.E.	2	8	XIII	12	
229	NBC 5651	76 × 45 × 19	I.E.	2	8	XIII	(broken)	
230	NBC 8445	74 × 43 × 12	I.E.	3	9	IV	16	
231	NBC 8454	82 × 46 × 14	I.E.	3	9	VII	10	
232	NBC 7658	64 × 42 × 13	I.E.	3	9	VII	18	
233	NBC 7670	78 × 44 × 13	I.E.	3	9	VII	25	
234	NBC 5688	70 × 42 × 16	I.E.	3	9	IX	26	
235	NBC 7175	58 × 37 × 15	I.E.	3	9	XI	14	
236	NBC 7269	66 × 42 × 13	I.E.	4	10	III	4+	
237	NBC 7556	66 × 39 × 11	I.E.	4	10	V	6	
238	NBC 8139	59 × 41 × 14	I.E.	4	10	V	30	
239	NBC 6387	50 × 34 × 13	I.E.	4	10	VI	26	
240	NBC 7268	67 × 36 × 12	I.E.	4	10	VIII	21	
241	NBC 7559	63 × 37 × 11	I.E.	5	11	V	23	
242	NBC 7199	69 × 39 × 12	I.E.	5	11	VI	(broken)	
243	NBC 9462	56 × 34 × 10	I.E.	5?	11?	VII	14	
244	NBC 6450	75 × 42 × 12	I.E.	5	11	VII	17	
245	NBC 7672	77 × 40 × 13	I.E.	6	12	X	26	
246	NBC 7558	69 × 37 × 12	I.E.	6	12	XI	24	
247	NBC 6477	31 × 30 × 13	I.E.	7	13	V	24	
248	NBC 7557	64 × 37 × 13	I.E.	7	13	V	30	
249	NBC 8025	60 × 35 × 13	I.E.	7	13	VI	5	
250	NBC 7135	68 × 38 × 13	I.E.	7	13	VI	27	

TEXT	MUSEUM NUMBER	MEASUREMENTS IN mm	REIGN	YEAR VC	YEAR MVDM	MONTH	DAY	SUBJECT MATTER
251	NBC 8444	76×37×10	I.E.	7	13	VII	8	
252	NBC 8443	80×37×13	I.E.	7	13	VIII	27	
253	NBC 7548	58×33×12	I.E.	7	13	IX	14	(seal illegible)
254	NBC 7158	45×36×12	I.E.	7	13	XIII	2	
255	NBC 6361	41×35×12	I.E.	8	14	VI	3	
256	NBC 7486	49×35×12	I.E.	8	14	VI	17+	
257	NBC 7144	45×36×12	I.E.	8	14	VI	28	
258	NBC 5622	40×33×13	I.E.	8	14	VII	6	
259	NBC 5619	48×33×15	I.E.	8	14	VII	22	
260	NBC 8852	38×32×11	I.E.	8	14	VII	(broken)	
261	NBC 7092	39×32×12	I.E.	8	14	VIII	22	
262	NBC 6362	36×31×13	I.E.	8	14	XII	18	
263	NBC 8520	40×30×10	I.E.	9?	15?	I	18	
264	NBC 5624	38×30×17	I.E.	9	15	I	19	
265	NBC 6369	43×39×11	I.E.	9	15	II	28	
266	NBC 7416	39×33×12	I.E.	9	15	III	10+	
267	NBC 8499	39×34×15	I.E.	9	15	IV	25	
268	NBC 5623	42×32×16	I.E.	9	15	IX	29	
269	NBC 7493	39×30×11	I.E.	9	15	X	7	
270	NBC 7156	39×31×12	I.E.	9	15	X	11	
271	NBC 6446	54×36×12	I.E.	10	16	X	7	
272	NBC 5654	57×38×16	I.E.	11	17	V	17	
273	NBC 8888	52×38×12	I.E.	14b	20	V	18	
274	NBC 6397	48×35×13	I.E.	15	21	IX	26	(seal illegible)
275	NBC 7394	52×35×13	I.E.	15	21	XII	22	(seal illegible)
276	NBC 7648	59×37×14	–		–	VII	8	
277	NBC 7170	59×43×17	–		–	VII	16	
278	NBC 8906	70×44×12	–		–	VII	25	
279	NBC 7262	63×41×20	–		–	VII	27	
280	NBC 8024	63×42×14	–		–	VII	28	
281	NBC 8026	53×37×15	–		–	VII	30	
282	NBC 8945	58×42×14	–		–	VIII	3	
283	NBC 7216	55×42×16	–		–	VIII	11	
284	NBC 8027	58×40×15	–		–	VIII	22	
285	NBC 7450	55×39×16	–		–	IX	9	
286	NBC 8887	55×39×15	–		–	IX	16	
287	NBC 7215	57×40×20	–		–	IX	24+	
288	NBC 8028	53×37×12	–		–	IX	28	(Cf. 289)
289	NBC 7189	50×37×13	–		–	IX	28	(Cf. 288)
290	NBC 7657	52×40×14	–		–	X	4	
291	NBC 6448	57×39×12	–		–	X	10	
292	NBC 8023	58×48×13	–		–	X	20	

TEXT	MUSEUM NUMBER	MEASUREMENTS IN mm	REIGN	YEAR VC	YEAR MVDM	MONTH	DAY	SUBJECT MATTER
293	NBC 8022	55×38×15	–		–	X	23	
294	NBC 7661	60×40×15	–		–	X	30	
295	NBC 8953	58×38×13	–		–	XI	1	
296	NBC 7652	59×42×20	–		–	XI	10	
297	NBC 7472	55×40×14	–		–	XI	19	
298	NBC 7474	46×36×13	–		–	XI	22	
299	NBC 7574	51×35×14	–		–	XI	23	
300	NBC 8939	48×36×12	–		–	XI	26	
301	NBC 7185	53×39×11	–		–	XI	30	
302	Ash. 1932-400	50×36×14	–		–	XII	21	
303	NBC 7479	52×38×13	–		–	XIII	7	
304	NBC 7717	56×36×14	–		–	(broken)	5	
305	NBC 7167	58×41×13	–		–	(broken)	22	
306	Ash. 1932-254	49×37×16	–		–	(broken)	(broken)	
307	Ash. 1932-379	51×34×12	–?		–?	(broken)	(broken)	
308	NBC 8944	81×45×13		(broken)		(broken)	6	
309	NBC 8299	72×40×14		(broken)		(broken)	17	
310	NBC 7536	75×43×15		(broken)		(broken)	(broken)	
311	NBC 8500	35×29×10	–		–	VI	28	(short type)
312	NBC 8508	34×30×11	–		–	VI	29	(short type)
313	NBC 7791	44×35×15	–		–	?	–	reedworkers (iti síg-^{d}In[anna])
314	NBC 7555	70×43×14	–		–	–	–	days absent

Texts in Transliteration

TEXT	REIGN	VC	MVDM	MONTH	DAY	SUBJECT MATTER
1. Lindblom High School 1	I.E.	7	13	VI	19	bitumen (duplicate of 107)
2. Lindblom High School 2	–		–	VI	25	worker list (short type)
3. Mr. Sheldon	I.E.	11b	17	II	–	skins

INDICES

PERSONAL NAMES

f. = father; s. = son

A-a, ad-KID, 280:18; 285:15; 287:19; 288:19; 289:19; 290:14; 291:18; 292:17; 293:17.

A-al-la-mu, Al-la-mu*, nagar, 222:7*; 228:7; 229:8*; 230:6; 232:9; 233:8; 234:8; 235:6; 250:5; 270:3; 271:3; 309:5; 310:10.

Ab-ba-mu, 172:5.

A-bi-ma, 186:9.

A-bi-ša-ru-um, nagar, 252:9; 271:6; 309:12.

A-bu-bu, f. of *Bu-qú-šum,* 128:seal; 129:seal; 137:seal; 177:seal.

A-bu-um, 128:1, 12.

A-bu-um-ilī, nagar, 252:10; 253:6; 264:4; 272:4.

^{d}*Adad-ba-ni,*
1. ašgab, 212:8; 213:7; 214:8; 215:8; 217:6; 218:8; 219:6; 230:11; 231:14; 240:11; 242:12; 244:10; 248:13; 253:10; 270:8; 273:2; 274:3; 275:4; 277:9; 278:9; 279:7; 281:7; 284:9; 286:9; 287:8; 288:8; 289:7; 291:8; 292:9; 293:9; 297:6; 298:8; 299:7; 300:9; 301:9; 303:9; 305:7; 306:9; 309:21; 310:13;
2. šu, 44:4;
3. kišib, 49:6;
4. gìr, 40:12.

^{d}*Adad-ellatī,*
1. ašgab, 233:18; 234:13; 235:11; 236:12; 276:7; 280:8; 282:8; 283:7; 284:10; 285:10; 287:10; 288:10; 289:10; 290:10; 291:10; 292:9; 305:9; 308:16′;
2. 314:16.

^{d}*Adad-ra-bí,*
1. ašgab, 208:9; 209:7; 210:7; 211:9; 216:9; 220:8; 221:9; 223:11; 224:11; 225:9; 226:11; 227:11; 228:14; 229:17; 236:13; 237:14; 240:13; 242:15; 243:7; 244:14; 245:14; 248:14; 276:8; 280:9; 282:7; 283:8; 285:9; 290:9; 294:9; 295:8; 296:8; 304:8; 307:8; 308:15′;
2. 181:3; 314:17.

A-da-làl, ašgab, 222:11; 230:10; 231:13.

Ad-da-gi-na, ašgab, 237:16; 238:7; 241:18; 246:20; 249:14; 250:15; 251:19; 252:21; 275:6; 308:10′.

Ad-da-kal-la,
1. ašgab, 233:21; 234:15; 235:13; 236:15; 237:15; 238:6; 241:13; 308:11′;
2. ì-sur, gìr, 163:7;
3. 49:3; 50:4.

A-gu-a, 186:9.

A-ḫa-am-ar-ši, dub-sar, gìr, 159:7.

A-ḫa-ni-šu,
1. ad-KID, 248:25; 250:20; 252:28; 265:10; 272:11; 275:11; 309:29;
2. gìr, 92:5.

Aḫ-da-nu-um, f. of *Ma-am-na-da-du,*160:6.

A-ḫu-a-ṭāb, ašgab, 249:15; 251:18; 252:19; 256:9; 257:6; 258:5; 261:6; 262:5; 265:6; 267:5.

A-ḫu-ba-a,
1. f. of Ur-^{d}Lugal-bàn-da, 64:seal; 65:seal; 69:seal;
2. túg-du$_{8}$, 276:24; 277:22; 278:26; 279:25.

A-ḫu-ṭāb,
1. nagar-lugal, 230:31;
2. 59:5; 63:5; 77:9.

A-ḫu-wa-qar, nagar, 248:9.

A-ku-ki, gìr, 157:3.

*A-ku-um, A-ku-ma**,
1. ašgab, 222:10; 228:15*; 229:13; 231:15*; 240:12; 242:11; 244:11; 245:12; 248:12; 253:9; 310:14*;
2. nagar-lugal, 230:32*.

A-lí-šu-nu, šà-tam, gìr, 118:7.

A-lí[ ], 124:seal b.

A-mur-É-a,
1. ad-KID, 208:20; 209:11; 210:11; 211:12; 216:14; 220:19; 221:19; 222:18; 231:25; 233:34; 236:25; 240:21; 243:11; 272:12; 274:8; 275:10; 276:12; 280:16; 282:18; 283:15; 285:13; 290:13; 291:13; 294:12; 295:11; 296:16; 303:12; 304:19; 307:12; 310:22;
2. 58:5; 313:1.

A-wi-lum-ma,
1. ad-KID, 228:19; 229:26; 230:15; 234:26; 235:17;
2. túg-du$_8$, 250:31; 251:46;
3. gìr, 33:8;
4. 174:4.

Ba-ab-ḫa-l[i?], 47:6.

B[A.D]AM-*ì-lí,* sipa-ur-ra, gìr, 101:4.

Ba-ga, Ba-a-ga*,
1. nagar, 233:6; 236:4; 239:3; 240:3; 242:2; 244:4*; 248:8*; 250:7*; 251:8*; 264:5; 272:5*; 309:8*;
2. nagar-lugal, 230:30.

*Ba-ga-tum, Ba-a-ga-tum**, nagar, 271:11; 309:16*.

Ba-la-la, gu$_4$-gaz, 121:2.

Be-lí-a-ma-ar, ad-KID, 276:18; 277:19; 278:17; 279:19; 280:19; 282:19; 283:19; 285:20; 290:20; 305:19.

Be-lí-šar, gìr, 113:7.

BI.Ú-*be-lí,* gìr, 120:4.

Bu-qú-šum,
1. s. of *A-bu-bu,* 128:seal; 129:seal; 133:seal; 137:seal; 177:seal; 202:seal;
2. gìr, 130:42; 137:9; 138:2; 153:15; 154:16; 155:17; 159:18; 160:16.

Bu-zu-zu, nagar, 248:5; 251:3.

Da-da-AN, gìr, 48:12.

^{d}*Da-mu-na-ṣi-ir,* gìr, 160:9.

Da-làl-ilī, ad-KID, 210:17.

Dan-^{d}*Amar-*^{d}*Sîn,* túg-du$_8$, 237:26; 238:16.

Dan-ni, túg-du$_8$, 250:27; 251:44.

Dan-nu-ri, 47:4.

Da-ru-du-um, f. of *Iq-bí-zum,* 160:4.

Diqdiqqu (AN.TI.URU.NAG),
1. gìr, 116:8;
2. 114:7.

DU$_7$ (PN?), sukkal Ì-si-in-na^{ki}, 48:5.

Du-šu-mu-um, nagar, 237:6; 241:5; 252:12; 271:10; 308:3′; 309:15.

É-a-ma-lik, 78:4, 8.

E-li-ra, Mar-tu, 118:5.

El-ni-ki, sagi, 155:6; 158:13.

^{d}En-líl-lá-me-en, 48:6.

^{d}*En-líl-ma-la-ak-šu,* kišib, 110:4.

^{d}*En-líl-ri-ṣú-šu,* gìr, 139:13.

En-um-É-a,
1. nagar, 230:4; 231:7; 233:11; 235:5; 245:3; 248:3; 249:4; 251:13; 255:3; 256:2; 257:2; 260:2; 267:2; 271:1; 272:1; 309:1;
2. gìr, 76:9;
3. 77:5, 6.

E-nu-zum, Mar-tu, 146:2.

Èr-ra-ašarid, 116:7.

*Èr-ra-ba-ni, Èr-ra-*DÍM*,
1. nagar, 208:3; 211:3; 214:3; 216:3; 218:2; 221:3; 222:4; 223:3*; 224:3; 225:3; 226:4; 227:4; 228:3; 229:3; 231:3; 232:4; 233:2; 234:3; 235:1; 237:4; 245:8; 249:6; 252:5; 263:4; 282:3; 283:2; 284:3; 285:3; 286:3; 290:3; 295:2; 297:3; 302:3; 308:2′; 310:3;
2. sipa-ur-ra, 101:5;
3. 46:5.

Èr-ra-dan, nu-kiri$_6$, 24:2; 25:4.
Èr-ra-ma-lik,
1. s. of Ur-ÉŠ[ ], 98:seal;
2. 98:9.
Eš$_4$-tár-an-dul-^{d}Iš-bi-Èr-ra, sagi, gìr, 151:7.
Eš$_4$-tár-ellatī, sagi, maškim, 137:5.
E-te-el-^{d}Iš-bi-Èr-ra, gìr, 139:7.
E-te-el-pù-um-É-a, 47:5.

Gal-zu-lu-lu, ašgab, 245:16; 253:13; 259:8; 268:8; 269:5; 274:5.
Gal-zu-na-lu$^?$-lu,
1. gìr, 82:12;
2. 58:1; 166:2.
Ga-ú-šum, 86:4.
Gìr-ì-sa, 58:3; 99:4.

Ha-la-la,
1. nagar, 228:5; 229:7; 233:7; 236:5; 239:4; 240:4; 242:7; 244:6; 252:6; 253:4; 272:6; 309:14;
2. nagar-lugal, 230:32.
HA.LA-ša, HI.LA-ša*,
1. s. of Ga[ ], 60:seal; 61:seal; 72:seal;
2. nagar, 250:9; 254:3; 256:6; 258:2; 261:2; 262:2; 263:6; 265:2; 268:2; 309:13;
3. túg-du$_8$, gìr, 3:6;
4. túg-du$_8$, 60:6, 8; 72:11; 208:25; 209:20; 210:20; 211:21; 212:20; 213:20; 214:21; 215:22; 216:22; 217:20; 218:21; 219:20; 220:21; 221:21; 222:26; 223:22!; 224:22; 225:22; 226:21; 227:22; 228:28; 229:29; 230:24; 231:28; 232:Rev.10; 233:38; 234:28; 235:26; 236:27; 237:22; 238:9; 239:14; 240:27; 241:28; 242:Rev.8′; 243:Rev.8′; 244:27; 248:31; 251:41; 255:5; 256:15; 257:13; 258:10; 259:14; 260:11; 270:13; 276:21; 277:23*; 278:22*; 279:22*; 280:21*; 281:21; 282:21; 283:21; 284:21; 285:22; 286:21; 287:21; 288:21; 289:21; 290:22; 291:21; 292:21; 293:20; 294:20; 295:20; 296:19; 297:19; 298:20; 299:20; 300:20; 301:20; 302:20; 303:20; 304:21; 305:21; 306:20; 307:20; 308:31′; 310:28;
5. ugula, 314:12*;
6. gìr, 93:2;
7. 61:3; 72:2; 73:6; 74:4; 75:5; 314:10*.
Ḫa-mi-mu-um, Mar-tu, 118:3.
Ḫu-un-te-[bi$^?$], 46:7.

I-ba-a-rí-iq, nagar, 250:3; 251:9.
Ib-ni-^{d}Adad, ad-KID, 309:30.
Ib-ni-^{d}Da-gan, ugula, 48:4.
I-da-be-lí, f. of *Ma-da-nu-uḫ,* 111:seal; 123:seal.
I-da-nu-um, 65:2.
I-din-^{d}Amurru, gìr, 124:4.
I-din-^{d}Da-gan, 45:8.
I-din-Èr-ra, nagar, 309:18.
I-din-ilī,
1. ad-KID, 222:22; 231:26; 236:23; 240:24; 242:14′; 245:24; 253:20; 272:14; 310:25;
2. túg-du$_8$, 240:31; 246:33; 252:36; 253:24;
3. šu, 173:13.
IGI.É.MAH, 94:3.
I-ḫu-uz-^{d}Da-gan, ì-rá-rá, gìr, 159:13.
Ik-šu-da, 48:8.
Ilī-ba-ni,
1. túg-du$_8$, 9:5; 208:23; 209:22; 210:21; 211:23; 216:24; 220:22; 221:22; 222:28; 223:23; 224:24; 225:24; 226:23; 227:23; 228:29; 229:29; 231:30; 234:32; 238:13; 239:17; 241:33; 242:Rev.12′; 243:Rev.10′; 244:31; 245:32; 248:32; 250:25; 251:38; 256:16; 271:18$^?$; 273:14; 304:22; 308:34′;
2. tur, túg-du$_8$, 236:29;
3. min, túg-du$_8$, 239:18;
4. GU, túg-du$_8$, 257:14;
5. lú Ma-rí, 113:4;
6. 54:5; 72:6.
Ì-lí-ki-a-bí, rá-gaba, gìr, 151:3.
Ì-lí-ma-lí-ki, 47:2.
Ì-lí-mi-ti, túg-du$_8$, 249:24; 251:39; 265:14; 274:16.

Ilī-ra-bí,
1. ad-KID, 212:12; 213:12; 214:14; 215:19; 217:12; 218:13; 219:17; 223:14; 224:14; 225:14; 226:14; 227:15; 228:25; 229:23; 230:21; 232:Rev.7; 233:25; 234:22; 235:20; 241:27; 244:18; 245:21; 248:23; 251:30; 252:31; 259:11; 263:15; 276:13; 280:14; 281:13; 282:15; 283:9; 285:14; 286:19; 290:15; 291:14; 294:13; 295:12; 296:17; 303:13; 308:29′;
2. 80:2; 313:3.

Ì-lí-sukkallum, gìr, 57:6.

Ì-lí-TAB.BA, *Ì-lí*-TAB.BA-*ì**, ad-KID, 212:13; 213:13; 214:14; 215:15; 217:16; 218:14; 219:12; 223:18; 224:18; 225:17; 226:17; 227:18; 228:21; 229:22; 230:17*; 232:Rev.3*; 233:24*; 234:20; 235:19*; 241:24*; 244:19*; 245:23*; 250:18*; 251:29; 252:24; 269:8*; 272:12*; 274:9*; 277:16; 278:20; 279:20; 281:14; 284:19; 286:14; 287:17?; 288:17; 289:17; 292:18; 293:14; 297:16; 298:17; 299:16; 300:18; 301:18; 302:17; 305:15; 306:17; 308:25′*; 309:31*.

Ì-lí-uṣ-ra-ni, dub-sar, 62:11.

Ìl-šu-ašarid, gìr, 109:6.

Ìl-šu-ba-ni,
1. gìr, 124:6;
2. 48:10.

Ìl-šu-e-er,
1. ad-KID, 67:3; 208:12; 209:10; 210:10; 211:11; 212:11; 213:11; 214:12; 215:13; 216:12; 217:11; 218:12; 219:11; 220:11; 221:12; 222:17; 223:13; 224:13; 225:13; 226:13; 227:13; 229:19; 230:14; 231:19; 232:Rev.1; 233:23; 235:16; 236:18; 237:18; 240:18; 241:20; 243:10; 244:17; 245:19; 246:23; 248:22; 249:17; 250:17; 252:23; 253:17; 254:10; 256:11; 257:8; 258:8; 259:10; 260:8; 263:13; 265:8; 266:8; 269:7; 272:10; 273:10; 274:7; 275:8; 276:11; 277:12; 278:12; 279:12; 280:11; 281:12; 282:11; 283:11; 284:12; 285:12; 286:12; 287:12; 288:12; 289:12; 290:12; 291:12; 292:12; 293:11; 294:11; 295:10; 296:10; 297:10; 298:11; 299:11; 300:11; 301:11!; 302:11?; 303:11; 304:11; 305:11; 306:11; 307:11; 308:21′; 309:27; 310:18;
2. gìr, 130:23, 26.
3. 314:26.

Ip-qú-ša,
1. ad-KID, 62:8;
2. šà-tam, gìr, 143:3;
3. 181:2.

Iq-bí-zum, s. of *Da-ru-du-um*, 160:3.

Ìr-mu, gudu$_4$, gìr, 103:4.

I-šar-a-ḫi, šà-tam, gìr, 143:5.

I-šar-be-lí, rá-gaba, gìr, 100:6.

I-šar-dajjān, *I-šar-dajjān-ì**, ad-KID, 212:16; 213:16; 214:17; 215:17; 217:14; 218:17; 219:18; 223:20; 224:19; 225:20; 226:15; 227:16; 228:22; 229:20; 230:20; 232:Rev.5*; 233:32; 234:25; 235:21; 237:20; 241:23*; 244:20*; 281:17; 286:17; 303:17; 308:28′*.

I-šar-ì-lí,
1. túg-du$_8$, 236:30; 238:14; 241:31; 244:30; 249:22; 252:37; 253:26; 276:23; 280:23; 282:23; 283:23; 287:22; 288:23; 289:23; 290:25; 292:23; 293:22; 297:20; 298:22; 299:23; 300:22; 301:22; 302:22; 306:22;
2. 72:5.

I-šar-lu-ba-lí-iṭ, gìr, 95:5; 96:9.

^{d}*Iš-bi-Èr-ra-ba-ni*, gu$_4$-gaz, gìr, 102:6.

^{d}*Iš-bi-Èr-ra-bēl-bēlī*, 78:6.

^{d}*Iš-bi-Èr-ra-dan*, túg-du$_8$, 252:38; 253:25; 271:19.

^{d}*Iš-bi-Èr-ra-ì-lí-ma-ti-šu*, ^{d}*Iš-bi-Èr-ra*-DINGIR.KALAM.MA*, gìr, 77:3*; 139:6; 155:14.

^{d}*Iš-bi-Èr-ra-na-da*, 45:6; 48:9.

^{d}*Iš-bi-Èr-ra-na-ra-am-*^{d}*Sîn*, 48:7.

^{d}*Iš-bi-Èr-ra-nu-úr-ma-ti-šu*, ^{d}*Iš-bi-Èr-ra-nu-úr-⟨ma-⟩ti-šu**,
1. ugula, 33:9*;
2. gìr, 136:5; 139:4; 140:7, 17; 141:6; 145:3.

^{d}*Iš-bi-Èr-ra*-zi-kalam-ma,
1. rá-gaba, gìr, 118:4;
2. gìr, 134:4;
3. 58:12.

Išdum-ki-in,
1. ašgab, 228:16; 229:14; 231:12; 241:17; 246:19; 248:16; 251:23; 273:5; 275:5; 308:18′;
2. gìr, 124:5;
3. 45:5.

Iš-me-É-a, 10:2.

I-tá-mi-šar, rá-gaba, gìr, 84:3.

I-ti-^{d}*Nin-gal*$^{?}$, muhaldim, gìr, 108:4.

Iz-kur-ilī, 45:7; 48:2.

Ki-bi-ir-a-ḫi, 45:4.

Ku-bu-lum,
1. ad-KID, 212:17; 213:17; 214:18; 215:14; 217:13; 218:19; 219:16; 223;19; 224:20; 225:19; 226:16; 227:17; 228;26; 229:25; 230:22; 232:Rev.8; 234:21; 235:24; 241:21; 244:24; 276:17; 280:13; 281:18; 282:13$^{!}$; 283:13; 285:19; 286:18; 290:19; 291:15; 294:18; 295:17; 296:12; 303:18; 307:17; 308:23′;
2. 80:4; 313:4; 314:24.

Kù-Eš$_4$-tár, ad-KID, 208:16.

Kù-^{d}Nanna,
1. ad-KID, 209:18; 210:16; 211:13; 216:20; 220:18; 221:18; 222:21; 231:21; 233:26; 236:24; 240:19; 242:Rev.3′$^{!}$; 245:27; 246:25; 249:19; 276:19; 277:20; 278:18; 279:18; 282:17; 283:18; 284:14; 294:14; 295:16; 296:13; 297:15; 298:16; 299:15; 300:17; 301:16; 302:15; 304:18; 305:12; 306:16; 307:18; 310:24;
2. túg-du$_8$, 251:40; 274:17;
3. dub-sar, gìr, 142:5;
4. 26:4$^{?}$; 80:11; 148:3; 314:22.

Kù-^{d}Nin-gal, 169:5.

Kur-ru-ub-Èr-ra,
1. šà-tam, gìr, 62:12; 107:4;
2. gìr, LHS 1:5.

Li-bur-be-lí,
1. kišib, 152:3, seal$^{?}$;
2. gìr, 133:11; 153:9;
3. 32:4; 38:4; 44:3; 272:16.

Lú-bala-ša$_6$-ga, ⟨Lú-⟩bala-ša$_6$-ga*,
1. lú-má-gal-gal, gìr, 137:4*;
2. gìr, 129:3.

Lú-^{d}Ba-ú, ašgab, 263:10; 266:6; 273:3; 309:23.

Lú-^{d}Da-mu, nu-kiri$_6$, 9:13.

Lú-^{d}En-ki, 37:3; 38:5; 40:8$^{?}$; 41:3; 69:2; 160:14.

Lugal-ab-ba,
1. ad-KID, 208:19; 209:17; 210:12; 211:19; 216:13; 220:12; 221:13; 231:22; 233:33; 240:20; 242:Rev.2′; 246:24; 257:9$^{?}$; 263:26; 277:13; 278:8; 279:13; 284:16; 287:13; 288:13; 289:18; 292:13; 293:12; 297:11; 298:12; 299:12; 300:12; 301:12; 302:12; 305:18; 306:12;
2. 80:6.

Lugal-ezen,
1. f. of ^{d}Nanna-ì-ša$_6$, 119:seal;
2. gìr, 139:11; 140:10.

Lugal-inim-gi-na, 78:11.

Lugal-ì-ša$_6$, Lugal-ì-sà*, Lugal-ì-sá**,
1. ašgab, 212:9*; 213:9*; 214:10*; 215:10**; 217:9*; 218:10*; 219:9*; 222:14*; 231:12*; 245:17; 253:11; 264:8; 281:10*; 302:7; 310:108;
2. nagar-lugal, 230:31*;
3. gìr, 139:17.

Lugal-kù-zu,
1. nagar, 245:2; 248:2; 249:3; 250:2; 251:11; 252:3; 256:3; 259:3; 260:3; 270:4; 272:3; 282:4; 283:4; 284:4; 285:4; 290:4; 293:4;
2. ašgab, 286:8;
3. ad-KID, 249:18;
4. 314:4.

Lugal-már-da, nagar, 271:7; 309:10.

Lugal-ša$_6$, ad-KID, 233:29.

Lugal-TAB-BA-ì, ad-KID, 299:12.

Lú-Gír-su^{ki}, muhaldim, gìr, 154:4.

Lú-^{d}Inanna, Lú-$^{\langle d\rangle}$Inanna*,
1. ašgab, 208:6; 209:5; 210:5; 211:6; 212:5; 213:5; 214:6; 215:6; 216:6; 217:5; 218:6; 219:5; 220:5; 221:6; 222:9; 223:6; 224:6; 225:6; 226:6; 227:6; 228:10; 229:10; 230:9; 231:10; 233:15; 234:10; 235:8; 236:9; 238:5; 239:9; 240:9; 241:11; 242:10; 243:5; 244:9; 245:11; 248:11; 249:10; 250:11; 251:15; 252:14; 253:8; 254:6; 256:7; 257:4; 258:4; 259:6; 260:5; 262:4; 264:7; 265:5; 266:5; 268:4; 269:3; 270:6; 271:14; 273:1; 274:1; 275:1; 276:6; 277:6; 278:6; 279:6*; 280:6; 281:6; 282:6; 283:6; 284:6; 285:6; 286:6; 287:6; 288:6; 289:6; 290:6; 291:6; 292:6; 293:6; 294:6; 295:5; 296:5; 297:5; 298:6; 299:6; 300:6; 301:6; 302:5; 303:6; 304:5; 305:5; 306:6; 307:6; 308:9′; 309:20; 310:10;
2. ad-KID, 208:14; 209:14; 211:16; 216:19; 220:17; 221:17; 243:Rev.6′; 265:11?;
3. gìr, 26:5;
4. 22:3; 93:6.
Lú-Kar-zi-da, 106:3.
Lú-^{d}Nanna,
1. ugula, 314:19;
2. gìr, 120:5.
Lú-^{d}Nin-gír-su,
1. nagar, 230:7; 233:5?; 236:7; 240:6; 309:6;
2. gìr, 153:11.
Lú-^{d}Nin-hur-sag, ašgab, 258:6; 259:7.
Lú-^{d}Nin-šubur,
1. šu-i, 62:5;
2. gìr, 4:8; 104:13; 133:8; 153:11; 175:4;
3. maškim, 124:7;
4. 150:13.
Lú-ša$_6$-ga, Lú-ša$_6$⟨-ga⟩*, gìr, 153:15*; 154:16; 155:17; 159:18; 160:16.
Lú-*ša-lim*, 4:4.
Lú-^{d}Šu-nir, ašgab, 271:15.

Ma-da-nu-úḫ,
1. s. of *I-da-be-lí*, 111:seal; 123:seal;
2. 111:Rev.3; 123:5.
Ma-am-na-da-du, s. of *Aḫ-da-nu-um*, 160:5.
Ma-nu-a-tum, géme Mar-tu, 146:1.
Maš-tur,
1. rá-gaba sagi, gìr, 115:3;
2. sagi, gìr, 125:3; 153:4.
Mu-na-nu-um, *Mu-na-núm**,
1. nagar, 222:6; 228:6; 229:5; 231:6; 232:5; 234:4; 235:2; 245:6; 248:4; 250:6; 251:10; 256:4; 271:4; 309:9; 310:7;
2. 48:3; 176:3; 314:27*.

Na-di,
1. nagar, 208:2; 211:2; 214:2; 216:2; 218:3; 221:2; 222:2; 223:2; 224:2; 225:2; 226:2; 227:2; 228:2; 229:2; 231:2; 232:2; 234:2; 237:2; 251:2; 255:2; 263:2; 265:3!; 266:2; 270:2; 271:2; 282:2; 283:3; 284:2; 285:2; 286:2; 290:2; 293:2; 295:3; 297:2; 302:2; 309:4; 310:2;
2. 186:12; 314:2!.
^{d}Nanna-ì-ša$_6$,
1. s. of Lugal-ezen, 119:seal;
2. kišib, 119:3.
^{d}Nanna-ki-ág,
1. šà-tam, gìr, 106:5;
2. šà-tam, 164:4;
3. gu-za-lá, gìr, 156:5; 161:5;
4. kišib, 2:5; 3:7; 4:7; 5:7; 6:5; 7:8; 13:6; 14:6; 15:6; 16:6; 17:6; 18:6; 19:6; 20:6; 21:5; 22:5; 23:8; 24:12; 25:8; 26:7; 27:6!; 28:6; 29:6; 30:6; 31:6; 32:7; 33:7; 34:7; 35:5; 36:5; 40:10; 41:6; 49:5; 50:6; 52:6; 53:9; Sheldon tablet:7;
5. gìr, 37:6; 38:8; 130:43; 138:5;
6. 8:8; 44:4; 60:7; 61:2; 62:15; 63:4; 64:2; 65:3; 66:3; 67:2; 68:5, 12; 146:4; 152:4.
^{d}Nanna-ma-ba, 23:5.
Nin-^{d}Nir-nu-da, 57:6.
Nu-ḫi-ilī, lú-kin-gi$_4$-a, gìr, 149:9.
Nu-úr-^{d}Adad,
1. ašgab, 297:8;
2. ad-KID, 208:18; 209:15; 210:14; 211:15; 220:15; 221:15; 222:20; 231:24; 233:30; 236:20; 240:23; 242:Rev.6′; 243:Rev.5′;

246:26; 253:19; 254:12; 257:10; 274:11; 275:12; 277:18; 278:19; 279:16; 284:13; 287:16; 288:16; 289:15; 292:15; 293:16; 297:13; 298:15; 299:18; 300:15; 301:15; 302:14; 305:13; 306:18; 309:33; 310:21.

Nu-úr-a-ša, sipa-ur-ra, gìr, 101:5.

Nu-úr-É-a,
1. ašgab, 212:6; 213:6; 214:7; 215:7; 216:10; 217:7; 218:7; 219:7; 220:9; 221:10; 223:9; 224:9; 225:11; 226:9; 227:10; 228:13; 229:11; 230:12; 231:16; 233:19; 234:14; 235:12; 236:14; 237:13; 239:10; 241:14; 244:12; 251:17, 22; 252:17; 268:5; 274:4; 275:3; 277:10; 278:7; 279:9; 281:9; 284:8; 286:7; 287:7; 288:7; 289:8; 292:8; 293:7; 298:7; 299:8; 300:8; 301:8; 302:9; 304:9; 305:6; 306:8; 308:17′; 309:22$^{?}$; 310:15;
2. ad-KID, 216:16;
3. túg-du$_8$, 230:27; 232:Rev.13; 233:41; 234:31; 236:28; 237:24; 240:30; 242:Rev.11′$^{?}$; 245:30; 249:23; 252:35; 274:14; 277:26; 278:25; 279:26; 284:23; 305:23; 309:36;
4. gìr, 71:4, 5;
5. 72:9; 314:8, 15;
6. tur, ašgab, 249:13; 250:14;
7. min, ašgab, 252:18;
8. GU, ašgab, 254:7.

Nu-úr-Èr-ra, ašgab, 240:14.

Nu-úr-Eš$_4$-tár,
1. gìr, 62:9;
2. 1:3; 183:8.

PI-*ú-tum,* maš-šu-gíd-gíd, 118:2.

Puzur$_4$-É-a, nagar, 234:7; 235:3; 237:7; 238:3$^{?}$; 241:6; 245:5$^{?}$; 252:8; 271:8; 308:4′; 309:11$^{?}$; 310:6.

Puzur$_4$-^{d}En-líl,
1. ad-KID, 208:17; 209:12; 220:13; 236:22; 243:Rev.3′; 251:34; 252:32; 298:14; 299:13$^{?}$; 302:18; 305:14;
2. gìr, 135:7$^{?}$;
3. 80:14.

Puzur$_4$-Eš$_4$-tár,
1. ad-KID, 208:17; 209:13; 210:18; 211:18; 216:18; 220:14; 221:14; 222:19; 231:23; 233:28; 236:19; 240:25; 243:Rev.2′; 253:18; 254:11; 259:12; 273:12; 277:15; 278:15; 279:14; 284:17; 287:14$^{?}$; 288:14; 289:13; 292:14; 293:13; 297:14; 298:13; 299:14; 300:14; 301:14; 305:16; 309:28; 310:20;
2. 80:15.

Puzur$_4$-^{d}Nin-kar-ak, ad-KID, 253:21; 274:10$^{?}$; 309:34.

Puzur$_4$-^{d}Nin-sun, gìr, 87:3.

Puzur$_4$-^{d}Sîn,
1. ad-KID, 210:13; 211:17; 216:17; 277:17; 278:16; 279:17; 284:15; 287:15; 288:15; 289:14; 292:19; 293:18$^{?}$; 297:12; 301:13; 309:32$^{?}$;
2. sukkal, maškim, 146:3.

Puzur$_4$-^{d}Šára, gìr, 46:2.

*Puzur$_4$-*Ú, 314:21.

*Puzur$_4$-*Ù.GUR, ad-KID, 245:26.

Ra-bí-ilī, nagar, 248:6; 271:5.

Ri-ip-ši-mu-ut, ì-rá-rá, gìr, 157:7.

^{d}Sîn-ba-ni, 45:3.

^{d}Sîn-na-ṣi-ir, gìr, 112:4.

^{d}Šamaš-ellatī, 12:4, 257:3.

Šar-ru-um-ba-ni, gìr, 55:5; 118:8.

*Še-li-bu-um, Še-li-bu**, ašgab, 233:20; 234:16; 235:14; 236:16; 240:15; 242:14; 244:13; 245:15; 248:15; 253:14; 268:6*; 273:6.

Šu-^{d}Adad
1. ad-KID, 208:13; 210:15; 211:14; 212:18; 213:18; 214:19; 216:15; 217:17; 218:15; 219:14; 220:16; 221:16; 222:23; 223:16; 224:16; 225:16; 226:18; 227:19; 231:20; 236:21; 240:22; 242:Rev.5′; 243:Rev.4′; 245:25; 276:15; 277:14; 278:14; 279:15; 280:17; 281:19; 282:16; 283:17; 284:18; 285:18; 286:15; 287:18; 288:18; 289:16;

290:18; 291:16; 292:16; 293:15; 294:17; 295:15; 296:15; 297:12; 298:18; 299:17; 300:16; 301:17; 302:16; 303:16; 305:17; 306:15; 310:24?;
2. min, 80:9;
3. šu, ad-KID, 209:16;
4. 80:7; 313:5.

Šu-É-a,
1. ašgab, 208:7; 209:6; 210:6; 211:8; 216:7; 220:6; 221:8; 223:7; 224:7; 225:7; 226:8; 227:7; 228:12; 229:12; 233:17; 234:12; 235:10; 236:11; 237:12; 241:12?; 243:6; 249:12; 250:13; 251:21; 252:16; 254:8; 268:7; 269:4; 272:9; 274:2; 275:2; 277:7; 278:8; 279:8; 284:7; 287:9; 288:9; 289:9; 292:7; 293:8?; 297:7; 298:9; 299:9; 300:7; 301:7; 302:6; 304:6; 305:8; 306:7; 308:14′; 309:24;
2. 314:14.

Šu-Èr-ra,
1. nagar, 229:6; 237:8; 242:5; 244:7; 251:4; 252:7; 271:9; 308:5′; 309:17;
2. túg-du$_8$, 208:22; 209:21; 210:22; 211:22; 216:23; 243:Rev.9′; 250:28?; 251:45; 277:25; 278:24; 279:24; 284:22; 292:22; 293:21; 297:21; 298:21; 299:21; 300:21; 301:21; 302:21; 305:22; 306:21;
3. 48:4; 72:7.

Šu-Eš$_4$-tár,
1. nagar, 208:4; 211:4; 214:4; 216:4; 218:4; 221:4; 222:3; 223:4; 224:4; 225:4; 226:3; 227:3; 228:4; 229:4; 231:4; 232:6; 234:5; 237:5; 276:3; 277:4; 278:4; 279:4; 280:4; 286:4; 287:4; 288:4; 289:3; 291:4; 292:4; 294:4; 296:3; 298:4; 299:4; 300:3; 301:3; 303:3; 305:4; 306:4; 308:6′; 310:8;
2. ad-KID, 212:14; 213:14; 214:15; 215:16; 218:16; 219:13; 223:15; 224:15, 18; 225:15; 226:13; 227:14; 228:20; 229:21; 230:16; 232:Rev.2; 233:27; 234:19; 235:18; 241:22; 244:22; 245:20; 248:24; 251:33; 252:25; 272:16; 280:12; 281:15; 282:12; 286:13; 291:17; 295:13; 296:11; 303:14; 307:15; 308:26′;
3. min, ad-KID, 215:20′; 217:18?; 219:15; 226:19; 227:20; 276:16; 280:15; 282:14; 283:16; 285:17; 290:17; 294:16;
4. šu, ad-KID, 217:15; 223:17; 224:17; 276:14; 281:16; 283:12; 285:16; 290:16; 291:19; 294:15; 296:14; 303:15; 307:16;
5. ^{šu}min, ad-KID, 212:15; 213:15; 214:16; 218:17; 286:16; 295:14;
6. gu$_4$-gaz, gìr, 102:6;
7. ugula uš-bar, 183:6;
8. 7:5; 34:3; 40:7; 55:4; 80:12; 313:2; 314:20, 23; Sheldon tablet:3.

Šu-^{d}Gu-nu-ra, ad-KID, 171:6.

Šu-ì-lí, šagina, gìr, 109:5.

Šu-ì-lí-šu, 190:9.

*Šu-la-núm, Šu-la-nu-um**,
1. ašgab, 222:15; 240:16*; 253:15; 262:6;
2. má-lah$_6$, gìr, 128:2; 129:7.

Šu-lu-lu,
1. nagar, 209:3; 210:2; 212:3; 213:3; 215:3; 217:3; 219:3; 220:3; 230:2; 231:5; 232:3; 233:4; 236:3; 239:5; 240:7; 242:6; 243:3; 244:3; 245:9; 249:7; 251:12; 252:4; 253:3; 259:4; 264:3; 276:4; 277:3!; 278:3; 279:3; 280:3; 281:3; 287:3; 288:3; 289:4; 291:3; 292:3; 293:3; 294:3; 296:2; 298:3; 299:3; 300:4; 301:4; 303:4; 304:3; 305:3; 306:3; 307:4; 309:7;
2. 314:1.

Šu-Ma-ma, sukkal, maškim, 128:13.

Šu-Ma-mi-tum,
1. gìr, 34:8?;
2. 22:2.

*Šu-^{d}Nin-kar-ak, Šu-^{d}Nin-kar⟨-ak⟩**,
1. kus$_7$, 107:3; LHS 1:3;
2. 2:3*!; 3:4; 4:5; 5:5; 6:3; 7:6; 11:3; 13:3; 14:3; 15:3; 16:3; 17:3; 18:3; 19:3; 20:3; 21:3; 24:9; 25:5; 27:3; 28:3; 29:3; 30:3; 31:3; 32:5; 33:5; 34:4; 35:3; 36:3; 53:7; 59:4; 96:7; 98:8; 99:3; 101:3*; 110:3*; 112:5; 119:2*; 124:8, 14; 129:9; 130:45; 133:12; 135:9; 136:6; 137:7; 149:11; 151:9; 153:12; 154:14; 155:15; 159:15; 178:4; 179:3; 180:3; Sheldon tablet:4.

Šu-^{d}Nin-šubur,
1. ašgab, 208:8; 209:8; 210:8; 211:7; 216:8; 220:7; 221:7; 223:8; 224:8; 225:8?; 226:7; 227:8; 228:11; 229:15; 233:16; 234:11; 235:9; 236:10; 237:11; 241:15; 243:8; 249:11; 250:12; 251:16; 252:15; 256:8; 257:5; 270:7; 277:8; 278:10; 279:10; 285:8; 290:7; 291:7; 294:7; 295:6; 296:7; 303:8; 304:7; 307:9; 308:13′;
2. 314:13.

Šu-^{d}Nisaba,
1. túg-du$_8$, 60:2; 212:23; 213:22; 214:23; 215:23; 217:23; 218:22; 219:22; 222:27; 223:25; 224:23; 225:23; 226:22; 227:24; 228:31; 231:29; 238:10; 240:29; 242:Rev.9′; 246:34; 248:30; 251:37; 277:24; 278:23; 279:23; 281:24; 284:24; 286:22; 305:24; 308:32′; 310:29;
2. 72:3; 314:7.

Šu-^{d}Nu-muš-da,
1. túg-du$_8$, 230:25; 232:Rev.11; 233:39; 234:29; 237:23; 239:15; 241:29; 244:28; 246:31; 274:15;
2. 72:8.

*Šu-*PAP.PAP,
1. túg-du$_8$, 60:4; 212:22; 213:21; 214:22; 215:24; 217:21; 218:23; 219:21; 230:26; 232:Rev.12; 233:40; 234:30; 237:25; 238:15; 240:28; 242:Rev.10′; 272:18; 276:22; 280:22; 281:28; 282:22; 283:22; 285:24; 286:23; 290:24; 291:23; 294:22; 295:22; 296:20; 303:21; 307:22;
2. 72:4.

^{d}Šu-^{d}Sîn-a-bi, ì-du$_8$, gìr, 127:12.

Šu-^{d}Šamaš, ašgab, 223:10; 224:10; 225:10; 226:10; 227:9.

Tu-ra-am-ì-lí, gìr, 144:4.

*U-bar-rum, U-bar-um**, *U$_4$-bar-ra***, 82:8**; 104:12*; 186:5.

Ú.GUR-*i-šar,* túg-du$_8$, 250:29; 251:43.

Ur-Al-la-mu,
1. s. of Ku[ ], 147:seal;
2. gìr, 103:8; 154:13;
3. 147:6.

Ur-^{d}Ba-ú, gìr, 160:7.

Ur-du$_6$-kù-ga, ad-KID, 252:26; 256:12; 266:9; 270:10.

Ur-^{d}Li$_9$-si-na[a], Ur-^{d}Li$_9$-si$_4$-na[b], Ur-Li-si-na[c], Ur-^{d}⟨Li-⟩si$_4$-na[d], Ur-^{d}Li$_9$-si[e], Ur-^{d}Li$_9$-si$_4$[f], Ur-^{d}⟨Li-⟩NIN-na[g], Ur-^{d}⟨Li-⟩si-na[h],
1. nagar, 208:1[d]; 209:1[d]; 210:1[d]; 211:1[d]; 212:1[d]; 213:1[d]; 214:1[d]; 215:1[d]; 216:1[d]; 217:4[d]; 218:1[d]; 219:1[d]; 220:1[d]; 221:1[d]; 222:1[b]; 223:1[d]; 224:1[d]; 225:1[d]; 226:1[d]; 227:1[d]; 228:1[b]; 229:1[?]; 230:1[d]; 231:1[g]; 232:1[?]; 233:1[a]; 234:1[b]; 236:1[b]; 237:1[f]; 238:1[f]; 239:1[?]; 240:1[f]; 242:1[f]; 244:1[d]; 245:1[f]; 248:1[f]; 249:1[f]; 250:1[f]; 251:1[f]; 252:1[f]; 253:1[f]; 254:1[f]; 255:1[?]; 256:1[e]; 257:1[f]; 258:1[f]; 259:1[f]; 260:1[f]; 261:1[f]; 262:1[f]; 264:1[f]; 265:1[f]; 266:1[f]; 267:1[f]; 268:1[f]; 269:1[f]; 270:1[f]; 271:12[f]; 276:1[a]; 277:1[a]; 278:1[a]; 279:1[a]; 280:1[a]; 281:1[?]; 282:1[a]; 283:1[a]; 284:1[a]; 285:1[a]; 286:1[d]; 287:1[a]; 288:1[a]; 289:1[a]; 290:1[a]; 291:1[b]; 292:1[?]; 293:1[a]; 294:1[a]; 295:1[a]; 296:1[a]; 297:1[a]; 298:1[a]; 299:1[a]; 300:1[a]; 301:1[a]; 302:1[a]; 303:1[a]; 304:1[?]; 305:1[a]; 306:1[a]; 309:3[f];
2. ugula, 314:6[c];
3. 123:4[h].

Ur-^{d}Lugal-bàn-da, Ur-^{d}⟨Lugal-⟩bàn-da*,
1. s. of *A-ḫu-ba-a,* 64:seal; 65:seal; 69:seal;
2. túg-du$_8$, 212:21; 215:25; 217:22; 218:24*; 222:29; 223:24; 224:25; 225:24; 226:24; 227:25; 228:30; 229:30; 231;31; 238:12; 239:16; 241:30; 244:29; 245:29; 246:30; 248:29; 249:21; 250:23; 251:36; 252:34; 253:23; 254:14; 256:14; 257:12; 259:13; 260:10; 265:13; 270:12; 271:17; 273:15; 274:13; 280:24; 281:22; 282:24; 283:24; 285:23; 286:24; 287:23; 288:22; 289:22; 290:23; 291:22; 294:21; 295:21; 296:21; 303:22; 307:21; 308:33′;

3. gìr, 35:6;
4. 9:15; 42:4; 43:3; 64:3; 65:4; 66:4; 69:3; 71:2; 75:2, 9?; 76:8; 81:6; 84:4; 85:5; 86:6; 314:9*.

Ur-dLÚ.LÀL?, gìr, 109:6.

Ur-mah, maškim, 129:8.

Ur-mes, ad-KID, 228:24; 229:23; 230:19; 232:Rev.6; 234:23; 235:22; 237:19; 241:25; 244:21; 245:23; 251:31; 252:27; 263:14; 265:9; 273:11; 275:9; 308:22′.

Ur-dNin-mug, ad-KID, 228:23; 229:24; 230:18; 232:Rev.4; 233:31; 234:24; 235:23; 241:26; 244:23; 248:26; 251:32; 252:29; 308:27′.

Ur-sig$_5$, nagar, 209:2; 210:3; 212:2; 213:2; 215:2; 217:2; 219:2; 220:2; 230:3; 233:3; 236:2; 239:2; 240:2; 242:8; 243:2; 244:2; 249:2; 252:2; 254:2; 259:2; 263:3; 264:2; 272:2; 281:2; 287:2; 288:2; 289:2; 291:2; 292:2; 294:2; 298:2; 299:2; 300:2; 301:2; 303:2; 304:2; 306:2; 309:2.

Ur-dSîn,
1. ašgab, 208:10; 212:7; 213:8; 214:9; 215:9; 217:8; 218:9; 219:13; 222:13; 231:11; 239:11; 240:10; 242:13; 244:15; 245:13; 253:12; 260:6; 273:8; 276:9; 280:7; 281:8; 282:9; 283:9; 285:7; 286:10; 290:8; 291:9; 294:8; 295:7; 296:6; 303:7; 307:7; 310:11;
2. nagar-lugal, 230:30;
3. muhaldim, 154:6.

Ur-ša$_6$-ga,
1. nagar, 276:2; 277:2; 278:2; 279:2; 280:2; 305:2;
2. 314:3.

Ur-dŠu-bu-la, gìr, 75:11.

Ur-dŠul-pa-è,
1. gìr, 120:4; 133:4;
2. 120:8.

Ur-dTIR, ašgab, 309:25.

Ur-Tum-ma-al, muhaldim, gìr, 154:2.

Ù.SUH$_5$?-*i-šar,* gìr, 33:8.

Warad-Èr-ra,
1. s. of *Ì-lí-ma*[ ], 203:seal;
2. lú-kas$_4$, 78:5, 10.

*Zi-la-ku-um, Zi-la-kum**, nagar, 222:5; 228:8*; 230:5*; 231:8*; 233:13*; 234:6*; 235:4*; 236:6*; 238:2; 239:6; 240:5; 242:3; 244:5; 310:5*.

Zi-nu-um, 188:7.

DIVINE NAMES

^{d}*Adad,* 83:14; in the names ^{d}*Adad-*, *Ib-ni-*, *Nu-úr*, *Šu-*.

^{d}Amar-^{d}Sîn, in the name *Dan-*.

^{d}*Amurru,* in the name *I-din-*.

^{d}Ba-ú, in the name Lú-.

^{d}*Da-gan,* 83:11; 105:3; 109:4; 121:8; 122:6; 150:17; 248:10; 249:8; 250:21; 251:7; in the names *Ib-ni-*, *I-din-*, *I-ḫu-uz-*.

^{d}Da-mu, 92:11; in the names ^{d}Da-mu-, Lú-.

É-a, in the names É-a-, *A-mur-*, *E-nu-um-*, *E-te-el-pù-um-*, *Iš-me-*, *Nu-úr-*, *Puzur*$_4$-, *Šu-*.

^{d}En-ki, 30:7; 168:8; in the name Lú-.

^{d}En-líl, 103:2; 110:seal; 133:3; 153:$3^{?}$; 158:3; 162:9; in the names ^{d}En-líl-, Puzur$_4$-.

Èr-ra, in the names *Èr-ra-*, *I-din-*, *Kur-ru-ub-*, *Nu-úr-*, *Šu-*, *Warad-*.

Eš$_4$*-tár,* in the names *Eš*$_4$*-tár-*, Kù-, *Nu-úr-*, *Puzur*$_4$-, *Šu-*.

^{d}*Gu-nu-ra,* in the name *Šu-*.

^{d}Inanna, 70:3; 155:5; 169:4; 193:12′; in the name Lú-.

^{d}*Iš-bi-Èr-ra,* 155:5; in the names ^{d}*Iš-bi-Èr-ra-*, *E-te-el-*.

^{d}*Latarak,* in the name Ur-.

^{d}Li$_{(9)}$-si$_{(4)}$(-na), in the name Ur-.

^{d}Lugal-AM, 155:5.

^{d}Lugal-bàn-da, in the name Ur-.

^{d}Lugal-már-da, 173:10.

Ma-ma, in the name *Šu-*.

Ma-mi-tum, in the name *Šu-*.

^{d}Mes-lam-ta-è-a, 160:8.

^{d}Nanna, 122:7; 176:2; in the names ^{d}Nanna-, Kù-, Lú-.

^{d}Nin-gal, in the names *I-ti-*, Kù-.

^{d}Nin-gír-su, in the name Lú-.

^{d}Nin-hur-sag, 188:3; in the name Lú-.

^{d}Nin-in-si-na, 46:11; 92:12; 108:3; 159:10; 211:2.

^{d}Nin-kar-ak, in the names Lú-, *Puzur*$_4$-.

^{d}Nin-mug, in the name Ur-.

^{d}Nin-urta, 90:$2^{?}$.

^{d}Nin-sun, in the name *Puzur*$_4$-.

^{d}Nin-šár-nun-na, 75:7.

^{d}Nin-šubur, in the names Lú-, *Šu-*.

^{d}Nir-nu-da, in the name Nin-.

^{d}Nisaba, in the name *Šu-*.

^{d}Nu-muš-da, in the name *Šu-*.

^{d}*Sîn,* 121:10; 122:10; 147:1; in the names ^{d}*Sîn-*, ^{d}*Iš-bi-Èr-ra-na-ra-am-*, *Puzur*$_4$-.

^{d}*Šamaš,* in the names ^{d}*Šamaš-*, *Šu-*.

^{d}Šára, in the name *Puzur*$_4$-.

^{d}Šu-bu-la, in the name Ur-.

^{d}Šul-pa-è, in the name Ur-.

^{d}Šu-nir, in the name Lú-.

^{d}*Šū-*^{d}*Sîn,* in the name ^{d}*Šū-*^{d}*Sîn-*.

^{d}Utu, 108:2.

GEOGRAPHICAL NAMES

COUNTRIES AND TOWNS

Dilmun^{ki}, 129:2.
Elam, 124:3.
Gír-su^{ki}, in the name Lú-Gír-su^{ki}.
Kára-har^{ki}, 149:8.
Kar-zi-da, in the name Lú-Kar-zi-da.
Kiš^{ki}, 149:7.
Má-gan, 143:2.
Ma-rí^{ki}, 113:4; 237:9.
Me-luh-ha, 114:3.
Mu-úr^{ki}, 233:12.
Nibru^{ki}, 112:2; 118:6; 283:23.
Unug^{ki}, 124:2.
Ùr-ra, 99:2; 115:2.

FIELDS AND RIVERS

a-šà ši-tum-me, 100:5.
a-šà ezen-sar, 244:15; 247:5; 308:7′, 19′, 30′.
^{i_7}íl-íl, 229:L.E.

TEMPLES

é-^{d}*Da-gan,* 105:3; 109:4; 121:8; 122:6; 150:17; 248:10; 249:8; 250:21; 251:7.
é-^{d}Da-mu, 92:11.
é ^{d}*En-líl-lá,* 153.3$^{?}$.
é-^{d}Inanna, 169:4.
é-^{d}Lugal-már-da, 173:10.
é-^{d}Nin-hur-sag, 188:3.
é-^{d}Nin-in-si-na, 108:3; 211:2.
é-gibil ^{d}Lugal-AM ^{d}Inanna ^{d}*Iš-bi-Èr-ra,* 155:5.

TERMS

^{giš}A.BA, 97:6.
a-GAR-nag-a, dehaired, 23:3, 4.
^{giš}A.HA-nu-úr-ma, . . . pomegranate, 24:1; 25:1.
a-rá-x-kam, for the xth time, 9:3, 6; 51:2, 4, 6; 63:2, 4, 6, 7; 102:2, 3; 182:2, 4, 6, 8.
a-tu_5, *rimkum*, bathing;
a-tu_5-lugal, bathing of the king, 189:4.
á, *idum*, rent, hire, 87:2.
á-gi_6-ba-a, at night, 142:3.
á-šu-du_7-a, implements, 150:13.
^{giš}AB.BA Me-luh-ha, 114:4.
abul, *abullum*, gate, 148:2.
ad-KID, *atkuppum*, reedworker, 62:8; 67:3; 171:6; 208-312 *passim*; LHS 2:3;
1. ki-ad-KID, place of the reedworkers, 313:7;
2. kin-ad-KID, work of the reedworkers, 170:7.
aga-uš, *rēdûm*, soldier, 149:7; 171:4.
^{giš}al-ak, to do work with the pickaxe, 244:6, 15; 247:6?; 308:7′, 19′, 30′;
ki-^{giš}al, place of the work with the pickaxe, 209:15.
^{giš}al-gar, musical instrument, 87:1.
Al-la-ḫa-ru, *alluḫarum*, a mineral dye, 130:5, 34?;
1. a-*al-la-ḫa-ru lí-iq-tum*, selected liquid? *alluḫarum*-dye, 33:1;
2. ŠU.URU.GÁ a-*al-la-ḫa-ru*, 33:2.
amar, *būrum*, young animal, 12:2.
^{giš}ar-gibil, ^{giš}ar-gú-gibil*, *argibillum*, a wooden structure, 90:6; 96:3*.
^{giš}asal, *ṣarbatum*, poplar, 88:2; 95:3; 188:1;
asal-tur, small poplar, 88:5.

^{gi}AŠ.SI,
1. ^{gi}AŠ.SI-gibil, 189:1, 4;
2. ^{gi}AŠ.SI-sumun, 189:2, 6;
3. ^{gi}kid AŠ.SI-gibil, 189:8;
4. ^{gi}kid-AŠ.SI-sumun, 189:9.
ašgab, *aškāpum*, leatherworker, 208-312 *passim*; LHS 2:2;
kin-ašgab, work of the leatherworkers, 130:19.

^{giš}ba-zu, 120:1?.
babbar, *peṣûm*, white, 83:8; 127:6; 130:11, 14; 153:8; 159:8; 177:2; 178:2; 192:2.
bàd, *dūrum*, wall, 252:12, 21; 310:5, 6, 12;
en-nu bàd, guard of the wall, 251:8, 21, 39.
^{gi}banšur, *paššūrum*, table, 78:3, 7, 9; 80:1; 90:3?; 102:1; 108:1; 115:1; 170:1; 187:2;
^{gi}banšur-sikil, a pure table, 113:3.
bar-da-^{giš}-ig, *bardûm ša daltim*, crossbar of a door, 126:2.
^{giš}*bu-kà-nu-um*, *bukānum*, pestle, 188:5.
^{dug}bur-zi, *pursûm*, *pursītum*, bowl, 167:2; 168:4, 6; 190:8;
sìla-bur-zi, bowl of one sila, 174:3; 184:5.

dabin, *tappinnum*, flour, 98:3; 185:7.
^{giš}dal, *tallum*, traverse beam, 109:2; 156:3; 188:16.
dam, *aššatum*, wife, 91:3.
^{giš}DÙ.EN, 105:2; 109:2; 173:11.
du_8-ši-a, green, 83:12; 117:1, 3, 6, 8; 130:2; 132:2.
du_{10}-ús, *narmakum*, bathroom, 4:2; 151:2.

dub-sar, *ṭupšarrum*, scribe, 62:11; 124:seal a? and b?; 128:seal; 129:seal; 133:seal; 137:seal; 142:4; 159:7; 177:seal; 200:seal; 202:seal; 203:seal.

dug, *karpatum*, vessel,
1. dug 11 sìla, vessel of 11 sila, 173:6;
2. dug 30 sìla, vessel of 30 sila, 167:3; 168:2; 190:10;
3. dug 30 sìla kaš-gin-šè, vessel of 30 sila for ordinary beer, 167:5-6;
4. dug 30 sìla kaš-ú-sa-sig$_5$, vessel of 30 sila for good second quality beer, 167:8;
5. dug 30 sìla ŠU.AL.LA, 167:7;
6. dug-da-al, large vessel(?), 190:6;
7. dug-nag-lugal, drinking vessel for the king, 153:10;
8. dug-sig$_7$-bala, vessel for vinegar, 168:1;
9. dug-sìla-bàn-da, vessel of a small(?) sila, 190:7;
10. dug-sízkur, vessel for offerings, 167:1; 168:3; 173:2; 190:2;
11. dug-ŠÀ.É, 174:1;
12. dug-ŠÀ.GI, 190:1, 11;
13. dug-tu$_7$, soup jar, 103:5;
14. dug-zag-lal dug-nag-lugal, waterproof drinking vessel for the king, 110:2-3; 133:6-7.

^{kuš}dùg-gan, *tukkannum*, bag, 103:LE; 159:1;
1. ^{kuš}dùg-gan ti-bala, courier's pouch, 159:4; 162:4;
2. ^{kuš}dùg-gan ti-bala sila$_4$-máš, courier's pouch of kid leather, 130:15;
3. ^{kuš}dùg-gan-túg, duffle-bag, 157:1; 160:1, 10; 165:1;
4. ^{kuš}dùg-gan-tur, small bag, 128:9;
5. ^{kuš}udu-dùg-gan, sheep-leather bag, 83:13;
6. ^{kuš}udu-dùg-gan-ti-bala, sheep-leather courier's pouch, 159:3.

dul$_4$, *katāmum?*, to cover, 83:4, 9; 94:1; 105:4; 109:3; 150:9, 12.

dumu-lugal, *mār šarrim*, prince, 77:7; 97:5.

dumu-níta-šagina, *mār šakkanakkim*, son of the governor, 92:10.

dumu-SAL, *mārtum*, daughter, 150:13.

^{gi}dur, *ṭurrum*, reed band, 158:11.

^{gi}dúr, *šubtum*, seat, 87:9.

^{giš}dúr-gar, *durga(r)rûm*, stool, 77:8.

e-rí-na, waterproof(?), 157:5;
e-rí-na-íl-me, 273:7.

^{kuš}e-sír, *šēnum*, sandal, 83:6, 17; 181:7;
1. ^{kuš}e-sír é-ba-an, pair of sandals, 128:7; 149:1;
2. ^{kuš}e-sír é-ba-an du$_8$-ši-a, pair of green sandals, 117:6;
3. ^{kuš}súhub-e-sír, 33:3.

é, *bītum*, house, 228:14; 229:5, 19, 26, 27, 29;
1. é-dam, house of the wife, 91:3;
2. é-du$_6$-la, storage house, 9:12; 53:4;
3. é-dumu-lugal, house of the prince, 77:7;
4. é-dumu-níta-šagina, house of the son of the governor, 92:10;
5. é-gal, palace, 24:6; 58:12?; 91:5; 117:11; 136:3; 139:14; 140:14; 141:5; 144:3; 151:6; 155:Rev.2′; 159:10; 166:4; 171:5; 175:3; 188:10, 14; 189:5;
6. é-gal-gibil, new palace, 158:7; 161:4;
7. é-gal-lugal, king's palace, 127:11;
8. é-géme-níg-àr-ra, house of the milling women, 98:7;
9. é-gibil, new house, 94:2; 155:5; 183:2; 257:2;
10. é-GIŠ.LÚ?, 59:3;
11. é-gu$_4$, house of the oxen, 90:6;
12. é-gu$_4$-niga, house of the fattened oxen, 156:4;
13. é-ì-rá-rá, house of the oilpressers, 239:7; 245:7; 250:8; 263:8;
14. é-kišib-ba, storage house, 1:2; 2:2; 3:3; 5:4; 6:2; 8:5; 11:2; 13:2?; 14:2; 16:2; 17:2; 18:2; 19:2; 20:2; 21:2; 28:2; 29:2; 30:2; 31:2; 33:4; 35:2; 36:2; 37:2; 53:6; 143:6; 158:6; 159:6;

15. é-kišib-ba giš-kin-ti simug-‹e-› ne, storage house of the workshop of the blacksmiths, 170:5;
16. é-lú-Ùr-ra, house of the man from Urra, 99:2;
17. é-*mu-na-aḫ-tum* for é-*mānaḫtum*?, workplace, 154:8;
18. é-muhaldim, kitchen, 168:7;
19. é-nar, house of the singers, 256:6;
20. é-nar ki U_4-bar-ra, house of the singers from Ubarra, 82:8;
21. é-nar-SAL ki U-bar-um, house of the female singers from Ubarrum, 104:12;
22. é-nin, house of the lady, 96:6; 151:2;
23. é-Puzur$_4$[ ], house of Puzur-[ ], 191:16;
24. é-SAL, women's house, 95:2; 97:7;
25. é-sagi!, house of the cupbearers, 151:5;
26. é-uš-bar, house of the weavers, 42:3; 43:2;
27. é-uz-ga, house of fattening sheep, 147:5; 154:1; 155:9.

é-ba-an, *tāpalum*, pair, 85:2; 117:1, 6; 128:7; 149:1.

gišÉ.ZABAR, 150:6.

ébih, *ebīḫu*, heavy rope, 81:1;

1. ébih-síg-gin, heavy rope of ordinary wool, 136:1;
2. ébih-síg-ud$_5$, heavy rope of goat's wool, 76:1, 4; 161:1;
3. ébih éš-ur-mah-šè, heavy rope for a lion's leash, 84:1.

en-nu, *maṣṣartum*, guard duty, 251:8, 21, 39.

ésir, *iṭṭûm*, bitumen, 1:1; 62:1, 3; 92:2, 4, 6, 7, 9; 93:5; 97:4, 9; 98:6; 100:2; 103:3, 6; 104:11; 105:1; 130:39; 156:3; 158:5, 8, 12; 173:2, 6, 9, 12; 193:4′, 8′, 11′;
ésir-é-a, bitumen, 2:1; 6:1; 14:1; 15:1; 16:1; 17:1; 18:1; 19:1; 20:1; 27:1; 28:1; 29:1; 30:1; 31:1; 36:1; 37:1; 41:1; 52:1; 62:10; 92:1; 97:1; 106:1; 107:1; 109:1; 127:9; 128:1; 129:1, 4; 133:2; 134:1; 135:1; 137:1; 138:1, 4; 151:1, 4; 153:2, 6; 154:7, 11; 155:4, 8; 156:1; 162:7; 169:1; 170:1; 181:1; LHS 1:1.

éš, *eblum*, *ašlum*, rope,

1. éš-níg-U.NU-a-síg-ud$_5$, rope of goat's wool thread, 114:3;
2. éš-síg-ud$_5$, rope of goat's wool, 75:1, 4;
3. éš-ur-gi$_7$-ra, dog's leash, 101:2;
4. éš-ur-mah, lion's leash, 84:1.

ÉŠ/ŠU.NÍG.UR, 68:8.

kušèš, cover(?),
kušèš má-kaskal-ta gur-ra, cover(?) of a boat returning from a trip, 157:5.

gaba-ri, *gabarû*, copy, 7:8; 8:8; 11:5; 13:5; 14:5; 15:5, LE; 16:5; 17:5; 18:5; 19:5; 22:4; 23:7; 24:11; 25:6; 26:6; 27:5; 28:5; 29:5; 30:5; 31:5; 33:7; 34:6; 36:6; 41:5; 49:4; 50:5; 52:5; 83:LE; 103:LE; 104:LE; 105:LE; 109:LE; 116:LE; 117:LE; 126:LE; 172:LE; 196:2; LHS 1:LE; Sheldon tablet:6, LE;
gaba-ri-dub-ba, copy of the original tablet, 2:6; 3:8; 4:9; 5:8; 6:6; 32:8; 35:7; 37:7; 38:7; 40:11; 53:10.

gada, *kitûm*, linen, 132:2.

gál, *bašûm*, to be,
ì-gál, are in it, 196:2!; 204:3.

gar/gá-gá-dè, *uḫḫuzum*, to apply, 10:6; 33:3?; 85:3; 90:5; 128:7, 9; 129:2; 137:3; 163:5; 177:4; *šakānum*, to place, 100:5; 121:5; 122:2; 159:5; 163:6.

gašam, *apkallum*, craftsman, 222:33.

GAZ-ésir, pestle to crush bitumen, 187:8.

géme Mar-tu, Amorite slave-girl, 146:1.

géme níg-àr-ra, milling woman, 98:7.

gi, *qanûm*, reed, 222:23; 231:21; 232:Rev.7′; 235:2; 242:13, 14;

1. gi-ra, type of processed reed, 47:1;
2. sa-gi, reed bundle, 45:1!; 47:3!; 48:1, 9, 13; 58:1, 10;
3. gu-kilib-sa-gi, bale of reed bundles, 48:1, 3, 13.

gi-gur, *gigurrum* (?), reed basket, 59:2; 210:17;
1. gi-gur 30 sìla, basket of 30 sila, 185:3;
2. gi-gur 60 sìla, basket of 60 sila, 185:2;
3. gi-gur-da, large basket, 120:3, 7; 185:1;
4. gi-gur-dug-tu$_7$, basket for soup jars(?), 103:5;
5. gi-gur-IN, basket from Isin(?), 211:15, 16, 17, 18; 216:19; 217:13; 218:19; 226:17, 18, 19; 227:17, 18, 19; 243:13, 14, 15, 16, 17;
6. gi-gur-mušen, basket for birds, 210:15, 16, 18;
7. gi-gur-níg-gir$_8$-ra, strong basket, 147:2;
8. gi-gur-sag-gá-na, large basket, 147:3.

gi-íl, to carry reed, 245:32.

gi-mun, basket for salt, 104:5.

gi-muš, *gimuššu*, punting pole, 95:1; 96:1.

gi-níg-šu-luh, reed basket for a washing bowl, 87:8.

gi$_6$, *ṣalmum*, black, 104:3, 6, 7; 116:3; 128:5; 130:6; 149:3; 177:1; 178:1; 180:1.

gi$_6$-pàr, *gipa(r)ru*, Giparu, 167:9.

130:6; 149:3; 177:1; 178:1; 180:1.

gi$_6$-pàr, *gipa(r)ru*, Giparu, 167:9.

^{gi}gi$_{16}$, gi$_{16}$-reed, 166:1.

gíd, *mūraku*, length, 57:1, 2, 3; 81:2; 88:1, 2, 4; 91:1, 4; 96:1, 2, 3; 161:2; 193:6′, 7′.

^{gi}gíd, *malīlu*, flute, 103:1; 133:1; 158:1.

^{giš}gíd-da, *ariktum*, spear, 92:7; 125:2.

^{giš}gigir, *narkabtum*, chariot, 73:6; 83:6; 86:3; 91:5?.

gir, *kirrum*, large vessel, 128:1; 151:5; 156:2;
1. gir-du$_{10}$-ús é-nin-a, vessel for the bathroom of the house of the lady, 151:2;
2. gir-gu-la, large vessel, 134:2;
3. gir ki-a-nag nin-a, vessel for the libation of the lady, 138:7;
4. gir má URU.LA.KI, vessel of the . . . boat, 137:2.

gìr, *ša šēp*, conveyor, *passim*.

^{giš}gìr-gub, *girigubbu*, footbench, 114:4; 150:3; 187:6.

giš-hum, *gišḫummu*, bench,
giš-hum-má-lugal, bench of the royal boat, 25:3.

giš-kin-ti, workshop, 3:2; 9:8; 24:8; 32:3; 38:3; 50:3; 52:4; 164:3; 170:5; 208:15; 230:29; 233:9; 237:3; 241:7?, 16?, 32; 242:4; 245:4, 31; 246:Rev.9, 14; 248:7, 21; 249:5, 20; 250:4, 19; 251:5, 20, 27?; 252:11, 20, 29; 254:4; 256:5; 261:3, 7; 263:5; 266:3; 267:3; 273:4; 308:1′, 12′, 24′.

giš.KUR ^{giš}gišimmar, date palm . . . , 91:2.

giš-nú, *eršum*, bed, 79:5; 90:2, 5; 113:1; 187:1;
1. giš-nú-^{giš}hašhur, bed of apple-tree wood, 53:3;
2. giš-nú-^{giš}íldag, bed of poplar wood, 53:1?;
3. giš-nú-nin, lady's bed, 74:1;
4. giš-nú-^{giš}ù-suh$_5$, bed of fir-tree wood, 53:2;
5. giš-nú-umbin-gu$_4$, bed with ox-shaped legs, 150:5.

giš.TUR, 193:5′.

giš-ùr, *gušūrum*, roofbeam, 109:2; 120:2; 188:4, 6, 9, 12, 16.
1. giš-ùr-*a-sa-am*, fitting(?) roofbeam, 188:11;
2. giš-ùr asal, roofbeam of poplar wood, 88:1; 95:3; 188:1;
3. giš-ùr dal, traverse roofbeam, 188:16.

^{giš}gišimmar, *gišimmarum*, date-palm, 91:2; 92:1;
^{giš}gišimmar UŠ×SA, 92:3.

gu-dim$_4$-ba-gada, type of linen,
gu-dim$_4$-ba-gada du$_8$-ši-a, green . . . linen, 132:2.

gu-kilib-sa-gi, bale of reed bundles, 48:1, 3, 13.

$^{giš/urudu}$gu-za, *kussûm*, chair, 92:6; 162:8?; 187:3;

1. ^{giš}gu-za má-gan, chair from Magan, 143:2;
2. ^{giš}gu-za-SAL, woman's chair, 150:2;
3. ^{giš}gu-za si-ús, stuffed chair, 143:1, 4; 150:1;
4. ^{giš}gu-za sír-da é-ba-an, a pair of sedan chairs, 85:2;
5. ^{giš}gu-za šu-nígin, chair for the assembly, 113:2;
6. ^{giš}gu-za ú?-tu lugal-ka, 10:5;
7. ^{giš}gu-za zag-ús, armchair, 83:14; 150:15.

gu-za-lá, *guzalûm*, thronebearer, 156:5; 161:5.

gu_4, *alpum*, ox, 90:6?; 150:5; see under kuš-; gu_4-niga, fattened ox, 156:4.

gu_4-gaz, ox slaughterer, 102:6; 121:2.

$gudu_4$, *pašīšum*, priest, 103:4.

gur, *târum*, to return, 157:5.

gur_7, *kārum*, granary, 167:10; 174:5; 195:5; 225:3, 15, 16; 265:11?.

^{gi}gurdub (GÁ×GI), reed basket, 235:22, 23, 24; 242:Rev. 2′, 3′, 4′, 5′, 6′; 244:21, 22, 23; 251:30, 31, 32, 33, 34.

guruš, 53:5.

guškin, *ḫurāṣum*, gold, 75:7; 114:5; 116:2.

^{gi}hal, *ḫallu*, reed container, 99:1;

1. ^{gi}hal AB.BA, 173:5;
2. ^{gi}hal *mu-du-lum*, reed container for salted meat?, 170:3;
3. ^{gi}hal síg, reed container for wool, 170:2.

^{na_4}HAR šu sè-ga, *erûm qadum narkabišu*, millstone with its upper stone, 187:4.

^{giš}hašhur, *ḫašḫūrum*, apple-tree, 53:3.

ḫu-pu-um, *ḫuppum*, basket, 90:4; 95:4?; 188:13; 193:3′; 195:4.

ì, *šamnum*, oil, 32:1; 44:1; 130:3, 7, 16, 33; 150:10, 16, 18; 160:12;

1. ì ba-a-dé, strained oil, 130:9;
2. ì ba-ab, 150:11;
3. ì-du_{10}-ga, fine oil, 157:4; 160:2;
4. ì-giš, sesame oil, 38:1; 49:1?; 50:1; 83:1;
5. ì-udu, mutton fat, 51:1, 3.

ì-du_8, *atûm*, doorkeeper, 127:12.

ì-rá-rá, *raqqûm*, oil presser, 157:7; 159:13; 239:7; 245:7; 250:8; 263:8.

ì-šur, *ṣāḫitum*, preparer of sesame oil, 163:7.

^{giš}ig, *daltum*, door, 76:7; 77:7; 83:11; 89:1; 97:3; 153:1; 158:7?; 159:10; 169:4; 178:3; 179:2; 180:2; 186:7, 10; 188:2, 8;

1. ^{giš}ig-abul, gate's door, 148:2;
2. ^{giš}ig-díb, door with panels, 70:3; 81:4; 192:3;
3. ^{giš}ì-dul_4, door covered with oil, 94:1;
4. ^{giš}ig mi-rí-za, door made of small boards, 127:1; 172:3;
5. ^{giš}ig-suh_4, door of reed matting, 92:9; 96:4; 155:1; 175:1; 193:9′, 13′;
6. ^{giš}ig-suh_4 tur, small door of reed matting, 97:3;
7. bar-da-^{giš}ig, crossbar of a door, 126:2.

^{giš}íldag, *ildakku*, poplar tree, 51:1; 53:1?; 125:1.

im, *ṭuppum*, tablet, 162:LE; 205:16; im-sar-ra, inscribed tablet, 100:4; 155:Rev.1′; 158:4; 206:12.

im-babbar, *gaṣṣum*, gypsum, 13:1; 100:3; 127:10.

im-KÙ.GI, *lēru*, mineral color, 5:2; 51:7; 83:5, 9; 130:8, 35; 150:8, 15.

ír, *tazzimtum*, lamentation, ír gu-la, great lamentation, 190:12.

IŠ abbreviation of kin-sahar, earthwork, 277:3, 4, 7, 8, 9, 10, 17, 18, 24, 25, 26; 297:2, 3, 6, 7, 8, 12, 13, 14, 15, 20, 21; 298:3, 4; 299:3, 4.

KA.AH, type of wool, 116:7.

^{kuš}ka-dù, *ermum*, cover, 83:10; 159:9.

KA-gìr, *padānum*, road, 107:2; LHS 1:2.

^{giš}ka-$kara_4$, *kanna/iškarakkum*, type of table, 150:4.

ka-tab, *katammum*, lid, 93:4; 110:2; 128:10; 133:6; 157:5; 160:13; 195:1;

ka-tab dug-nag-lugal, lid for the king's drinking vessel, 153:10.

^{giš}ká, *bābum*, gate, 109:2; 193:5′, 12′;
1. ká-é-gal, palace gate, 188:10;
2. ká é-gal-lugal, gate of the king's palace, 127:11;
3. ká é-gibil, gate of the new house, 155:5.

^{giš}kak-sal$_4$, *saparrum*, chariot or cart, 131:5.

kaskal, *ḫarrānum*, (business) trip, 149:8; 157:5; 284:10; 285:10; 287:10; 288:10; 289:10; 290:10; 291:10; 292:10; 305:10.

kaš, *šikārum*, beer,
1. kaš-gín, ordinary beer, 167:6;
2. kaš-ú-sa-sig$_5$, good second quality beer, 167:8.

kaš-dé-a, *qerītum*, banquet, festival,
1. kaš-dé-a dingir-re-e-ne, banquet of the gods, 167:11;
2. kaš-dé-a ^{d}En-ki, banquet of Enki, 168:8;
3. u$_4$-kaš-dé-a, day of the banquet, 171:3; 190:9.

kešda/kéš-dè, *rakāsum*, to bind, wrap, 90:7; 114:6; 164:2; 195:4$^?$.

ki-a-nag, place of libation, 138:7.

ki-kuš-gar-ra for ugnim? *ummānum*, army, 189:6.

ki-lá, weight, 68:9; 73:3, 5; 74:2; 76:2, 5; 81:3; 84:2; 86:2; 161:3; 163:2.

ki-sá-a, *kisûm*, part of the wall, 22:7; 81:5; 125:5; 192:4; 272:15.

ki-ti-tum, kitītum, fine wool, 79:1, 3.

^{gi}kid, *kītum*, reed mat, 185:4$^?$;
1. ^{gi}kid AŠ.SI-gibil, 189:8;
2. ^{gi}kid AŠ.SI-sumun, 189:9;
3. ^{gi}kid ^{giš}ig-é-gal-gibil, reed doormat of the new palace, 158:7;
4. ^{gi}gi$_{16}$-kid, mat of gi$_{16}$-reed, 166:1.

kin, *šiprum*, work, 82:11; 130:19, 22, 25; 170:7;
1. kin-sahar, earth work, see IŠ;
2. kin-til-la, finished work, 147:4; 150:9$^?$, 12.

kišib, *kunukkum*, seal, *passim*;
1. kišib-ra, to roll a seal, 130:3;
2. kišib-ra-a, sealed tablet, 159:5; 196:2$^?$.

ku$_4$, *erēbum*, to enter, 141:5; 189:5.

ku$_6$, *nūnum*, fish,
1. ku$_6$-sar, 103:4;
2. ku$_6$-ú-sa, 87:4.

kun-zi-da, *meḫrum*, weir, 208:3, 4, 7, 8, 9, 16, 17, 18, 19, 20, 21, 23, 24.

kurum$_7$-ak, *piqittum*, inspection, LHS 2:5; kurum$_7$-ak gašam-e-ne, inspection of the craftsmen, 222:32-33.

kus$_7$, *kizûm*, equerry, 107:3; LHS 1:3.

kuš, *maškum*, skin, 82:1;
1. kuš-a-GAR-nag-a, dehaired skin, 23:3, 4;
2. kuš-amar, skin of a young animal, 12:2;
3. kuš-du$_8$-ši-a, green skin, 117:3, 8;
4. kuš-du$_8$-ši-a-máš-gal, green full-grown goat skin, 130:13;
5. kuš-gu$_4$, oxhide, 7:1; 12:1; 23:1; 39:2; 40:1; 55:1; 68:2; 83:9; 127:3, 4; 130:28; 182:1, 3, 5;
6. kuš-gu$_4$-babbar, white oxhide, 83:8; 159:8; 178:2; 192:2;
7. kuš-gu$_4$-gi$_6$, black oxhide, 104:6; 178:1; 180:1;
8. kuš-gu$_4$-mu-2, hide of a two year old ox, 68:4;
9. kuš-gu$_4$-mu-2-babbar, white hide of a two year old ox, 127:6;
10. kuš-gu$_4$-mu-2-síg-mú, hairy hide of a two year old ox, 127:8;
11. kuš-gu$_4$-mu-3, hide of a three year old ox, 68:3; 127:5;
12. kuš-gu$_4$-síg-mú, hairy oxhide, 68:6; 127:7; 148:1;
13. kuš-gu$_4$-ú-háb, red oxhide, 83:7, 16; 117:2, 7; 128:3; 130:1; 149:2; 179:1; 192:1;
14. kuš-sag-gu$_4$, oxhide of prime quality(?), 39:1;
15. kuš-máš, goat skin, 83:4;

16. kuš-máš-du$_8$-ši-a, green goat skin, 83:12;
17. kuš-máš-gal, skin of a full-grown goat, 23:2; 39:5; 40:4; 55:3; 130:30; 162:3; 191:1; Sheldon tablet:1;
18. kuš-máš-gal-gi$_6$, black skin of a full-grown goat, 104:3, 7; 116:3; 130:6; 149:3; 177:1;
19. kuš-máš-gal-ú-háb, red skin of a full-grown goat, 104:8; 130:2;
20. kuš-máš-níta, skin of a male goat, 34:2; 39:6; 40:5; 130:31;
21. kuš-máš-níta-babbar, white skin of a male goat, 130:14;
22. kuš-sila$_4$, lamb skin, 40:6; 130:32;
23. kuš-sila$_4$-kin-gi$_4$-a, skin of a lamb for cultic purposes, 26:3;
24. kuš-sila$_4$-máš, skin of a kid, 39:7;
25. kuš-sila$_4$-ú-háb, red lamb skin, 56:1;
26. kuš-udu, sheepskin, 22:1; 23:4; 26:2; 34:1; 39:4; 40:3; 93:1, 3; 130:29; 152:1; 157:2; 159:2; 160:11, 13; 162:2; 191:5, 8, 9; 195:1, 2, 4, 6; Sheldon tablet:2;
27. kuš-udu-babbar, white sheepskin, 130:11; 153:8; 177:2;
28. kuš-udu-gi$_6$, black sheepskin, 128:5;
29. kuš-udu-síg-mú, hairy sheepskin, 23:4;
30. kuš-udu-ú-háb, red sheepskin, 128:8, 10;
31. kuš-udu-a-lum, *alum* sheepskin, 7:2; 26:1; 39:3; 40:2; 55:2; 162:1;
32. kuš-udu-a-lum-e-rí-na, waterproof(?) *alum* sheepskin, 157:5;
33. kuš-udu-a-lum-ú-háb, red *alum* sheepskin, 128:4;
34. kuš-zag-bar, leather scraps, 63:2.

lal, *šaqālum*, to weigh, 74:5; 76:8; 81:6; 84:5; 85:4; 86:4; 136:2.

la(l)u$_6$, *ribbatum*, arrears, 80:1, 3, 5, 10, 13, 16; 314:1, 5, 11, 18, 25, 27.

^{dug}lahtan, *laḫtānum*, beer vat, 173:1, 4;

^{dug}lahtan-gíd-da, pointed beer vat, 158:10.

lí-iq-tum, *liqtum*, selected, 33:1.

^{kuš}lu-úb, *luppum*, leather bag,

1. ^{kuš}lu-úb-gu$_4$-gal-sumun, large old oxhide bag, 68:1;
2. ^{kuš}lu-úb-sir, bag to carry metals, 71:6.

lú-kas$_4$, *lāsimum*, courier, 78:5, 10.

lú-kin-gi$_4$-a, *mār šiprim*, messenger, 149:9.

lú-má-gal-gal, 137:4.

lugal, *šarrum*, king, 4:3; 9:8; 10:5; 25:3; 33:3; 87:9; 110:3; 117:1; 118:9; 127:11; 129:6; 133:7; 153:10; 189:4; 190:12; 230:33; 295:19.

^{giš}ma-al-tum, *majjāltum*, bed, 150:7; 187:9.

^{gi}ma-an-sim, *nappītum*, sieve, 154:10; 211:19!;

1. ^{gi}ma-an-sim dabin, sieve for barley flour, 98:3; 185:7;
2. ^{gi}ma-an-sim níg-àr-ra, sieve for flour, 98:4; 185:8;
3. ^{gi}ma-an-sim zì-gu, sieve for pea-flour, 185:6;
4. ^{gi}ma-an-sim zì-gu-sig$_5$, sieve for fine pea-flour, 98:1;
5. ^{gi}ma-an-sim zì-gu-ús, sieve for ordinary pea-flour, 98:2.

ma-da-nu-um, *mandanum*, basket, 166:2.

^{gi}ma-sá-ab, *masabbum*, basket, 121:1, 3, 7, 9; 122:1, 5, 7, 9; 166:3; 171:1;

^{gi}ma-sá-ab tur, small basket, 170:4.

^{gi}MA.ŠA, 234:22, 23, 24.

má, *elippum*, boat, 157:5;

1. má-Dilmun^{ki}-gu-la, large Dilmun boat, 129:2;
2. má-^{d}En-ki, Enki's boat, 30:7;
3. má-gu-la-lugal, large royal boat, 129:6;
4. má-lugal, royal boat, 25:3; 295:19;
5. má-Ma-rí^{ki}, Mari boat, 237:9;
6. má-tur, small boat, 77:4; 88:6; 128:1;
7. má-URU.LA.KI$^{?}$, 135:5; 137:2;

8. ki-má-a-ka, the place of the boats, 246:Rev.3, 17.
má-lah$_4$, *malāḫum*, boatsman, 128:2; 129:7.
Mar-tu, *Amurrûm*, Amorite, 90:7; 118:3, 5; 121:4; 122:2; 146:2; 165;3?.
géme Mar-tu, Amorite slave-girl, 146:1.
máš, *urīṣum*, goat, see kuš-.
máš-da-ri-a, *irbum*, offering, 24:5.
máš-šu-gíd-gíd, *bārûm*, diviner, 118:2.
maškim, *rābiṣum*, inspector, 124:7; 128:13; 129:8; 135:6; 137:5; 146:3; 149:10; 159:13.
mu-du-lum, muddulum, salted meat, 170:3.
mu-túm, delivery, *passim*.
mu$_4$, *labāšum*, to cover(?), 77:8.
muhaldim, *nuḫatimmum*, cook, 108:4; 154:2, 4, 6.

^{giš}*na-aḫ-ba-tum, naḫbātum*, case, 8:1; 112:1; 116:1;
kuš-udu-*na-aḫ-ba-tum*, sheep-leather case, 195:2.
na-ap-tá-nu-um, naptanum, banquet, 166:4; ki-*na-ap-tá-nu-um*, place of the banquet, 102:5; 171:2.
na-kab-tum, nagabtum, place for domestic animals, 122:3.
na$_4$, *abnum*, stone, 22:2?.
nagar, *nagārum*, carpenter, 208-312:*passim*; LHS 2:1;
1. nagar-lugal, royal carpenter, 230:33;
2. kin-nagar, work of the carpenters, 82:11.
nar, *nārum*, singer, 82:8; 256:6;
nar-SAL, female singer, 104:12.
níg, thing, property, 121:4; 122:2; 130:40.
níg-àr-ra, flour, 98:4; 185:8.
níg-ba, *qīštum*, present, 83:6; 113:4; 118:9; 146:2.
níg-dab$_5$, *nindabûm*, offering, 167:4; 168:5, 7.
níg-ga, *makkūrum*, property, 53:5.
NÍG.GA.GA.TUM, 184:2.
níg-gál-la, materials, 170:6; 189:10.
níg-gir-ra, kneading(?), 97:2.
níg-gù-dé, provisions, 3:2; 24:7; 25:2; 32:2; 38:2; 50:2; 52:3.
níg-ka$_9$, *nikkassum*, account, 9:2, 7.
níg-kin-ezen, festival works, 261:4, 8, 10, 12.
níg-kud, *miksum*, custom dues, 15:2; 27:2; 41:2; 52:2.
NÍG.MAŠ, 184:1.
NÍG.NI.DU$_8$.HU.UM, 184:3.
níg-pi-lu$_5$-da, cult objects, 128:12.
níg-SUD?-a guškin, 75:7.
níg-šu-luh, washing bowl, 87:8.
níg-šu-tag$_4$-a, *šūbultum*, official present, níg-šu-tag$_4$-a Mar-tu, official present for the Amorites, 165:3.
níg-U.NU-a, thread,
1. níg-U.NU-a síg-gi, thread of the wool of the uligi-sheep, 74:3;
2. níg-U.NU-a síg-gin, thread of ordinary wool, 140:4!, 11; 141:3; 142:2; 144:2; 145:1;
3. níg-U.NU-a síg-gin-ga-ríg, thread of combed ordinary wool, 136:2;
4. níg-U.NU-a síg-ud$_5$, thread of goat's wool, 54:2; 71:1; 104:10; 114:3; 130:24, 40; 131:3; 139:1; 140:5, 8, 12; 141:1; 142:1; 144:1; 162:6; 163:4.
^{giš}NÍG.UMBIN-gu-la, 136:3;
^{giš}NÍG.UMBIN-gu-la-PA.HU, 44:2.
NIM, 45:8.
nimgir, *nāgirum*, herald, 164:1.
nin, *bēltum*, lady, 90:2; 96:6; 138:7; 151:2; 183:5; 257:5.
nu-gub/nu, absent, 208-312:*passim*.
nu-kiri$_6$, *nukaribbum*, gardener, 9:13; 24:2; 25:4.
^{giš}nu-KU, 89:2.
^{giš}nu-kuš, *nuku(š)šû*, door pivot, 89:3; 155:2; 169:2; 193:2′, 10′.
nu-ub-tuk, did not take place, 197:2; 198:2; 199:1; 200:1; 201:2, LE; 202:1; 203:1.
nu-úr-ma, *nurmû*, pomegranate, 130:10, 36;
1. nu-úr-ma-duru$_5$, fresh, moist pomegranate, 24:3;

2. A.HA-^{giš}nu-úr-ma, 24:1;
3. ^{giš}A.HA-nu-úr-ma, 25:1.

^{giš}PA.DA, 46:1, 4, 6, 9.
peš-murgu, date-palm spine, 78:12; peš-murgu-^{gi}banšur, table of date-palm spines, 78:7, 9.
^{gi}pisan, *piš/sannum*, basket, 147:1; 184:4; 191:4;
1. ^{gi}pisan-dub-ba, tablet basket, 100:1;
2. ^{gi}pisan-GAL.ZA.LUM, 87:6;
3. ^{gi}pisan-hal, basket, 8:3;
4. ^{gi}pisan-im-sar-ra, tablet basket, 158:4;
5. ^{gi}pisan-ku$_6$-sar, basket for . . . fish, 103:4;
6. ^{gi}pisan-ku$_6$-ú-sa, basket for . . . fish, 87:4;
7. ^{gi}pisan-*na-aḫ-ba-tum*, basket used as a case, 8:1; 112:1;
8. ^{gi}pisan-níg-gir$_8$-ra, strong basket, 154:1, 3, 5; 155:7;
9. ^{gi}pisan-ninda, bread basket, 187:5$^?$;
10. ^{gi}pisan-suh$_4$, basket of reed matting, 8:2;
11. ^{gi}sag-pisan-gíd-da, large long basket, 173:8.

ra, *maḫāṣum*, to beat, 124:3.
rá-gaba, *rakbum*, rider, 84:4; 100:7; 115:3; 118:4; 151:3.

sa, *gīdum*, catgut, 116:5; 117:5, 10; 130:18, 38; 149:6.
SA.EZEN, 65:2.
sa-gi, reed bundle, 45:1$^!$; 47:3$^!$; 48:1, 9, 13; 58:1, 10.
sá-du$_{11}$, *sattukkum*, regular offering, 103:2; 133:3; 158:3.
^{giš}sag-gul, *sikkūrum*, bolt, lock, 155:3; 169:3; 193:1′, 14′.
sagi, *šāqium*, cupbearer, 110:seal; 115:3; 119:seal; 125:3; 137:6; 151:5$^!$, 7$^?$; 153:4; 155:6; 158:13; 167:4; 168:5.
sahar, *eperum*, earth, see IŠ.
si, *malûm*, to fill, 82:7.
síg, *šipātum*, wool, 79:2, 4; 170:2;
1. síg-^{giš}ga-ríg-ak, combed wool, 42:1;
2. síg-^{giš}ga-ríg-ak 4-kam-ús, combed wool of fourth quality, 10:1, 3;
3. síg-gi, wool of the uligi-sheep, 73:1, 4; 74:3;
4. síg-gin, ordinary wool, 9:11; 42:2; 85:1; 136:1; 140:4$^!$, 11; 141:3; 142:2; 144:2; 145:1;
5. síg-gin-^{giš}ga-ríg, ordinary combed wool, 43:1; 136:2;
6. síg-gin-šu-peš$_5$, ordinary plucked wool, 86:2;
7. síg-peš$_5$-a, plucked wool, 4:1;
8. síg-ud$_5$, goat's wool, 3:1; 9:1, 10; 11:1; 21:1; 35:1; 54:2; 60:1; 61:1; 64:1; 65:1; 66:1; 69:1; 71:1; 72:1, 10; 75:1, 4; 76:1, 4; 101:1; 104:10; 106:2; 114:3; 130:24, 40; 131:3; 139:1; 140:5, 8, 12; 141:1; 142:1; 144:1; 161:1; 162:6; 163:4.
síg-mú, hairy, 23:4; 68:6; 127:7, 8; 148:1.
sig$_4$, *libittum*, brick, 216:8, 9, 10; 217:7, 8, 9, 14$^!$, 16, 17, 18, 21, 22, 23.
sig$_7$-bala, vinegar, 168:1.
sila$_4$, *puḫādum*, lamb, see kuš-.
simug, *nappāḫum*, smith, 170:5.
sipa-ur-ra, dog herdsman, 101:6.
sízkur, *niqûm*, offering, 115:2; 167:1; 168:3; 173:2; 190:2; sizkur-gur$_7$, offerings of the granary, 167:10; 174:5.
sub$_6$/su-ba*, to coat, 92:2*; 170:1.
^{kuš}súhub, *suḫuppatum*, boot, 250:31;
1. ^{kuš}súhub-e-sír, 33:3;
2. ^{kuš}súhub-lugal du$_8$-ši-a é-ba-an, pair of green royal boots, 117:1.
sukkal, *sukkallum*, messenger, 48:5; 128:13; 146:3.
sukkal-mah, *sukkalmaḫḫum*, high court official, 111:1′; 129:8; 135:6; 149:10; 159:13; 183:4.

šà-ba, in it, 163:3.

šà-bi-ta, out of which, 78:2; 82:4; 83:3.

šà-tam, *šatammum*, 62:12; 86:7; 106:5; 107:4; 118:7; 124:10; 130:40; 136:2; 143:5, 7; 164:4.

^{giš}ŠÀ.TAR, 82:6; 104:1.

šà-tuku$_5$, *šēlī'tum*, mattress, 66:2;

šà-tuku$_5$ sè-ga, stuffed mattress, 113:1.

šagina, *šakkanakkum*, governor, 92:10; 109:5.

^{dug}šáman, *šappatu*, bowl, 128:10;

1. ^{dug}šáman-ì, bowl for oil, 160:12;
2. ^{dug}šáman-ì-du$_{10}$-ga, bowl for fine oil, 157:4, 160:2;
3. ^{giš}šáman-nimgir, bowl for heralds, 164:1.

še-gín, glue, 5:1; 51:5; 63:3; 70:1; 82:3, 10; 90:1; 104:4, 9; 114:2; 116:4; 117:4, 9; 127:2$^?$; 128:6; 130:17, 37; 149:5; 162:5; 176:1; 177:3.

še-giš-ì, *šamaššammū*, sesame, 163:6.

ŠID.DA.LAL, 116:2.

šitim, *itinnum*, builder, 276:4; 277:2; 279:4; 280:4; 282:4; 283:3, 4; 284:4; 285:3, 4; 287:2, 3, 4; 288:2, 3, 4; 289:2, 3, 4; 290:3, 4; 292:1; 305:2, 3;

ki-šitim, place of the builders, 212:2; 215:4; 216:5; 217:4.

ŠU.DÍM, 208:2; 291:5; 292:5; 293:5; 294:5.

šu e-sír-bi šà-ba, its shoe-mold is included(?), 149:2.

šu-i, *gallābum*, barber, 62:5.

^{giš}šu-nir, *šurīnum*, *šurinnu*, emblem, 176:2.

šu-ti, *maḫārum*, to receive, *passim*.

ŠU.URU.GÁ A-*al-la-ḫa-ru*, 33:2.

^{giš}ŠU$_4$.A, *littum*, stool,

^{giš}ŠU$_4$.A du$_{10}$-ús, stool for the bathroom, 4:4.

ták-ši-ru-um, *takšīrum*, repair, 129:5; 135:2.

^{giš}taskarin, *taskarinnum*, boxwood, 88:5.

tu-ra, *marṣum*, ill, 208-312: *passim*.

tù-uk-šu, *tukšum*, shield, 97:8.

túg, *ṣubātum*, cloth,

1. túg-HU.LA-síg-gi$_4$, 73:2;
2. túg-NÍG.DUL-síg-gi GUL, 73:4;
3. túg-ŠE.LI.TUM-síg-gi, 73:1;
4. túg-U.ŠUDUN, 86:1.

túg-du$_8$, felter, 3:6; 9:5; 60:9; 72:11; 208-312 *passim*; LHS 2:4;

1. túg-du$_8$-^{kuš}súhub, felter of boots, 250:31;
2. kin-túg-du$_8$, work of the felters, 130:25.

tug-du$_8$-a, *kiššum*, felt, 33:3;

1. túg-du$_8$-a-babbar, white felt, 116:6;
2. túg-du$_8$-a-SU.A-síg-gin, . . . felt of ordinary wool, 85:1.

^{giš}tukul, *kakkum*, weapon;

^{giš}tukul-Mar-tu, Amorite weapon, 90:7.

túl, *būrtum*, cistern, 156:4.

ú-háb, red, 56:1; 83:7, 16; 104:8; 117:2, 7; 128:3, 4, 8, 10; 130:1, 12; 149:2; 179:1; 192:1.

ú-háb, *ḫūratum*$^?$, madder, 130:4.

^{giš}ù-suh$_5$, *ašūḫu*, fir tree, 53:2; 57:1, 2, 3, 4; 88:3$^?$; 91:1, 4; 95:1; 96:1, 3, 5; 175:2; 183:1; 186:5$^?$, 8, 11;

^{giš}ù-suh$_5$-gal, large fir tree, 96:2; 183:7.

UD.KI.AN.UD, 108:2.

udu, *immerum*, sheep, see kuš-.

ugnim, *ummānum*, army, 45:10; 47:8$^?$; 189:6$^?$.

ugula, *waklum*, overseer, 33:9; 48:4; 314:6, 12, 19, 26;

ugula uš-bar, overseer of the weavers, 183:6.

^{giš}umbin, *ṣuprum*, leg,

1. ^{giš}umbin-^{giš}dúr-gar, leg of a stool, 77:8;
2. ^{giš}umbin-giš-nú, leg of a bed, 90:5;
3. umbin-gu$_4$, oxshaped leg, 150:5.

^{kuš}ummu(d), *nādum*, waterbag, 110:1; 119:1; 133:5; 135:3!;
^{kuš}ummu(d)-máš-gal, waterbag of full-grown goat leather, 128:11; 130:12.
ur-gi$_7$, *kalbum*, dog, 101:2.
ur-mah, *nēšum*, lion, 84:1.
urudu, *erûm*, copper, 124:1; 132:1; 162:8.
uš-bar, *i/ušparum*, weaver, 42:3; 43:2; 183:6.
UŠ×SA, 92:3;
^{giš}UŠ×SA-ša$_6$, 193:6′, 7′.

^{giš}ZA.AN.KA/ZÀ.AN.KA, 163:1;
^{giš}ZÀ.AN.KA-giš-nú-nin, 74:1.
za-ḫi-ru-um, šāḫirum?, shoe straps, 149:4.
za-mi-ri-tum, zamirītum, household utensil or weapon, 67:1; 118:1; 124:1.

^{giš}zà-mi, *sammûm*, lyre, 104:2;
^{giš}zà-mi-sumun, old lyre, 82:5.

zag-bar, scraps, 63:2.

^{gi}ZAR.ZAR, 98:5; 154:9; 185:5.

zé-na, *zinûm*, midrib of frond of the date-palm, 78:1.

zi, to issue,
1. zi-ga, issue, *passim*;
2. ba-zi, issued, *passim*;
3. zi, to levy, 208-312: *passim*.

zì, *qēmum*, flour,
1. zì-gu, pea-flour(?), 185:6;
2. zì-gu-sig$_5$, good pea-flour(?), 98:1;
3. zì-gu-ús, ordinary pea-flour(?), 98:2;
4. zì-sig$_{15}$, coarse flour, 70:2.

CONCORDANCE OF MUSEUM NUMBERS

Museum Number	Text	Museum Number	Text
Ash. 1932–240	63	NBC 5608	42
Ash. 1932–241	149	NBC 5617	124
Ash. 1932–242	65	NBC 5619	259
Ash. 1932–243	135	NBC 5622	258
Ash. 1932–249	61	NBC 5623	268
Ash. 1932–250	64	NBC 5624	264
Ash. 1932–251	152	NBC 5629	19
Ash. 1932–252	23	NBC 5630	18
Ash. 1932–253	157	NBC 5631	88
Ash. 1932–254	306	NBC 5632	35
Ash. 1932–255	162	NBC 5638	24
Ash. 1932–257	33	NBC 5643	210
Ash. 1932–258	119	NBC 5645	129
Ash. 1932–259	110	NBC 5649	43
Ash. 1932–260	62	NBC 5651	229
Ash. 1932–261	114	NBC 5654	272
Ash. 1932–262	56	NBC 5669	103
Ash. 1932–379	307	NBC 5671	13
Ash. 1932–383	117	NBC 5688	234
Ash. 1932–384	40	NBC 6336	116
Ash. 1932–400	302	NBC 6358	108
Ash. 1932–401	82	NBC 6361	255
Ash. 1932–403	81	NBC 6362	262
Ash. 1932–405	7	NBC 6365	136
Ash. 1932–408	191	NBC 6369	265

Museum Number	Text	Museum Number	Text
NBC 6370	138	NBC 7065	142
NBC 6372	69	NBC 7070	15
NBC 6374	106	NBC 7073	126
NBC 6377	165	NBC 7077	30
NBC 6382	39	NBC 7078	94
NBC 6386	90	NBC 7085	6
NBC 6387	239	NBC 7091	36
NBC 6390	213	NBC 7092	261
NBC 6393	224	NBC 7094	107
NBC 6397	274	NBC 7098	11
NBC 6414	223	NBC 7099	67
NBC 6417	68	NBC 7109	115
NBC 6422	92	NBC 7110	199
NBC 6424	134	NBC 7118	44
NBC 6436	91	NBC 7120	27
NBC 6442	211	NBC 7121	22
NBC 6446	271	NBC 7122	143
NBC 6447	153	NBC 7131	34
NBC 6448	291	NBC 7135	250
NBC 6450	244	NBC 7136	228
NBC 6454	140	NBC 7140	158
NBC 6461	8	NBC 7142	151
NBC 6473	16	NBC 7144	257
NBC 6476	109	NBC 7155	183
NBC 6477	247	NBC 7156	270
NBC 6479	28	NBC 7158	254
NBC 6482	20	NBC 7164	3
NBC 6487	176	NBC 7167	305
NBC 7043	29	NBC 7168	215
NBC 7049	31	NBC 7170	277
NBC 7062	2	NBC 7173	206
NBC 7063	132	NBC 7175	235

Museum Number	Text	Museum Number	Text
NBC 7177	208	NBC 7357	100
NBC 7178	150	NBC 7362	169
NBC 7183	96	NBC 7365	14
NBC 7185	301	NBC 7366	49
NBC 7187	47	NBC 7368	122
NBC 7189	289	NBC 7388	217
NBC 7190	139	NBC 7391	168
NBC 7197	155	NBC 7394	275
NBC 7199	242	NBC 7396	133
NBC 7201	72	NBC 7398	185
NBC 7203	209	NBC 7400	57
NBC 7205	137	NBC 7404	172
NBC 7213	167	NBC 7412	4
NBC 7215	287	NBC 7416	266
NBC 7216	283	NBC 7417	145
NBC 7217	214	NBC 7418	144
NBC 7218	154	NBC 7429	163
NBC 7221	75	NBC 7442	186
NBC 7225	207	NBC 7450	285
NBC 7227	125	NBC 7452	197
NBC 7233	171	NBC 7454	97
NBC 7234	202	NBC 7456	120
NBC 7236	184	NBC 7457	187
NBC 7239	51	NBC 7459	76
NBC 7244	161	NBC 7463	95
NBC 7250	84	NBC 7468	46
NBC 7252	17	NBC 7471	164
NBC 7255	5	NBC 7472	297
NBC 7262	279	NBC 7473	127
NBC 7266	226	NBC 7474	298
NBC 7268	240	NBC 7475	219
NBC 7269	236	NBC 7479	303

Museum Number	Text	Museum Number	Text
NBC 7480	45	NBC 7602	204
NBC 7483	220	NBC 7608	102
NBC 7484	212	NBC 7609	141
NBC 7486	256	NBC 7620	79
NBC 7493	269	NBC 7621	203
NBC 7498	121	NBC 7624	201
NBC 7505	60	NBC 7629	200
NBC 7508	181	NBC 7639	118
NBC 7519	196	NBC 7640	188
NBC 7522	12	NBC 7643	112
NBC 7527	105	NBC 7648	276
NBC 7534	156	NBC 7652	296
NBC 7535	50	NBC 7653	216
NBC 7536	310	NBC 7656	189
NBC 7537	193	NBC 7657	290
NBC 7544	58	NBC 7658	232
NBC 7548	253	NBC 7659	48
NBC 7555	314	NBC 7661	294
NBC 7556	237	NBC 7664	205
NBC 7557	248	NBC 7670	233
NBC 7558	246	NBC 7672	245
NBC 7559	241	NBC 7673	59
NBC 7568	147	NBC 7717	304
NBC 7571	89	NBC 7721	71
NBC 7572	10	NBC 7732	86
NBC 7574	299	NBC 7742	177
NBC 7577	170	NBC 7743	198
NBC 7578	146	NBC 7745	99
NBC 7593	37	NBC 7746	178
NBC 7597	131	NBC 7747	180
NBC 7598	148	NBC 7752	182
NBC 7599	1	NBC 7760	190

Museum Number	Text	Museum Number	Text
NBC 7784	55	NBC 8468	173
NBC 7791	313	NBC 8475	225
NBC 7796	179	NBC 8478	218
NBC 8011	80	NBC 8484	38
NBC 8016	174	NBC 8486	87
NBC 8022	293	NBC 8489	9
NBC 8023	292	NBC 8492	222
NBC 8024	280	NBC 8496	54
NBC 8025	249	NBC 8497	73
NBC 8026	281	NBC 8499	267
NBC 8027	284	NBC 8500	311
NBC 8028	288	NBC 8503	66
NBC 8079	77	NBC 8504	175
NBC 8136	113	NBC 8508	312
NBC 8139	238	NBC 8510	192
NBC 8235	130	NBC 8520	263
NBC 8299	309	NBC 8521	70
NBC 8414	85	NBC 8852	260
NBC 8425	52	NBC 8887	286
NBC 8428	74	NBC 8888	273
NBC 8433	25	NBC 8906	278
NBC 8435	21	NBC 8939	300
NBC 8439	26	NBC 8944	308
NBC 8441	41	NBC 8945	282
NBC 8442	101	NBC 8946	221
NBC 8443	252	NBC 8952	53
NBC 8444	251	NBC 8953	295
NBC 8445	230	NBC 9177	93
NBC 8454	231	NBC 9224	123
NBC 8462	195	NBC 9227	111
NBC 8463	227	NBC 9282	32
NBC 8466	98	NBC 9462	243

Museum Number	Text
NBC 9931	128
NBC 9932	194
NBC 9995	83
NBC 10069	160
NBC 10073	159
NBC 10075	104
NBC 10076	166
ZRL (now HSM) 134	78
LHS 1	46
LHS 2	46
Mr. Sheldon tablet	46

CATALOGUE OF SEAL IMPRESSIONS

seal a:	124	seal B or M:	177
seal b:	124	seal M:	128
seal c:	64		129
	69		137
seal d:	60		200
	61		202
	72	seal O or c:	65
seal e:	147	seal T:	203
seal f:	98	illegible:	59
seal g:	111		63
	123		99
seal h:	152		135
seal i:	119		253
seal j:	110		274
seal B:	133		275

TEXTS IN TRANSLITERATION

LHS 1

Obv. 10 (sìla) ésir-é-a
KA-gìr-šè
Šu-^{d}Nin-kar-ak kus$_7$
šu ba-an-ti
gìr *Kur-ru-ub-Èr-ra*
Rev. u$_4$ 19-kam
iti kin-^{d}Inanna
mu en ^{d}Inanna máš-e
ì-pà
L.E. gaba-ri

LHS 2

4 nagar-me
5 ašgab-me
7 ad-KID
3 túg-du$_8$-me
kurum$_7$-ak
u$_4$ 25-kam
gub-ba-àm
19 guruš
iti kin-^{d}Inanna

Mr. Sheldon

13 kuš-máš-gal
4 kuš-udu
ki *Šu-Eš$_4$-tár*-ta
Šu-^{d}Nin-kar-ak
šu ba-an-ti
gaba-ri
kišib ^{d}Nanna-ki-ág
iti gu$_4$-si-su
mu bàd *Eš$_4$-tár-tá-ra-am-^{d}Iš-bi-Èr-ra*
ba-dù
L.E. gaba-ri

AUTOGRAPHED TEXTS

PLATE I

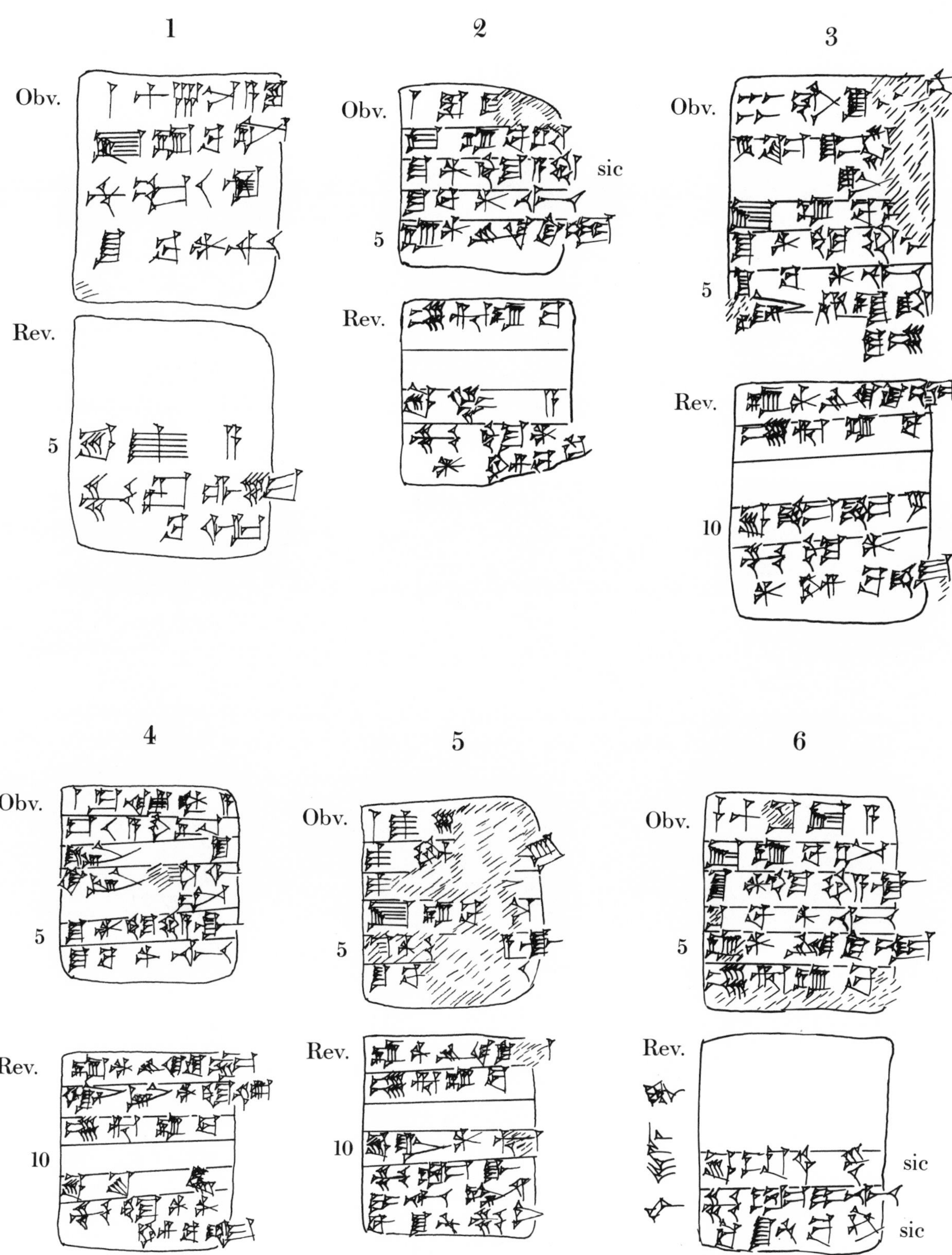
1
Obv.
Rev.
5
2
Obv.
sic
5
Rev.
3
Obv.
5
Rev.
10
4
Obv.
5
Rev.
10
5
Obv.
5
Rev.
10
6
Obv.
5
Rev.
sic
sic

PLATE II

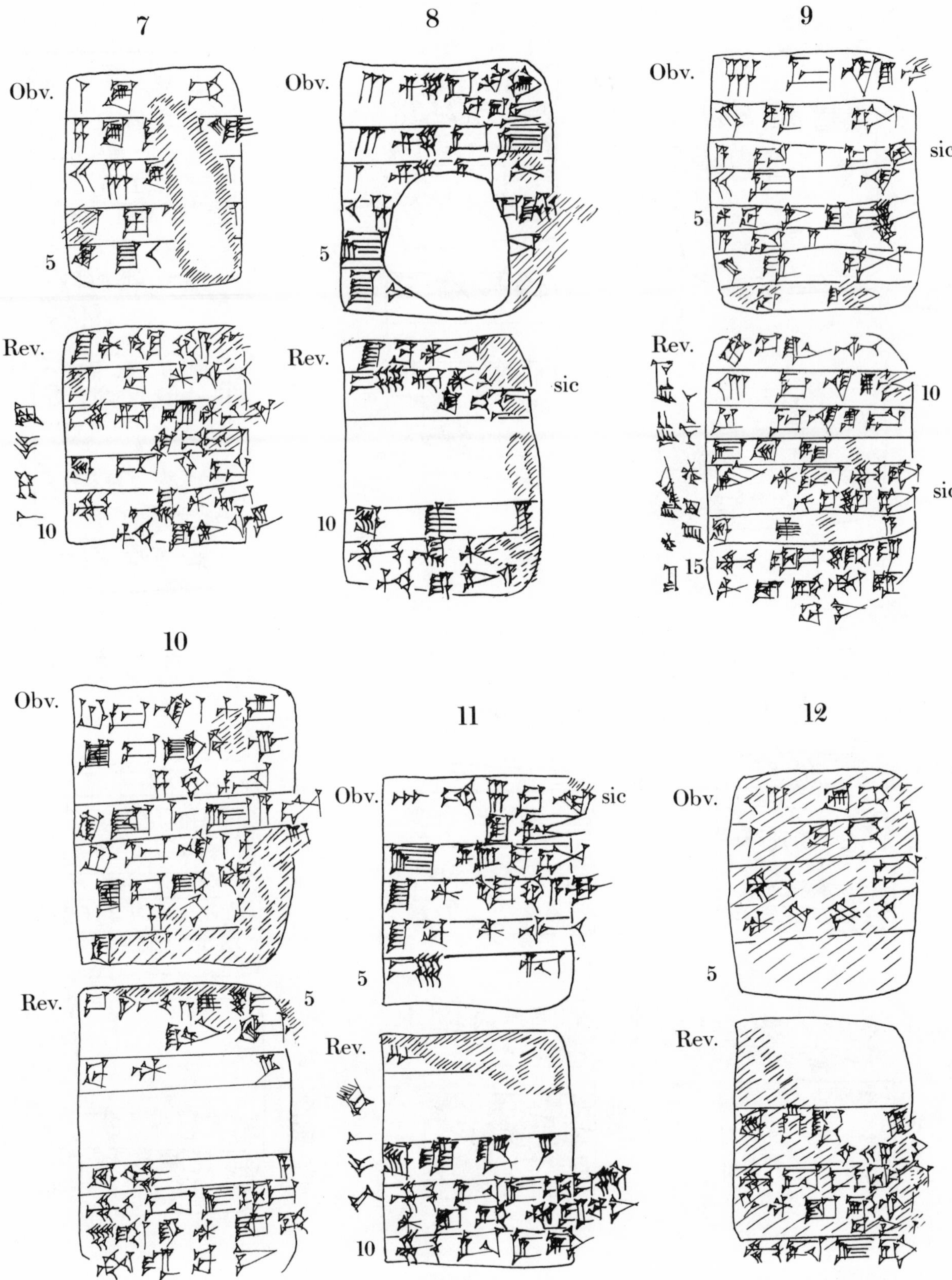

7
Obv.
Rev.
8
Obv.
Rev.
sic
9
Obv.
sic
Rev.
sic
10
Obv.
Rev.
11
Obv.
sic
Rev.
12
Obv.
Rev.

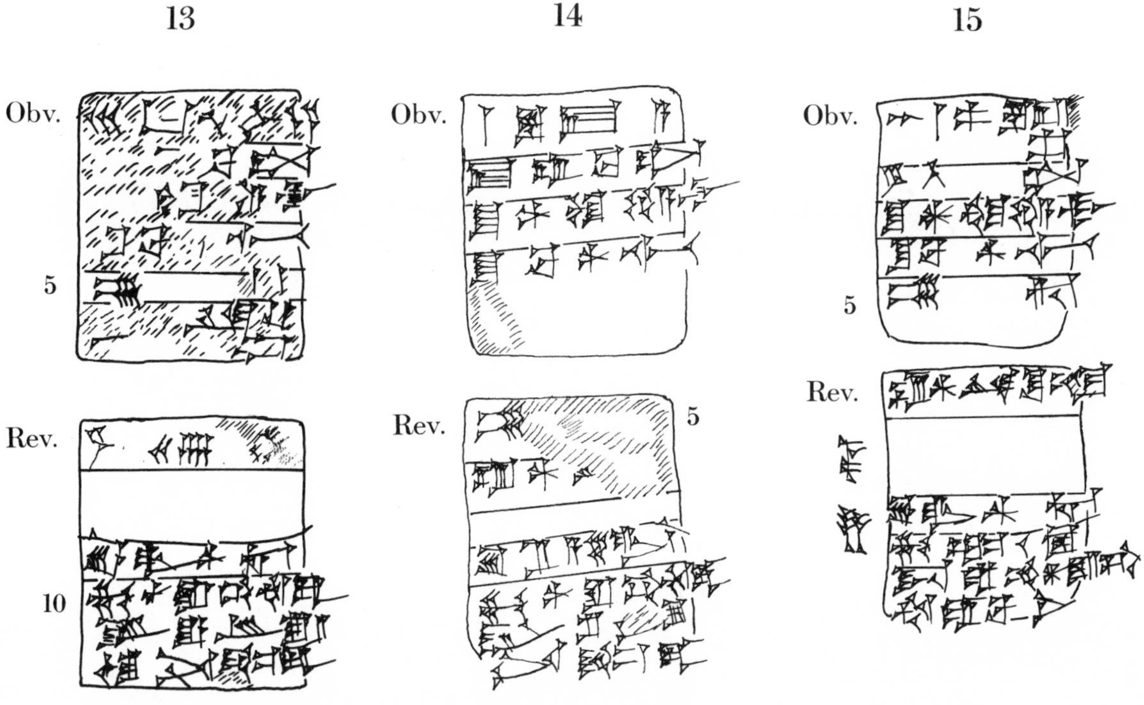

13
14
15
Obv.
Rev.
sic

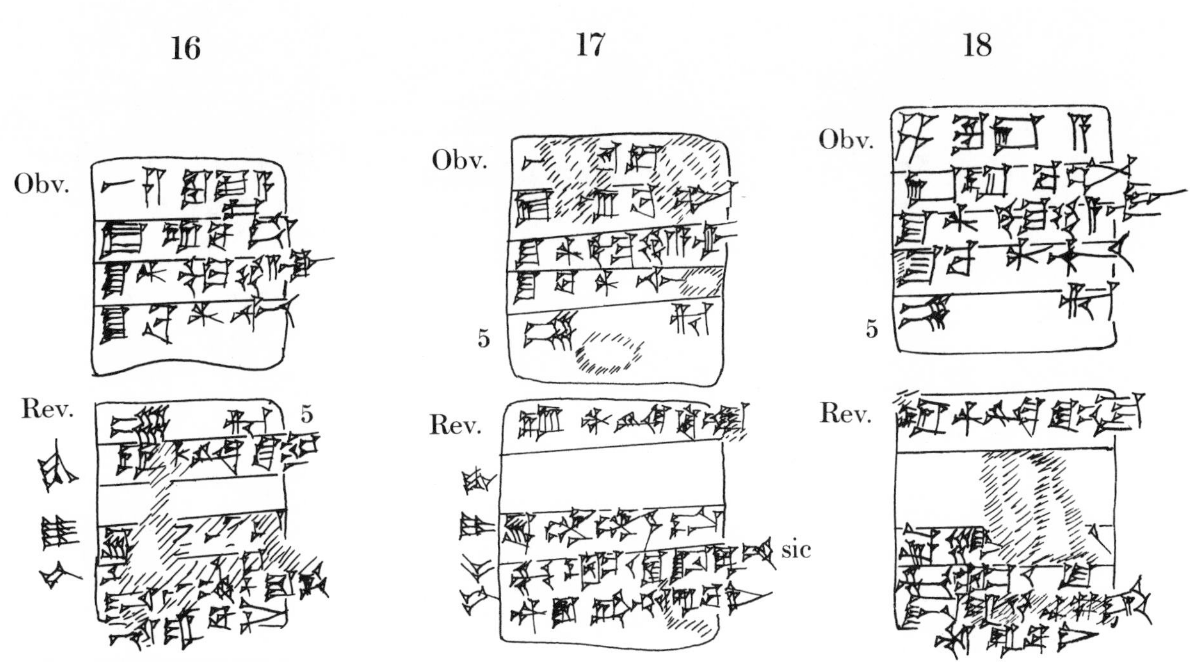

16
17
18
Obv.
Rev.
sic

PLATE IV

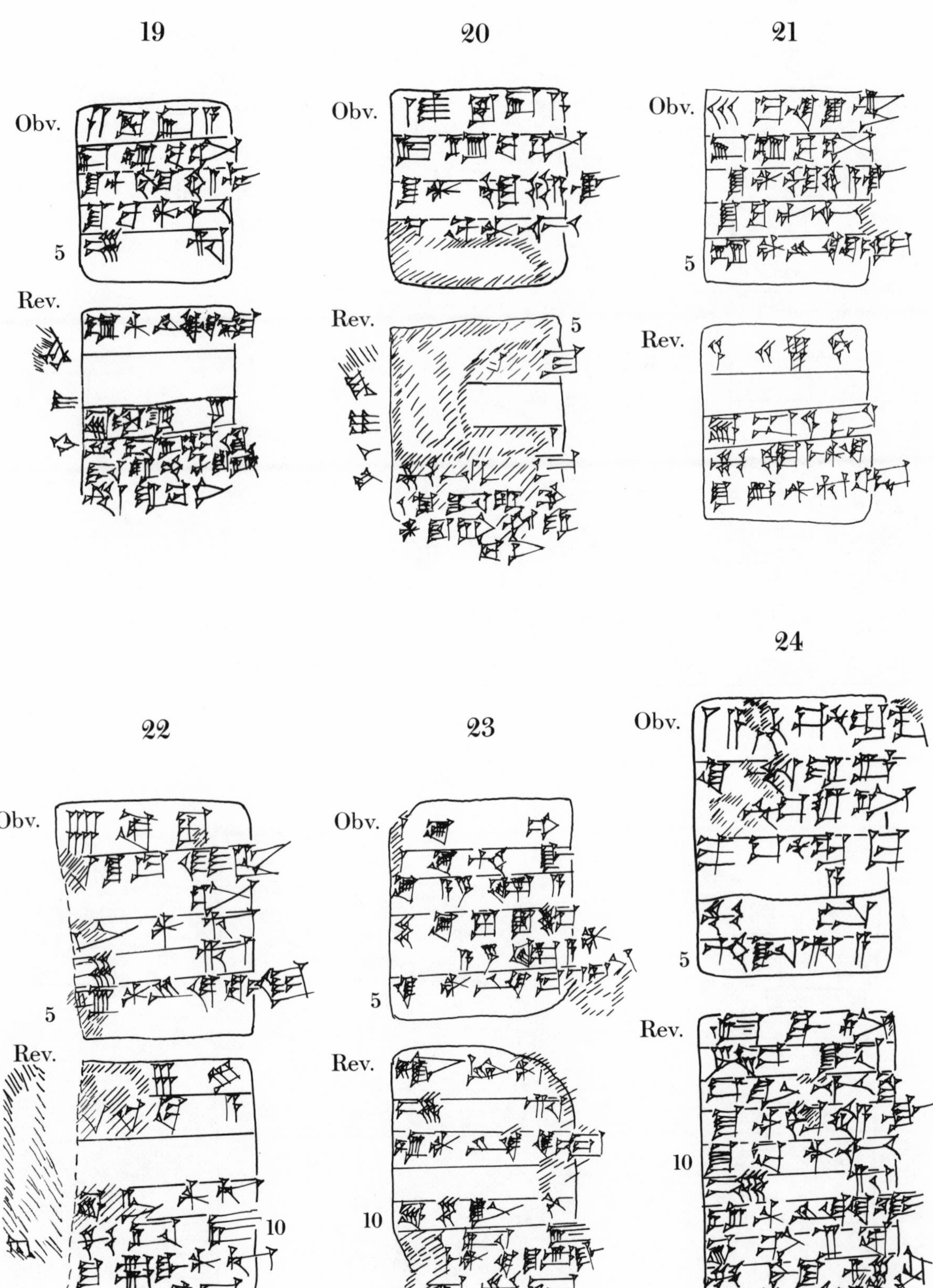

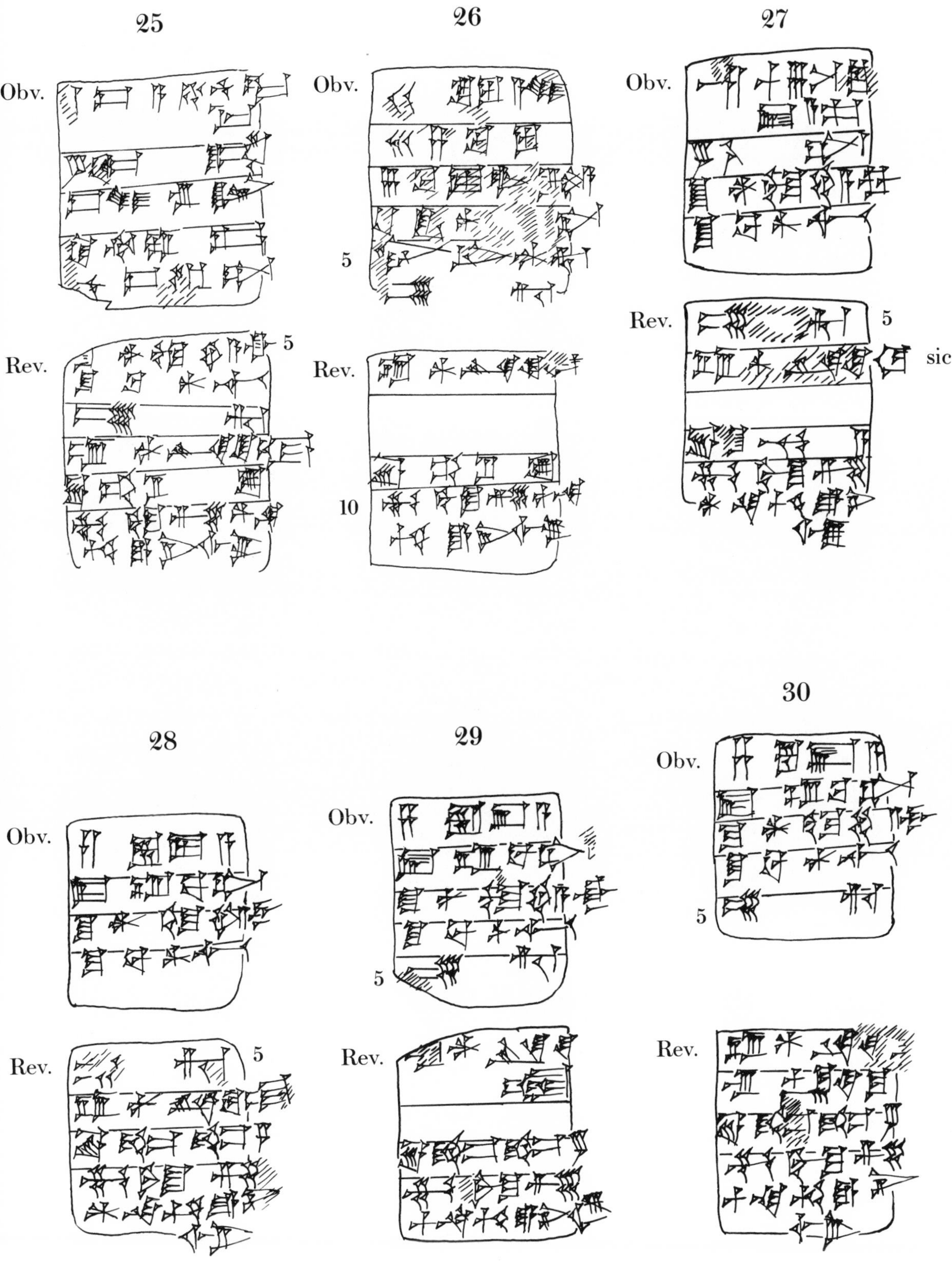
25
Obv.
Rev.
5
26
Obv.
5
Rev.
10
27
Obv.
Rev.
5
sic
28
Obv.
Rev.
5
29
Obv.
5
Rev.
30
Obv.
5
Rev.

PLATE VI

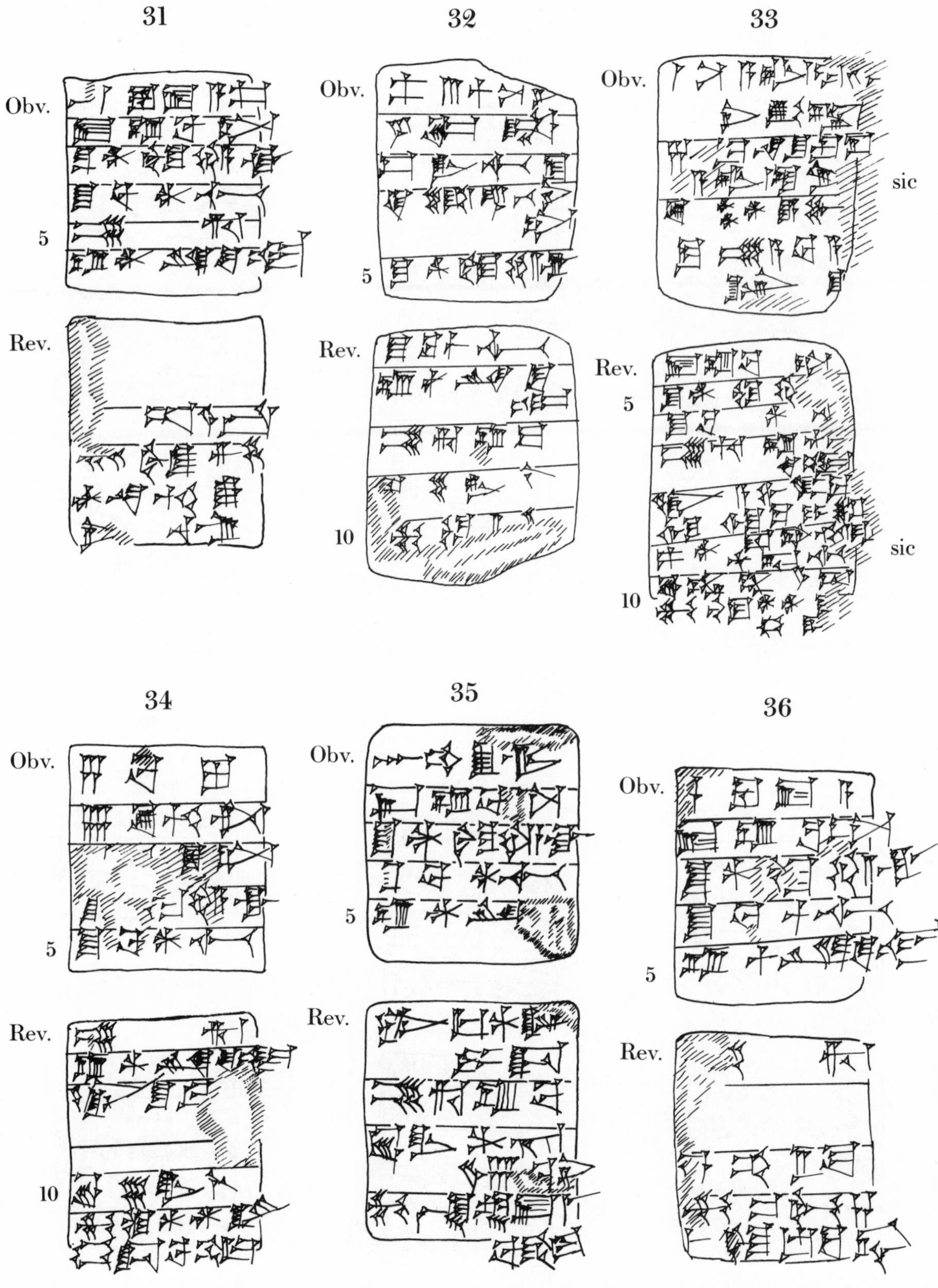

31
32
33
Obv.
Obv.
Obv.
sic
Rev.
Rev.
Rev.
sic
34
35
36
Obv.
Obv.
Obv.
Rev.
Rev.
Rev.

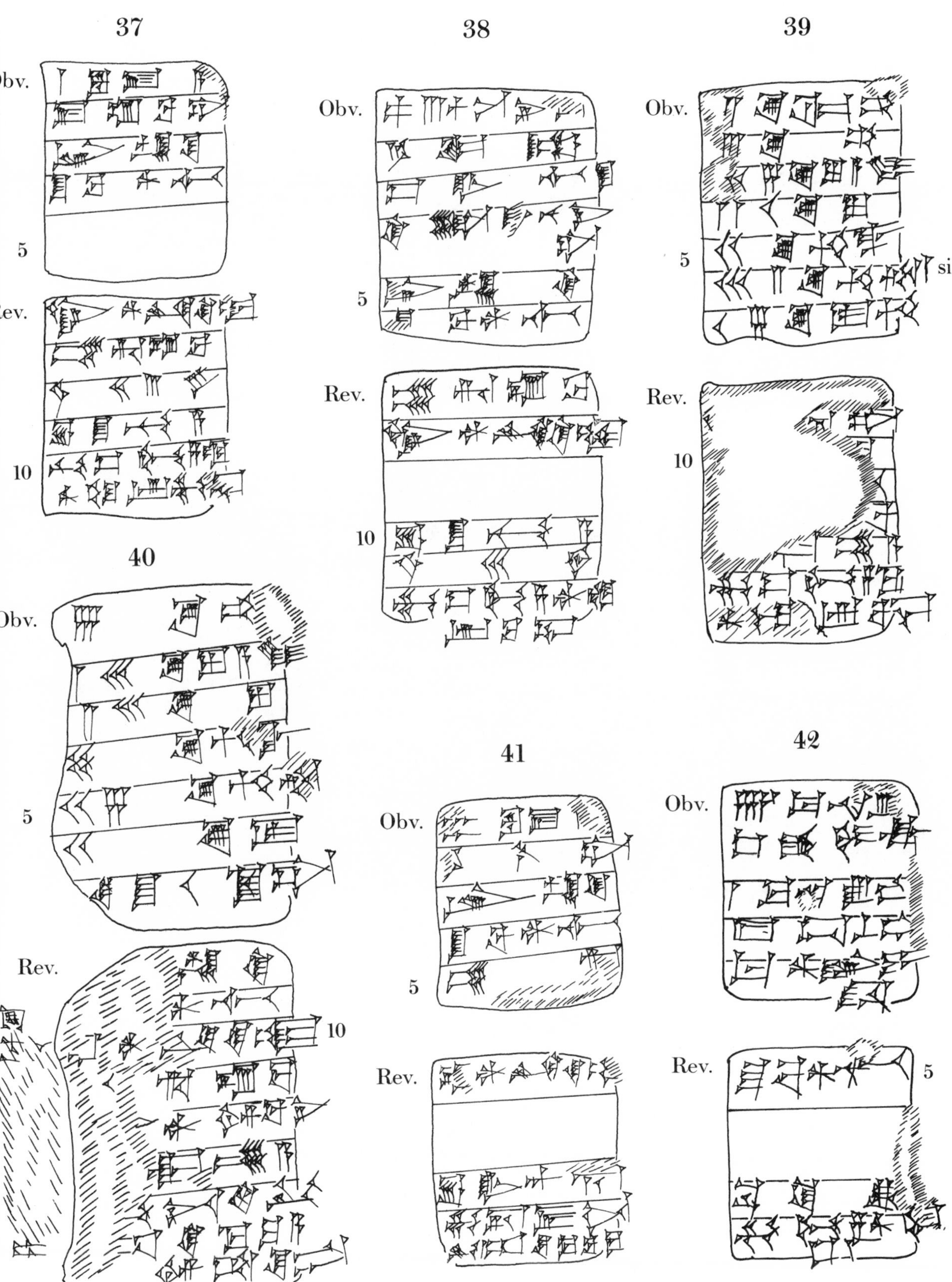
37
Obv.
5
Rev.
10
38
Obv.
5
Rev.
10
39
Obv.
5
sic
Rev.
10
40
Obv.
5
Rev.
10
41
Obv.
5
Rev.
42
Obv.
Rev.
5

PLATE VIII

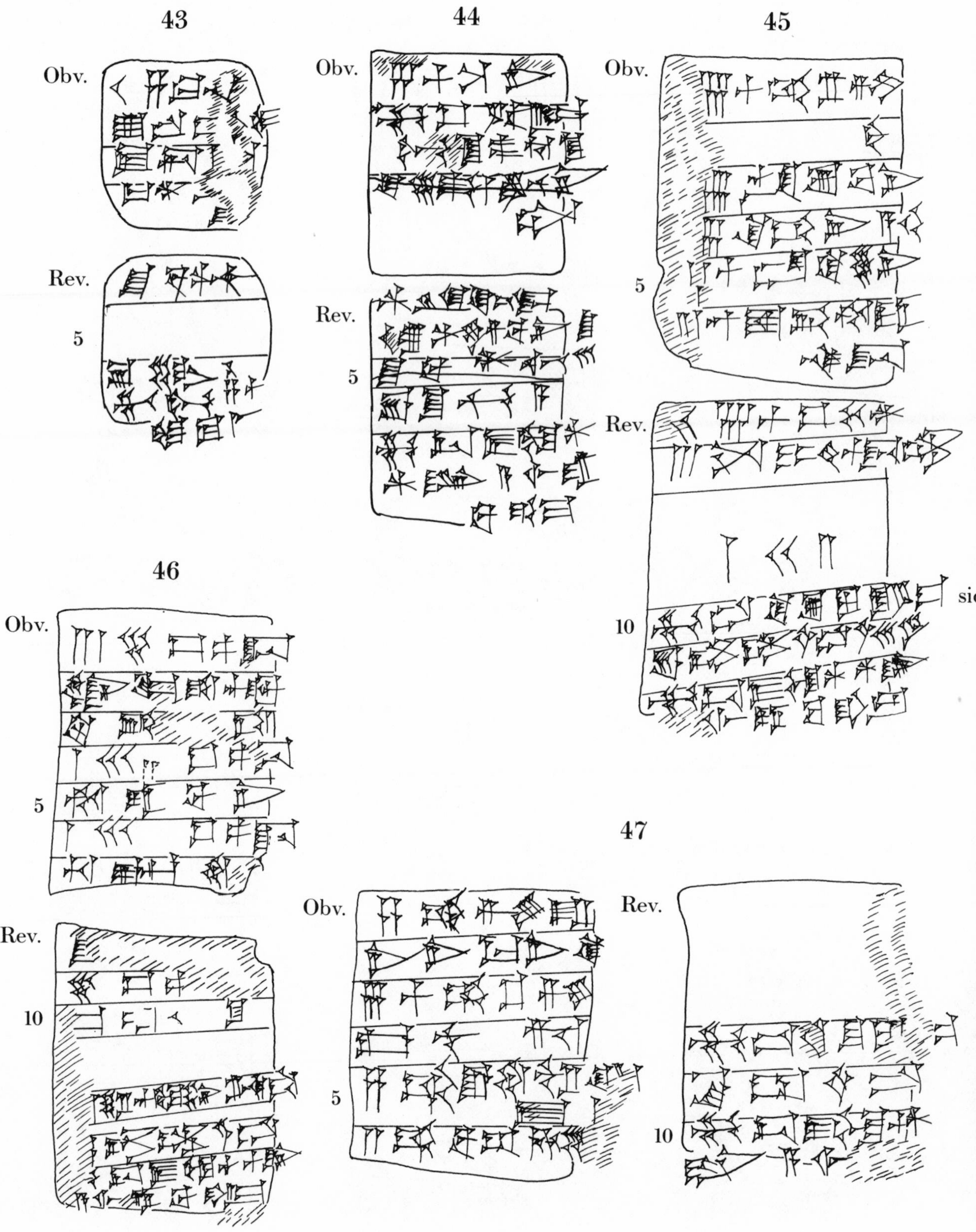

43
Obv.
Rev.
5
44
Obv.
Rev.
5
45
Obv.
5
Rev.
sic
10
46
Obv.
5
Rev.
10
47
Obv.
5
Rev.
10

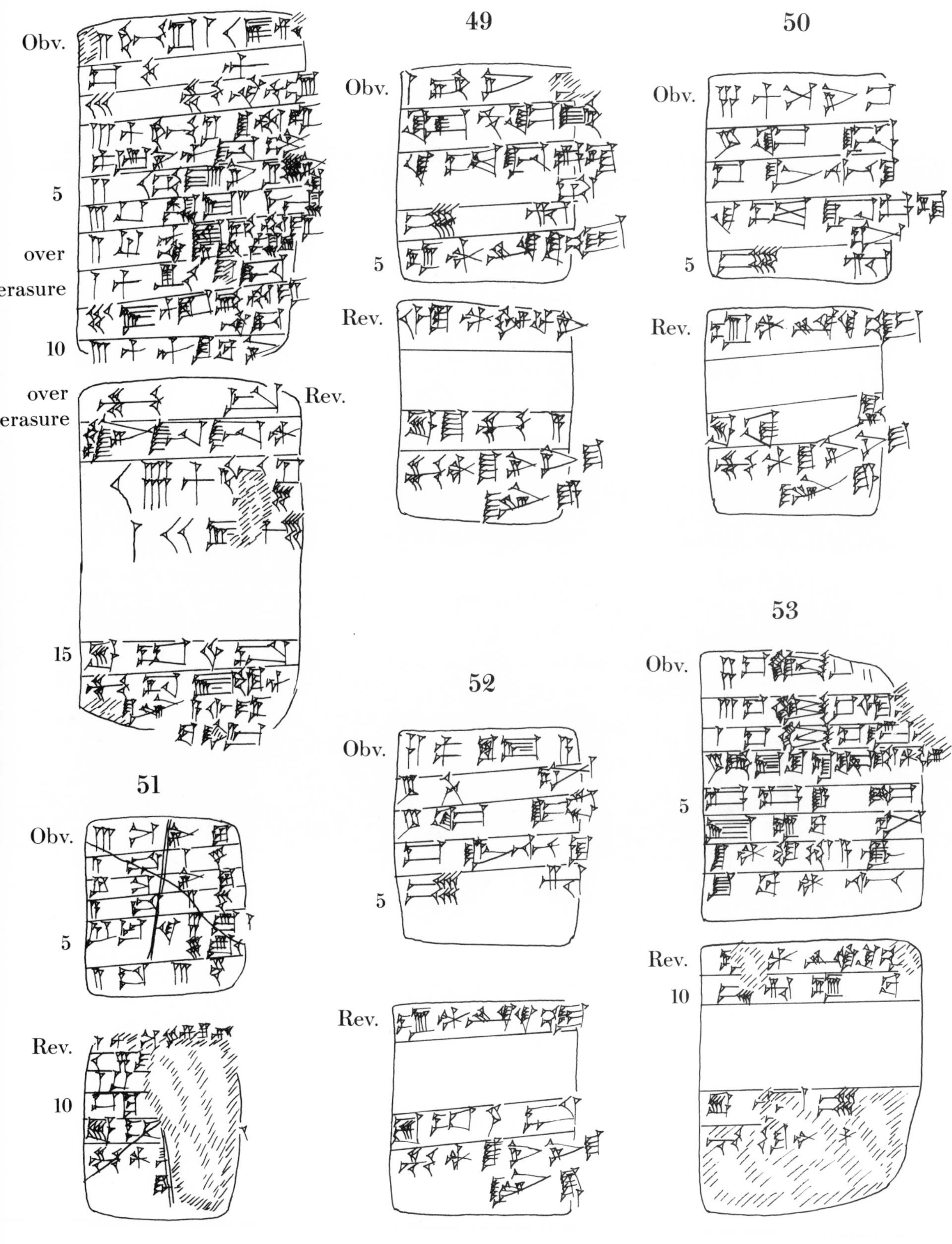
48
Obv.
over
erasure
over
erasure
Rev.
49
Obv.
Rev.
50
Obv.
Rev.
51
Obv.
Rev.
52
Obv.
Rev.
53
Obv.
Rev.

PLATE X

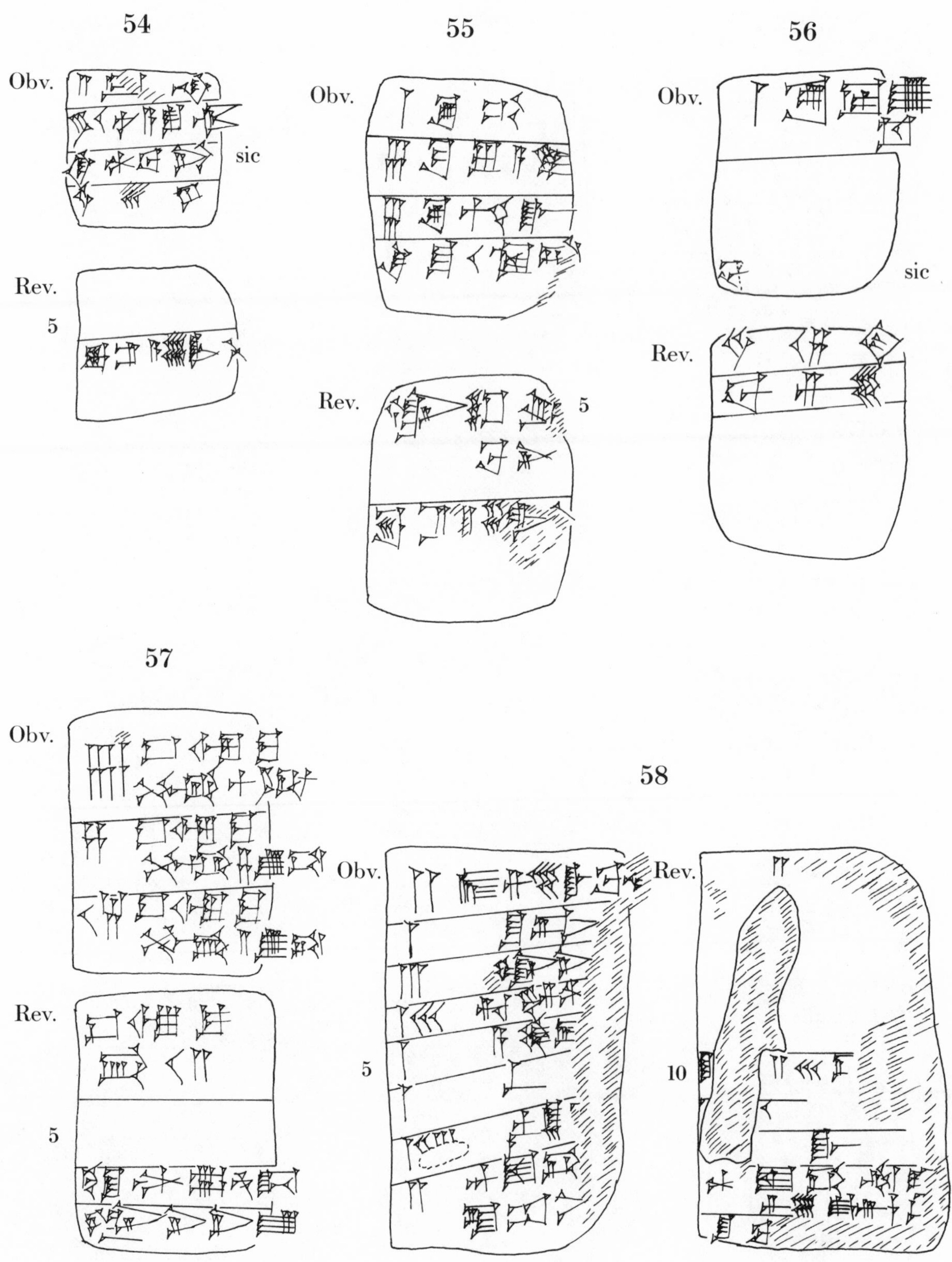

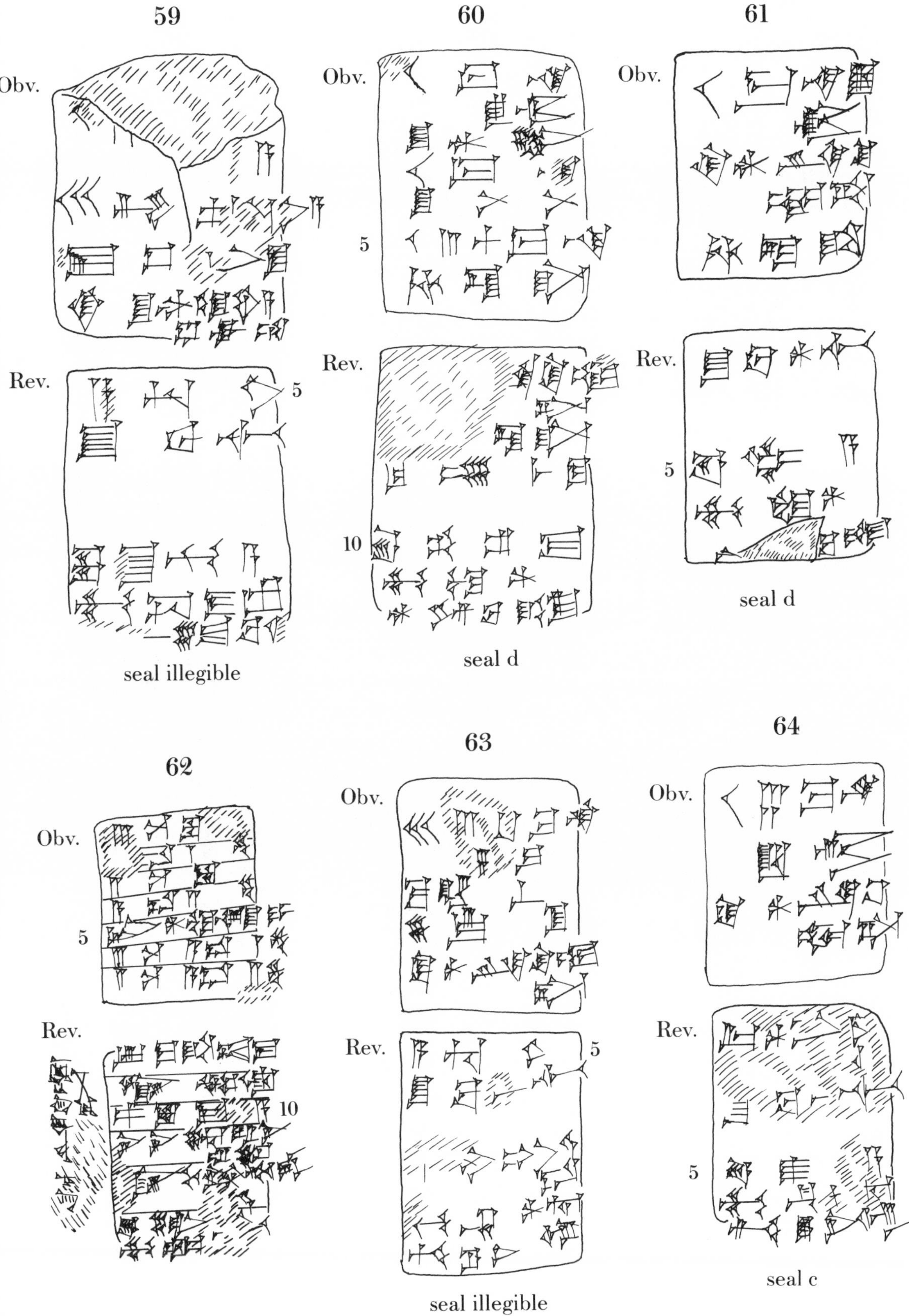
59
Obv.
Rev.
seal illegible
60
Obv.
Rev.
seal d
61
Obv.
Rev.
seal d
62
Obv.
Rev.
63
Obv.
Rev.
seal illegible
64
Obv.
Rev.
seal c

PLATE XII

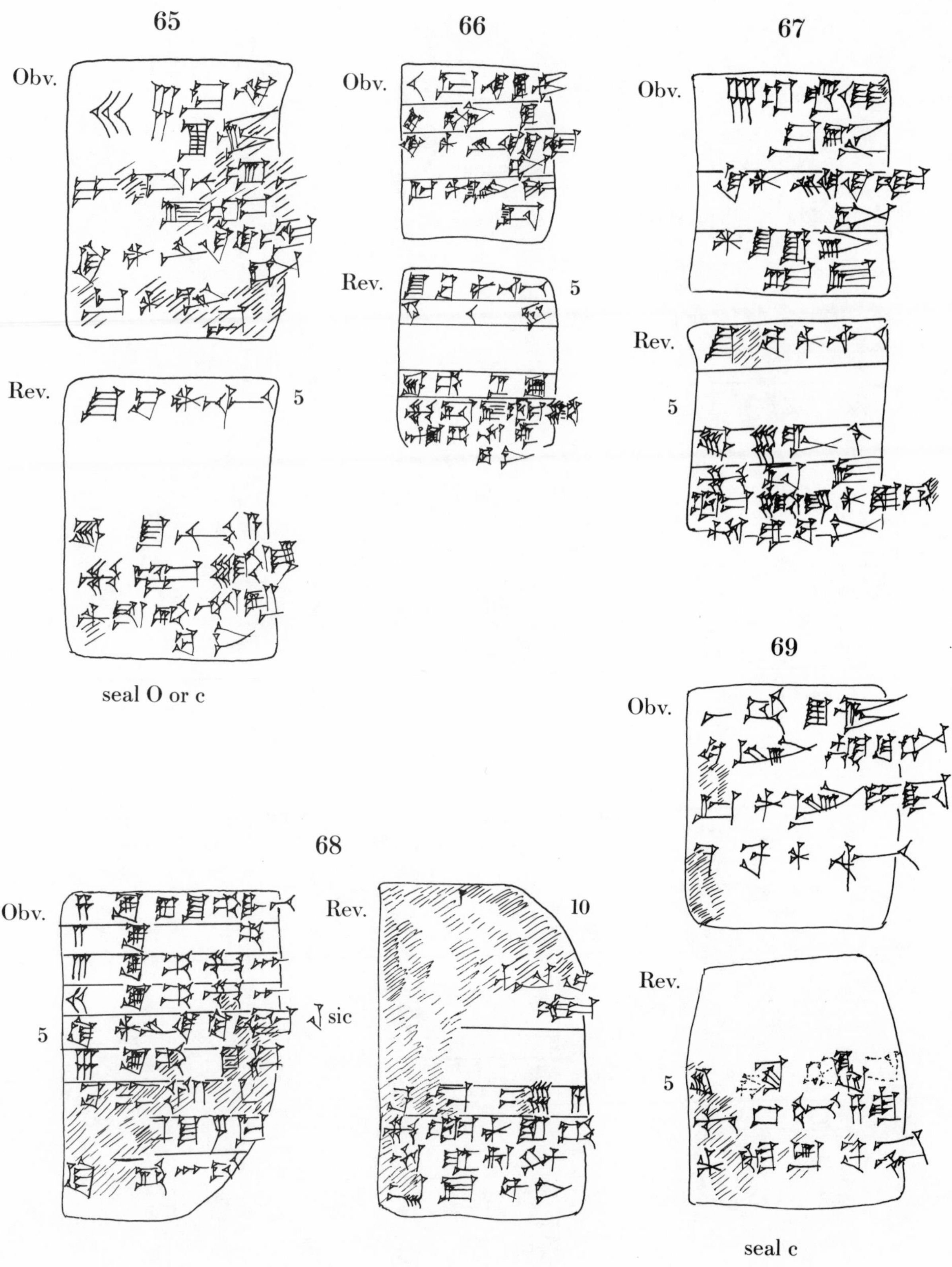
65
Obv.
Rev.
seal O or c
66
Obv.
Rev.
67
Obv.
Rev.
68
Obv.
sic
Rev.
69
Obv.
Rev.
seal c

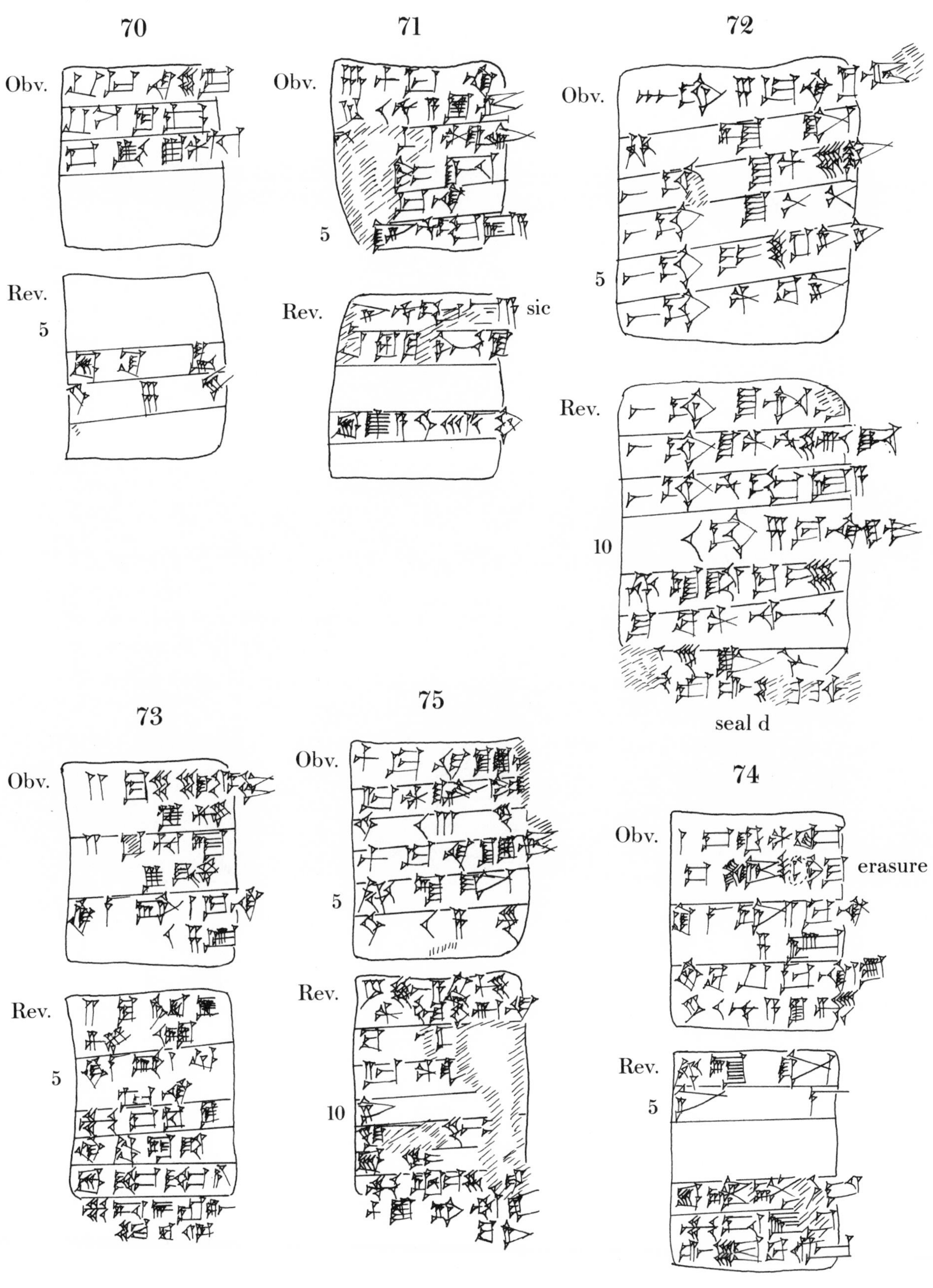
70
Obv.
Rev.
71
Obv.
Rev.
sic
72
Obv.
Rev.
seal d
73
Obv.
Rev.
75
Obv.
Rev.
74
Obv.
erasure
Rev.

PLATE XIV

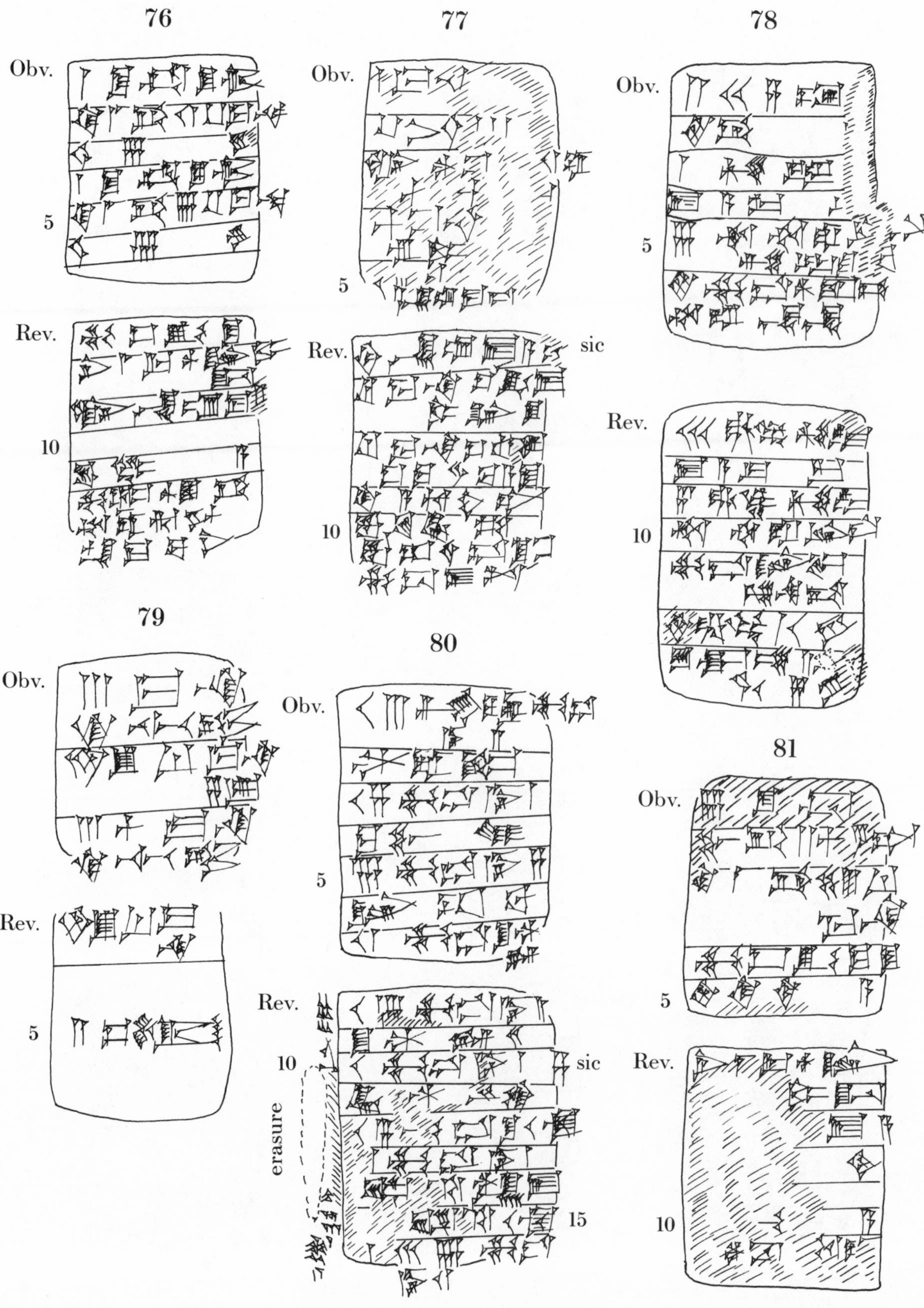
76
Obv.
5
Rev.
10
77
Obv.
5
Rev.
sic
10
78
Obv.
5
Rev.
10
79
Obv.
Rev.
5
80
Obv.
5
Rev.
10
sic
erasure
15
81
Obv.
5
Rev.
10

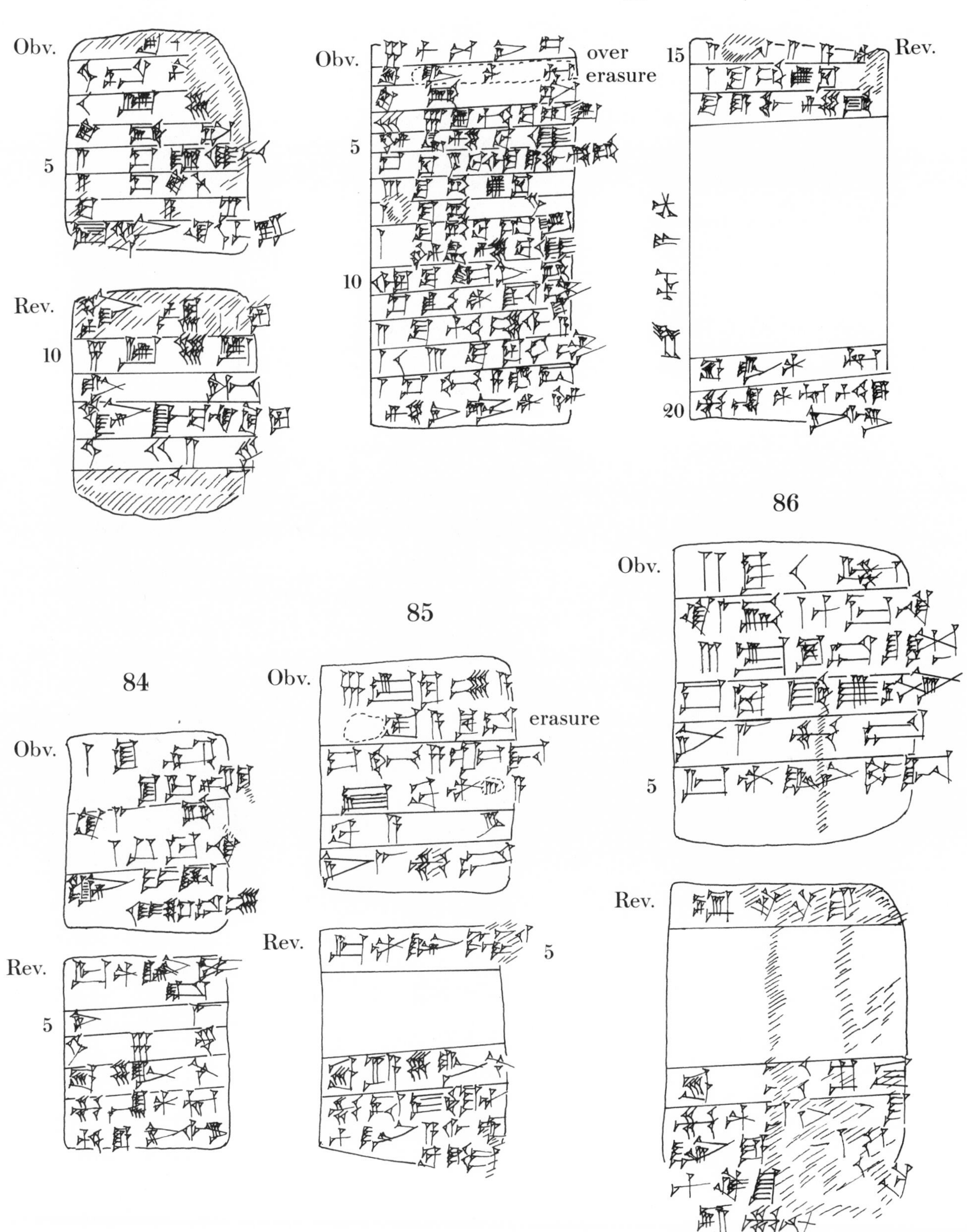
82
Obv.
5
Rev.
10
83
Obv.
over erasure
5
10
15
Rev.
20
84
Obv.
Rev.
5
85
Obv.
erasure
Rev.
5
86
Obv.
5
Rev.

PLATE XVI

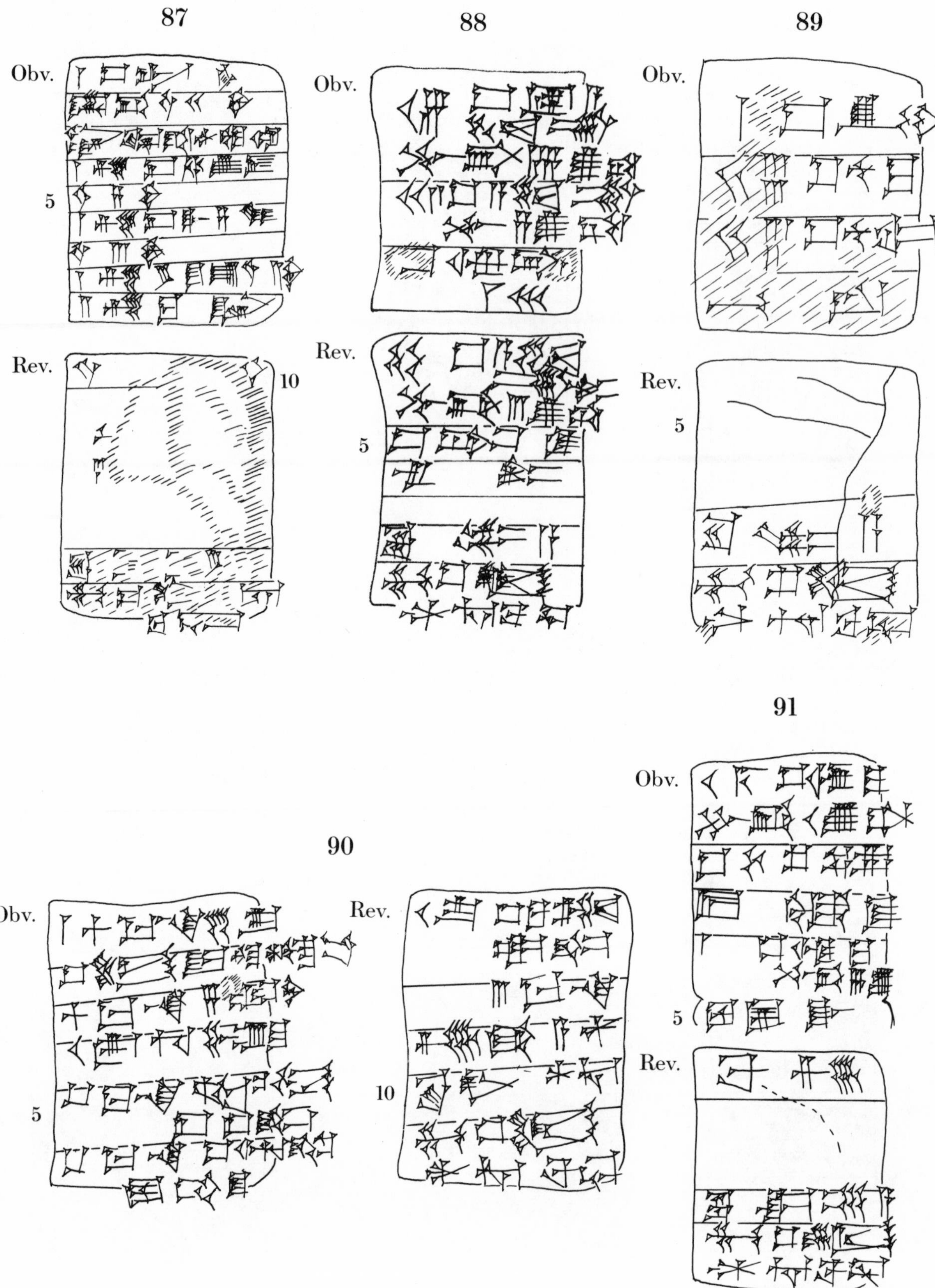

92

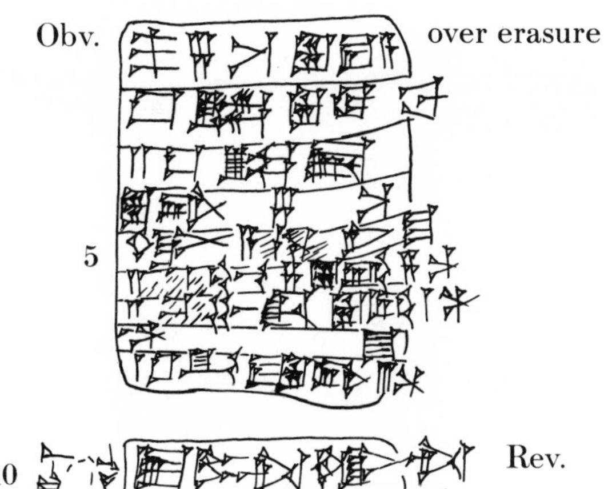
Obv.
over erasure

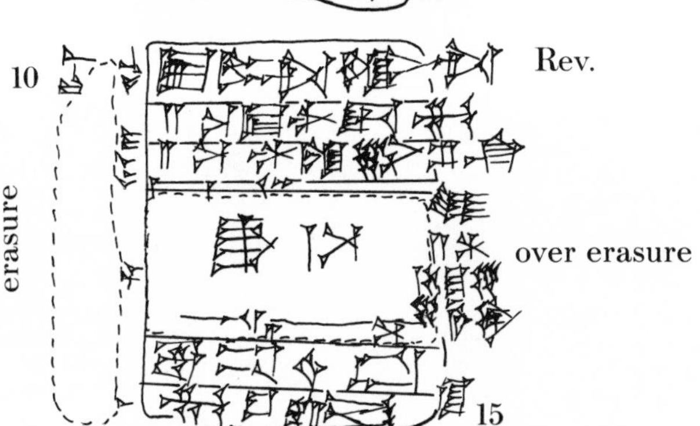
Rev.
erasure
over erasure

93

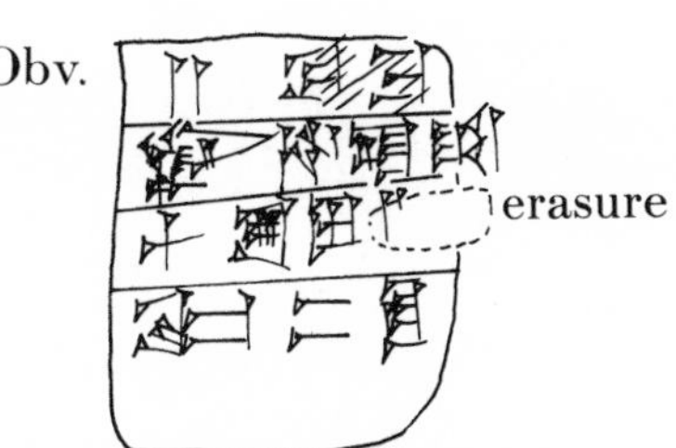
Obv.
erasure

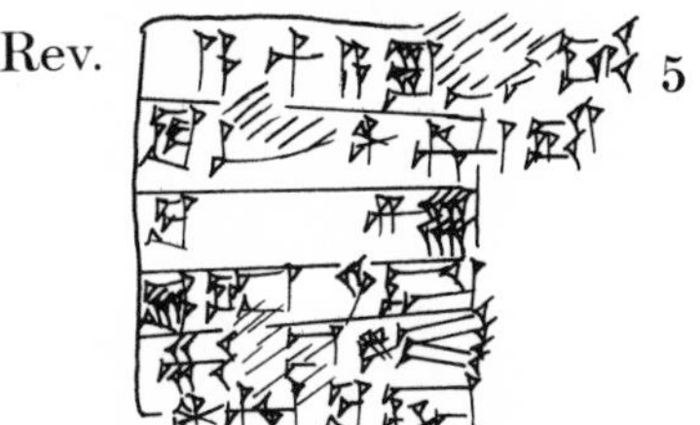
Rev.

94

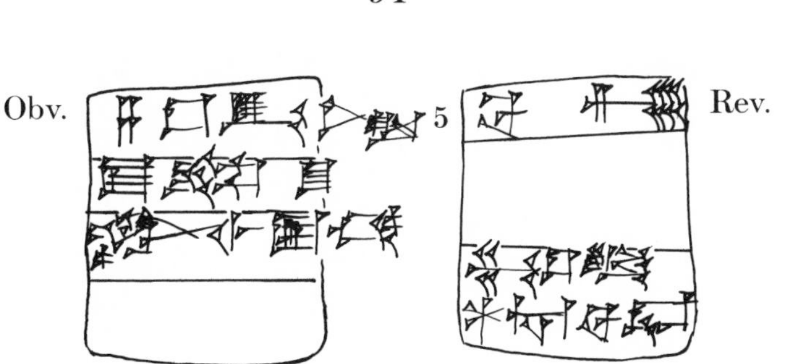
Obv.
Rev.

95

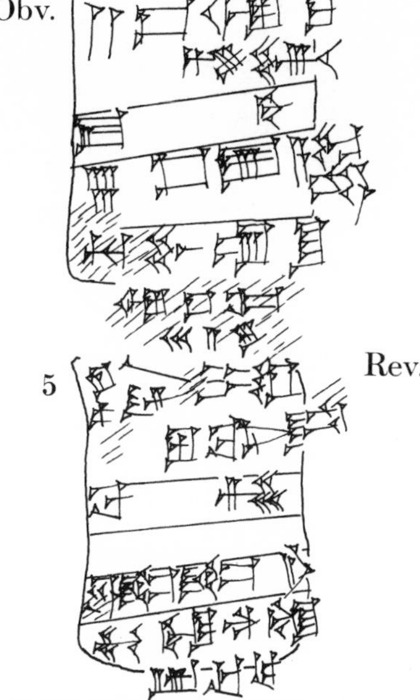
Obv.
Rev.

96

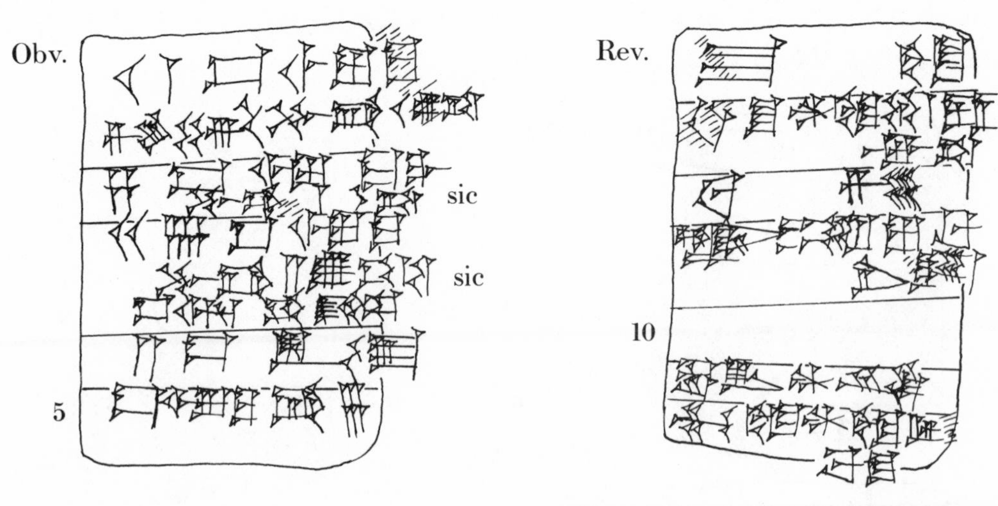

98

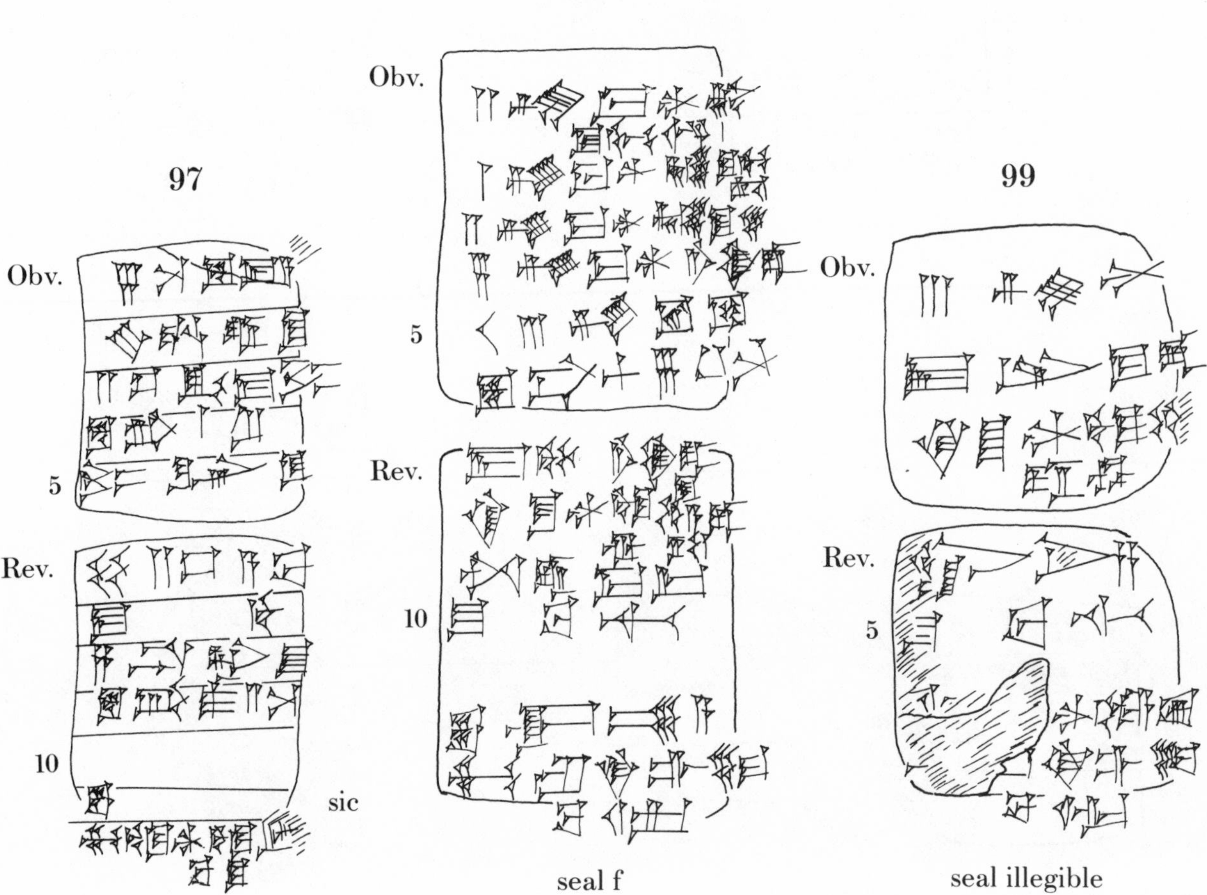

seal f

seal illegible

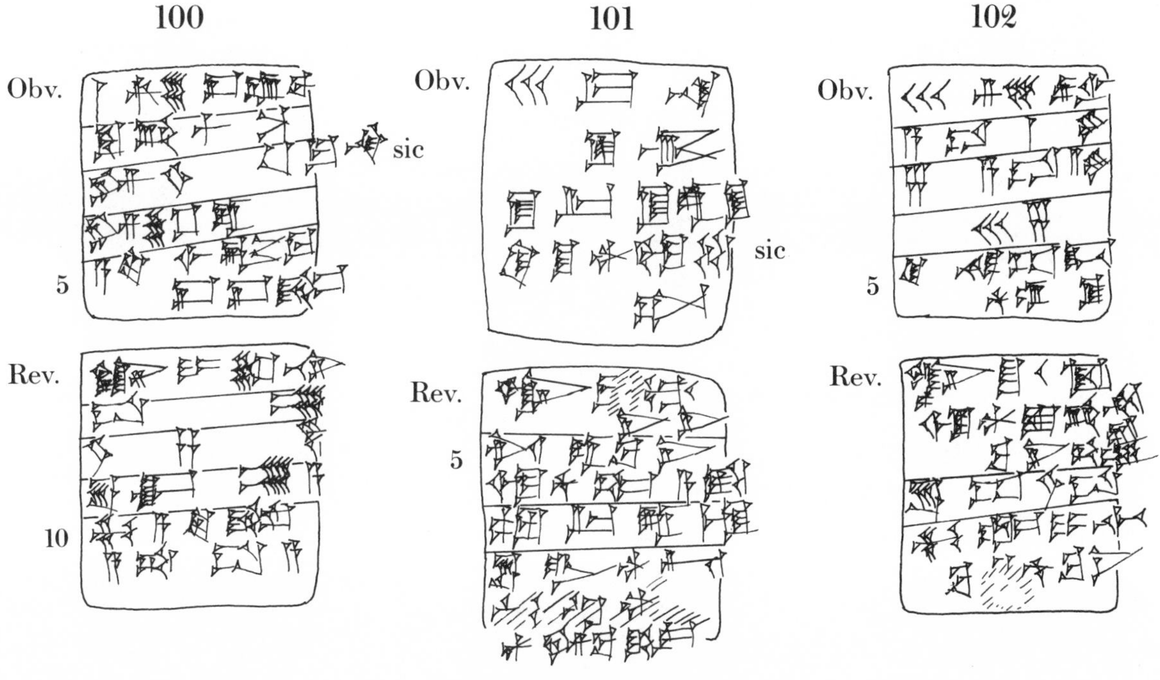
100
Obv.
sic
5
Rev.
10
101
Obv.
sic
Rev.
5
102
Obv.
5
Rev.

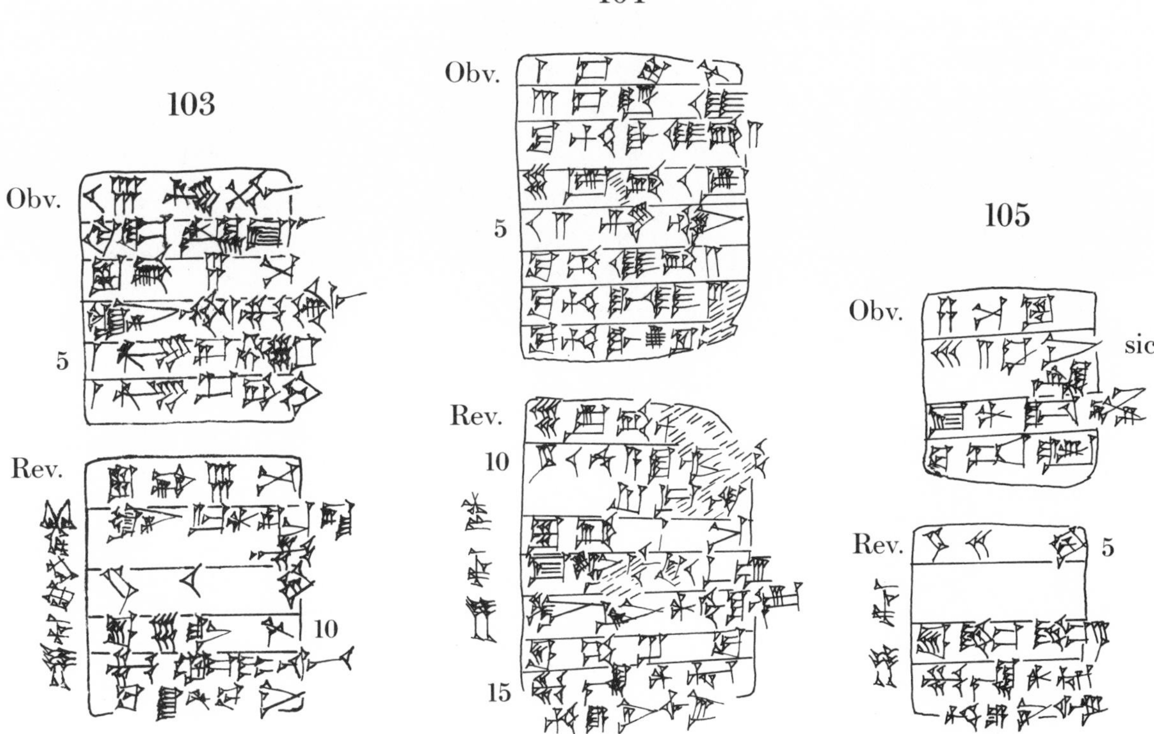
103
Obv.
5
Rev.
10
104
Obv.
5
Rev.
10
15
105
Obv.
sic
Rev.
5

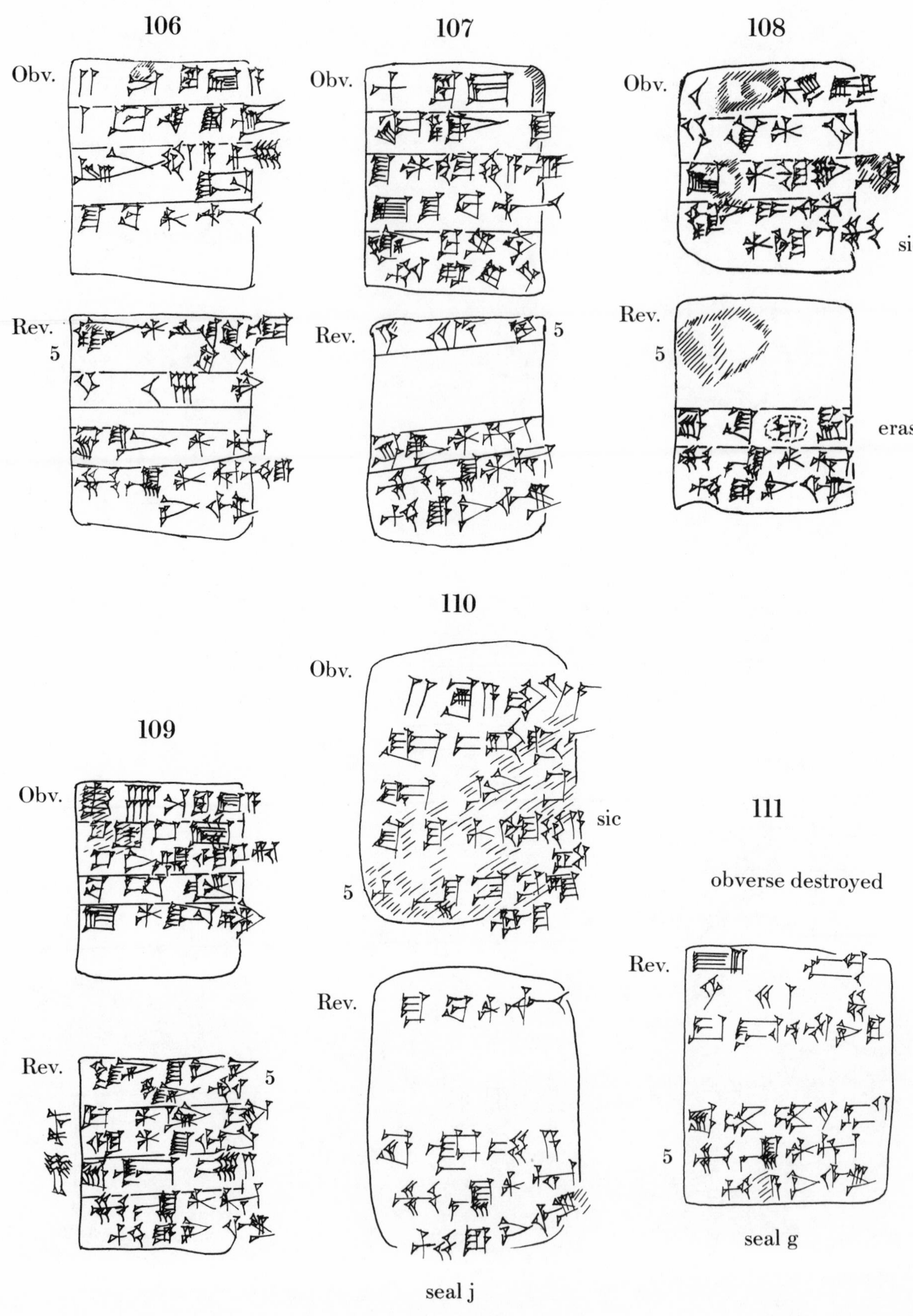
106
Obv.
Rev.
5
107
Obv.
Rev.
5
108
Obv.
sic
Rev.
5
erasure
110
Obv.
sic
5
Rev.
seal j
109
Obv.
Rev.
5
111
obverse destroyed
Rev.
5
seal g

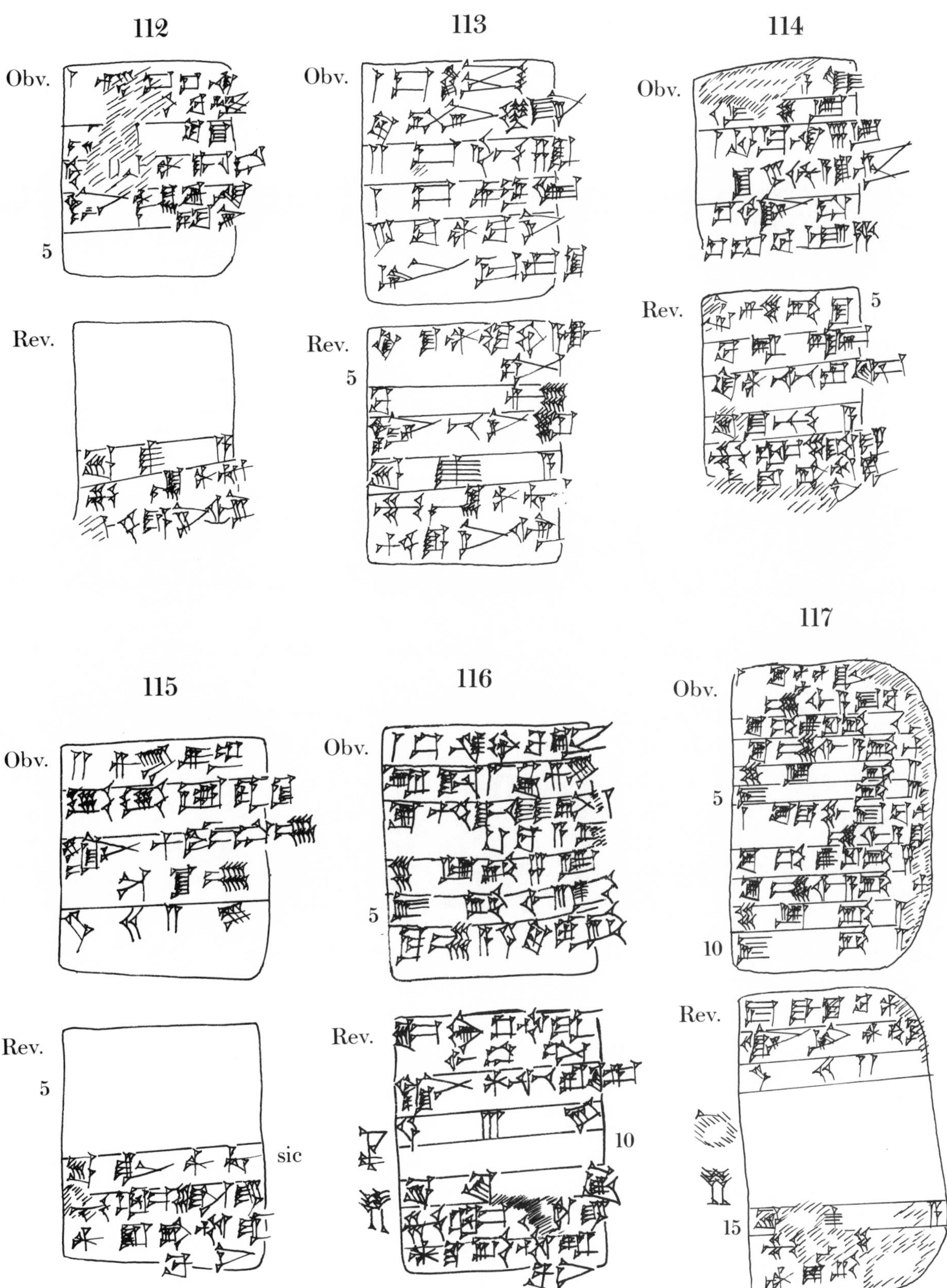
112
Obv.
5
Rev.
113
Obv.
Rev.
5
114
Obv.
Rev.
5
115
Obv.
Rev.
5
sic
116
Obv.
5
Rev.
10
117
Obv.
5
10
Rev.
15

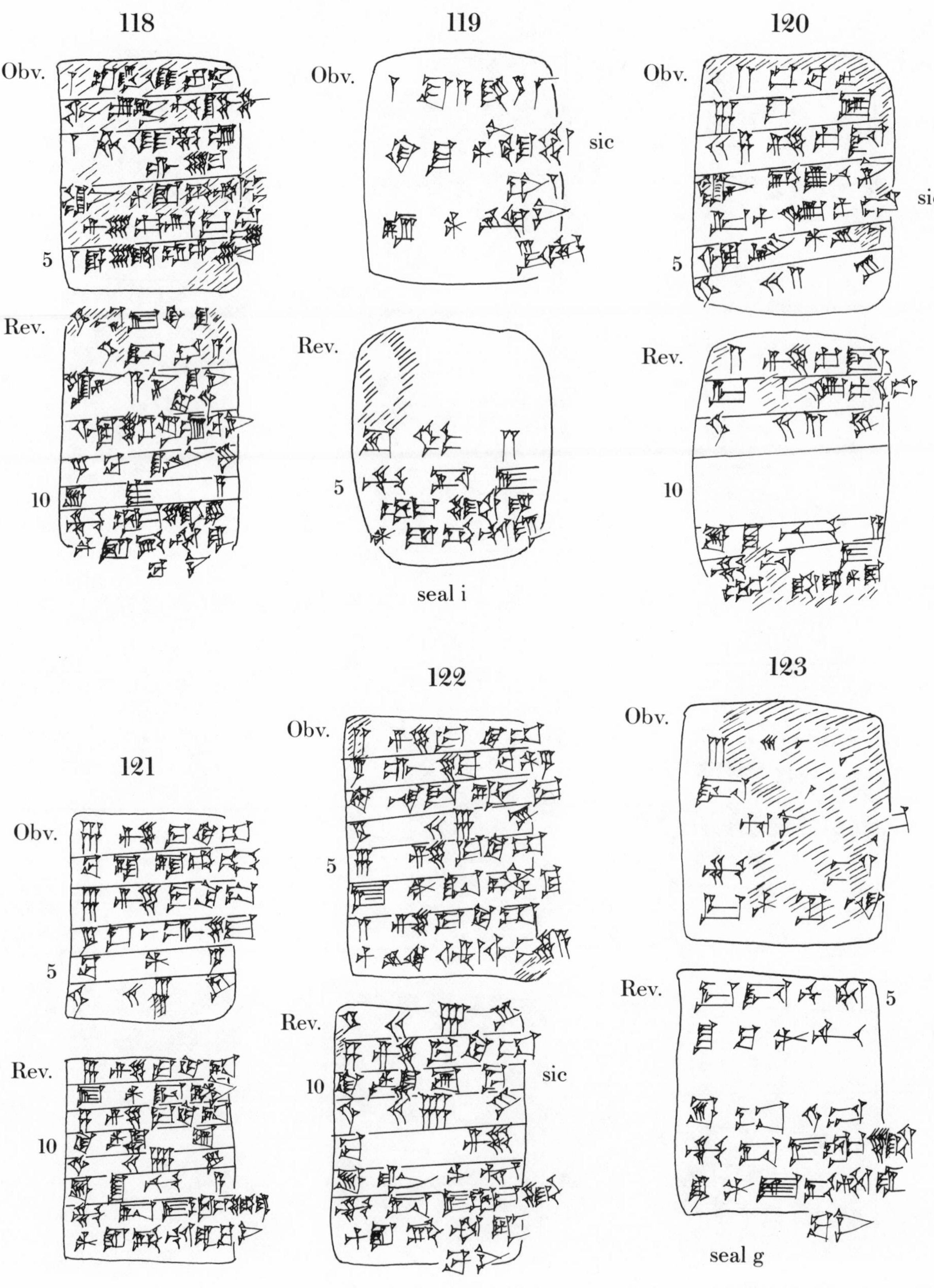
118
Obv.
5
Rev.
10
119
Obv.
sic
Rev.
5
seal i
120
Obv.
sic
5
Rev.
10
121
Obv.
5
Rev.
10
122
Obv.
5
Rev.
sic
10
123
Obv.
Rev.
5
seal g

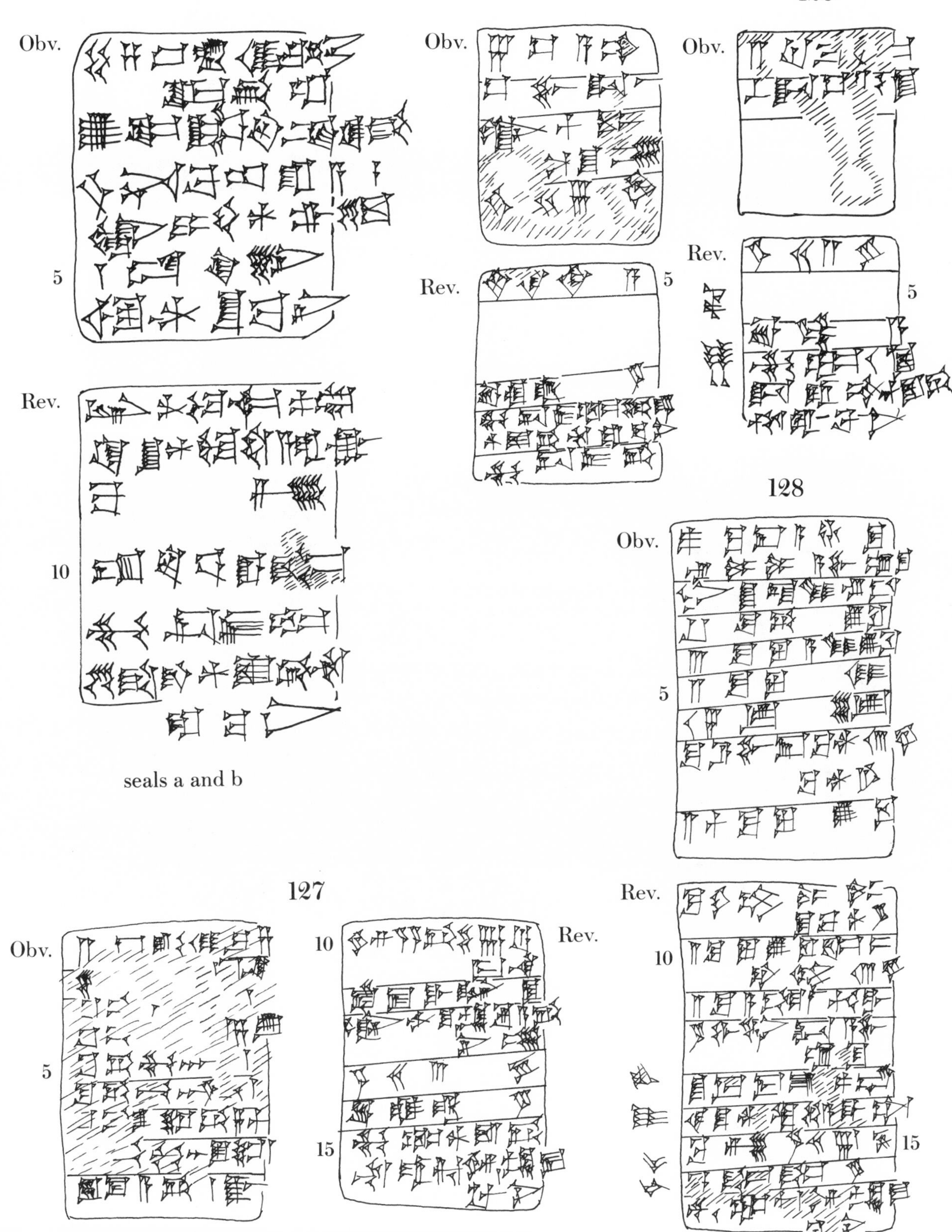
124
Obv.
Rev.
seals a and b
125
Obv.
Rev.
126
Obv.
Rev.
128
Obv.
Rev.
127
Obv.
Rev.

seal M

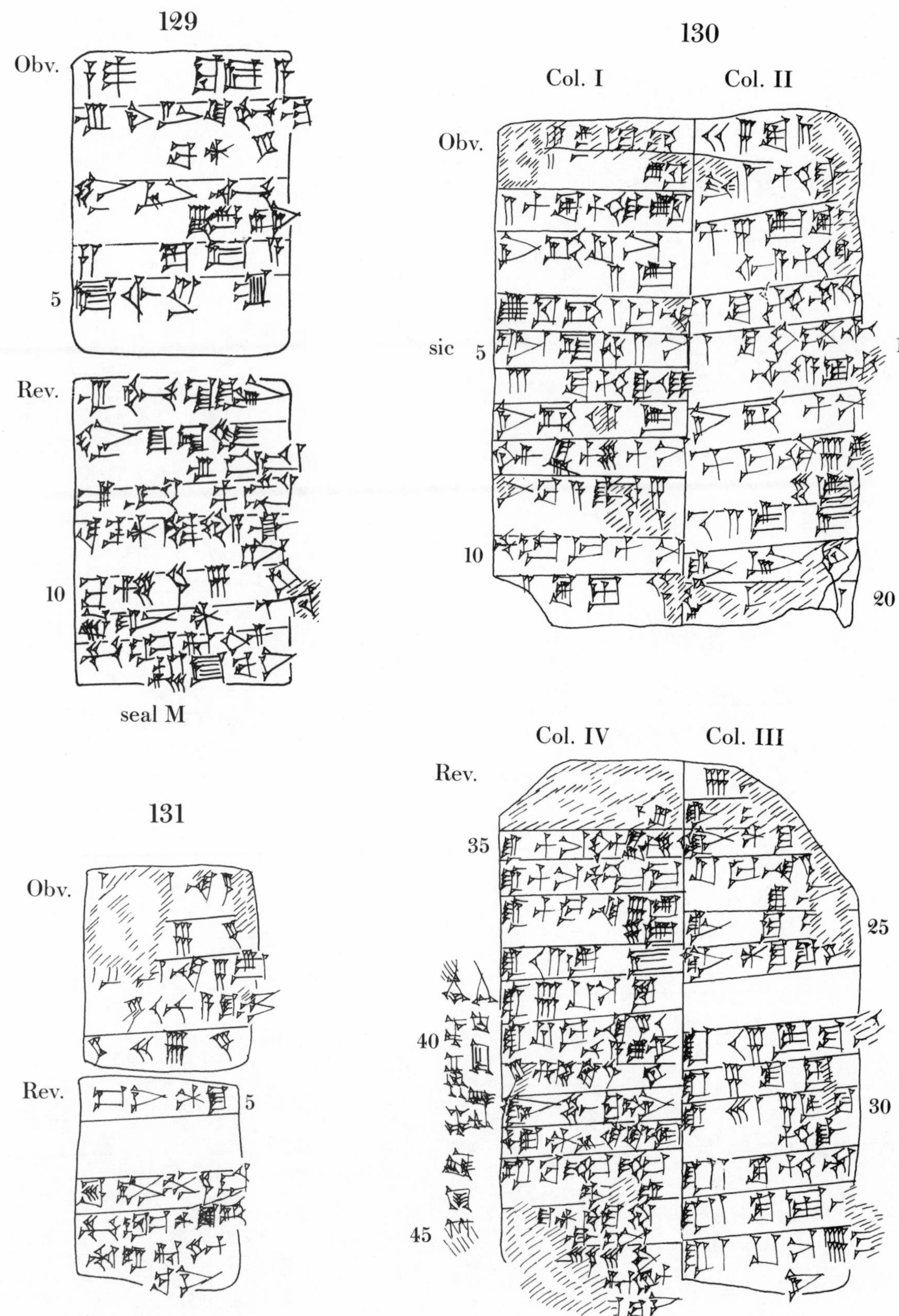
129
Obv.
Rev.
seal M
130
Col. I
Col. II
Obv.
sic
Col. IV
Col. III
Rev.
131
Obv.
Rev.

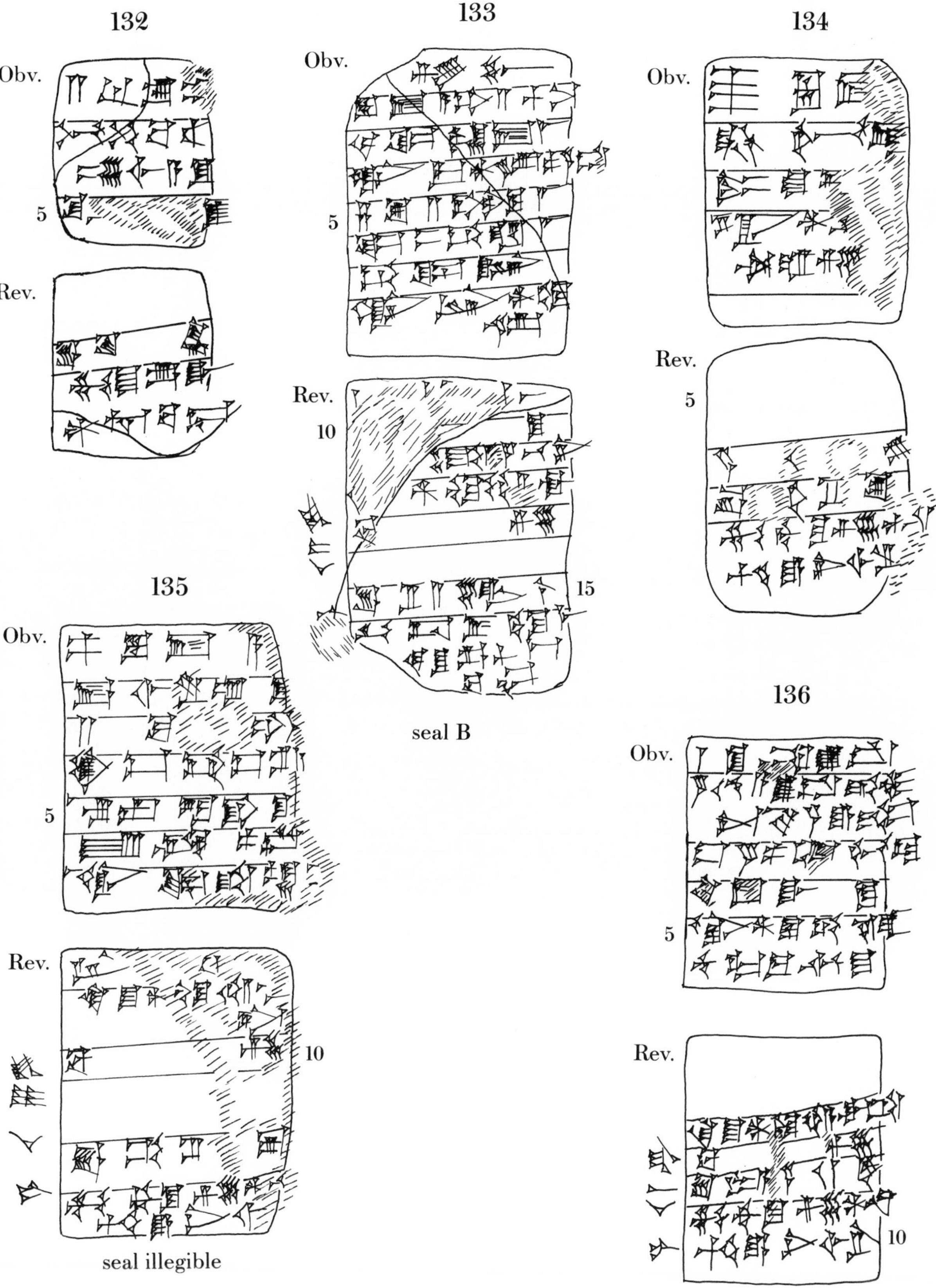
132
Obv.
Rev.
133
Obv.
Rev.
seal B
134
Obv.
Rev.
135
Obv.
Rev.
seal illegible
136
Obv.
Rev.

137

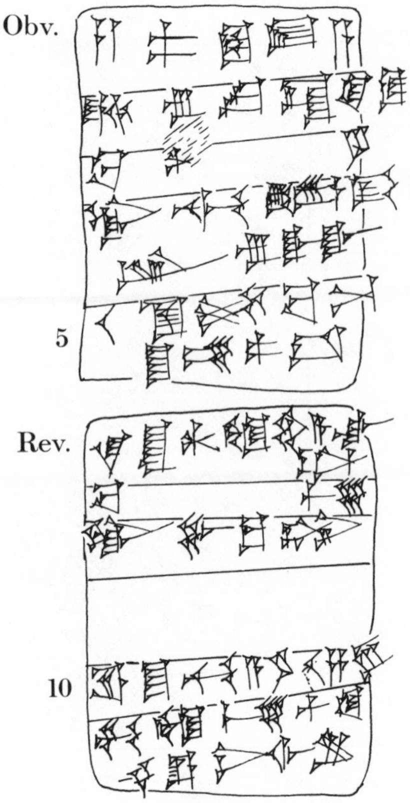

Obv.

sic

Rev.

seal M

138

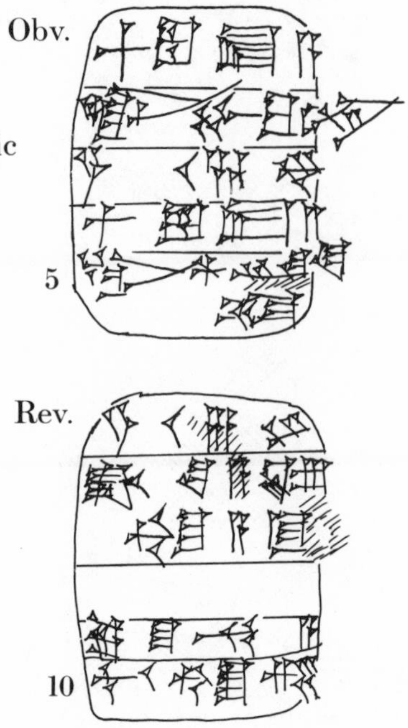

Obv.

Rev.

139

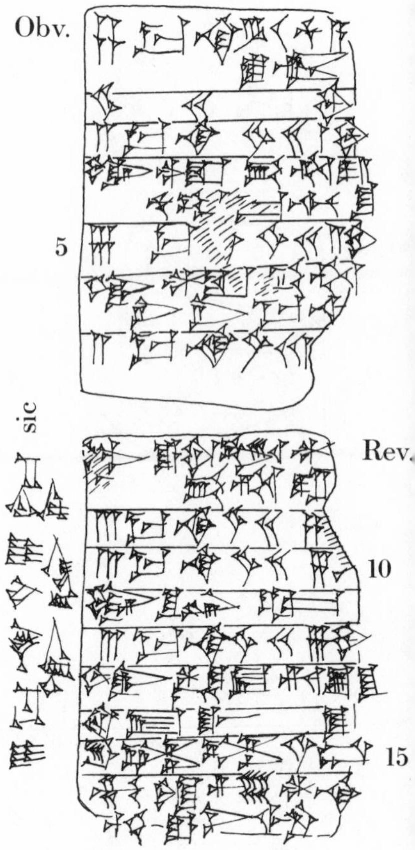

Obv.

sic

Rev.

140

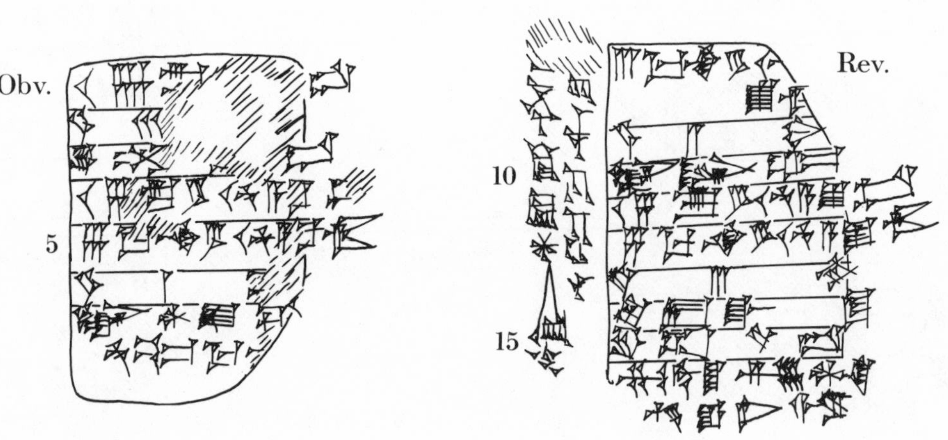

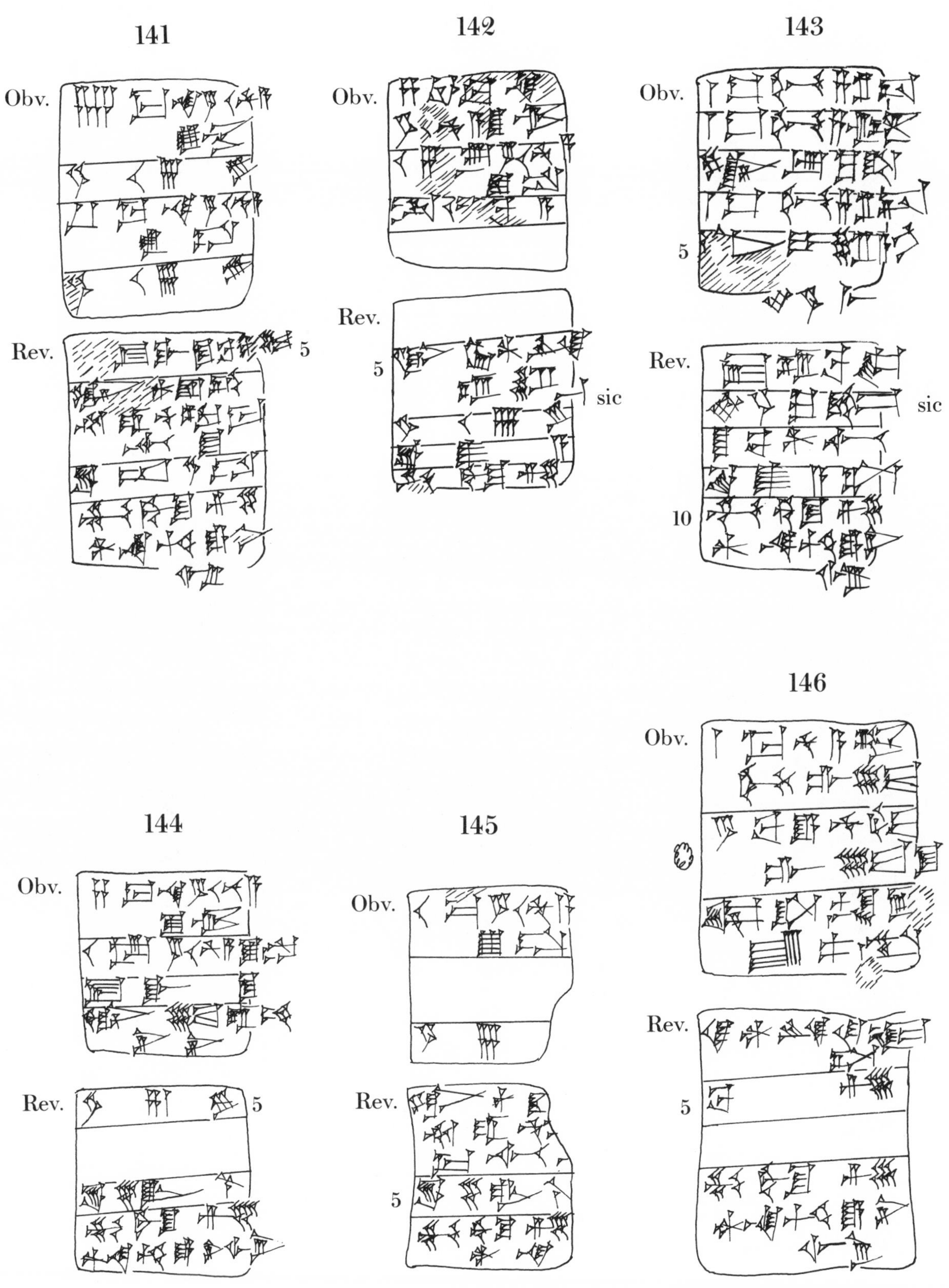
141
Obv.
Rev.
142
Obv.
Rev.
sic
143
Obv.
Rev.
sic
144
Obv.
Rev.
145
Obv.
Rev.
146
Obv.
Rev.

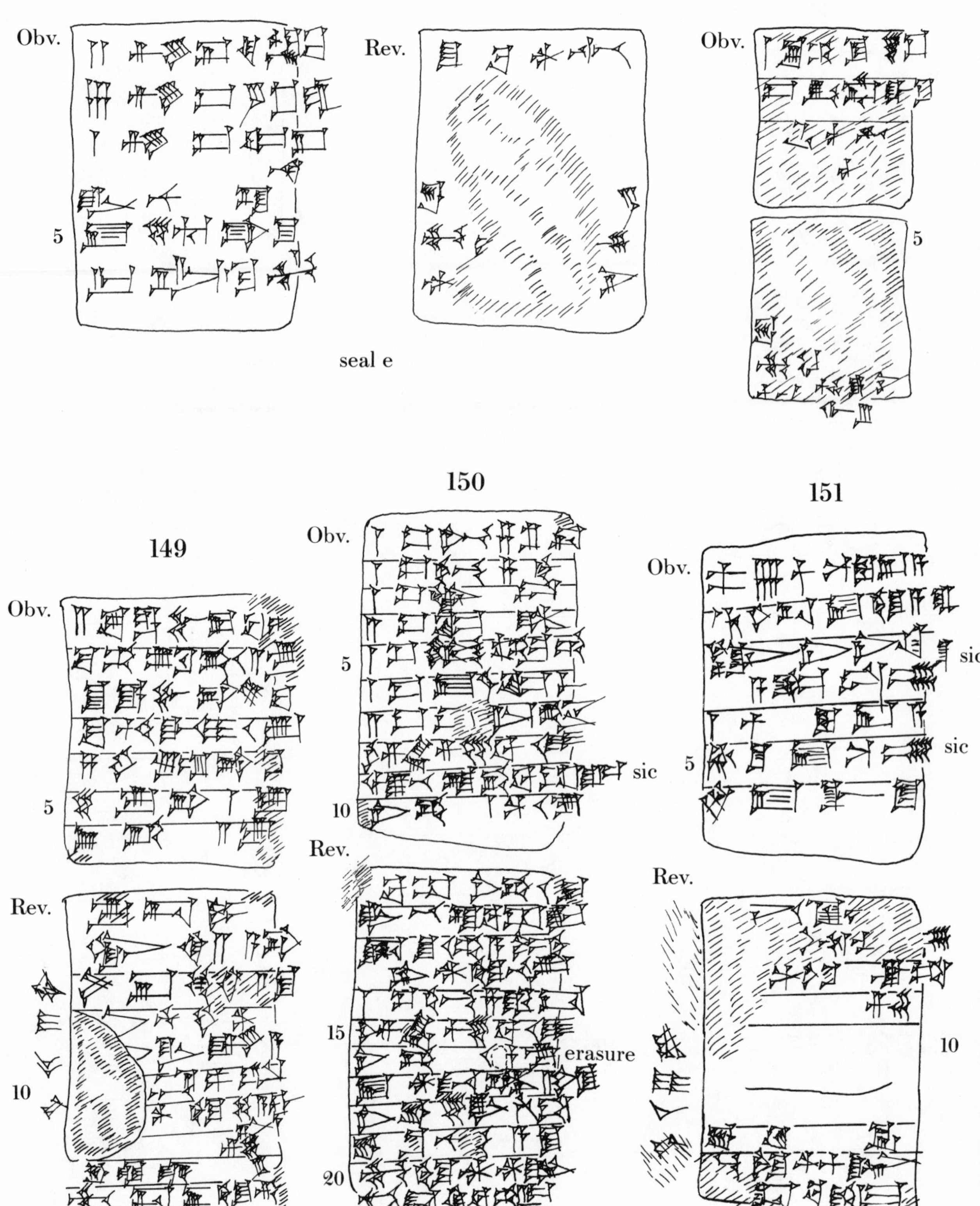
147
Obv.
5
Rev.
seal e
148
Obv.
5
149
Obv.
5
Rev.
10
150
Obv.
5
sic
10
Rev.
15
erasure
20
151
Obv.
sic
5
sic
Rev.
10

152

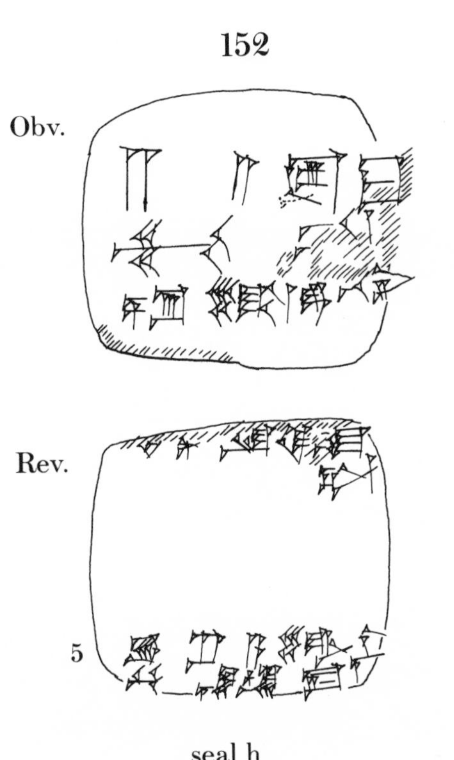

seal h

153

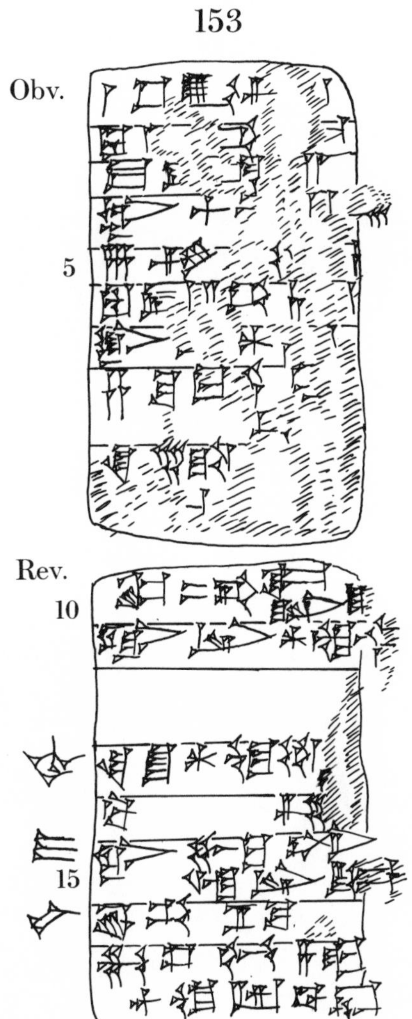

154

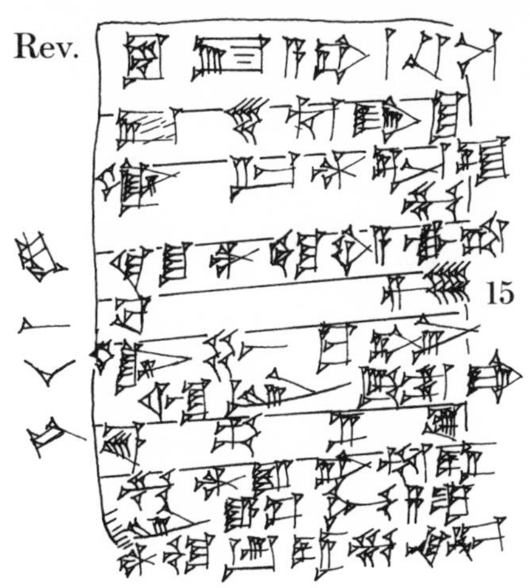

PLATE XXX

155

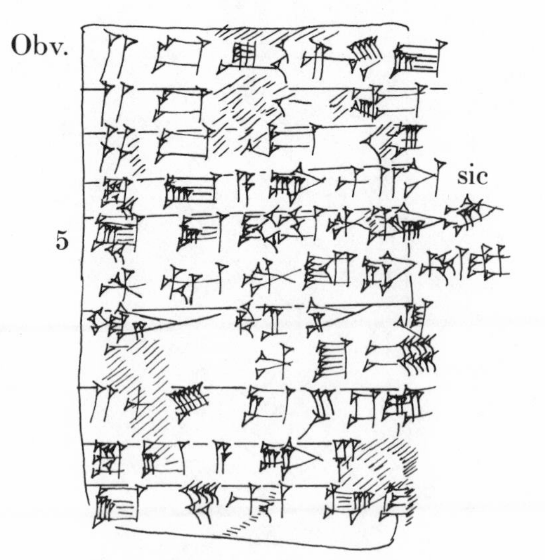

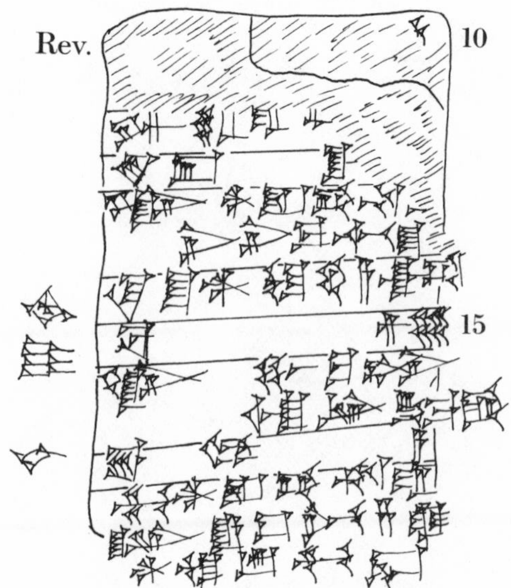

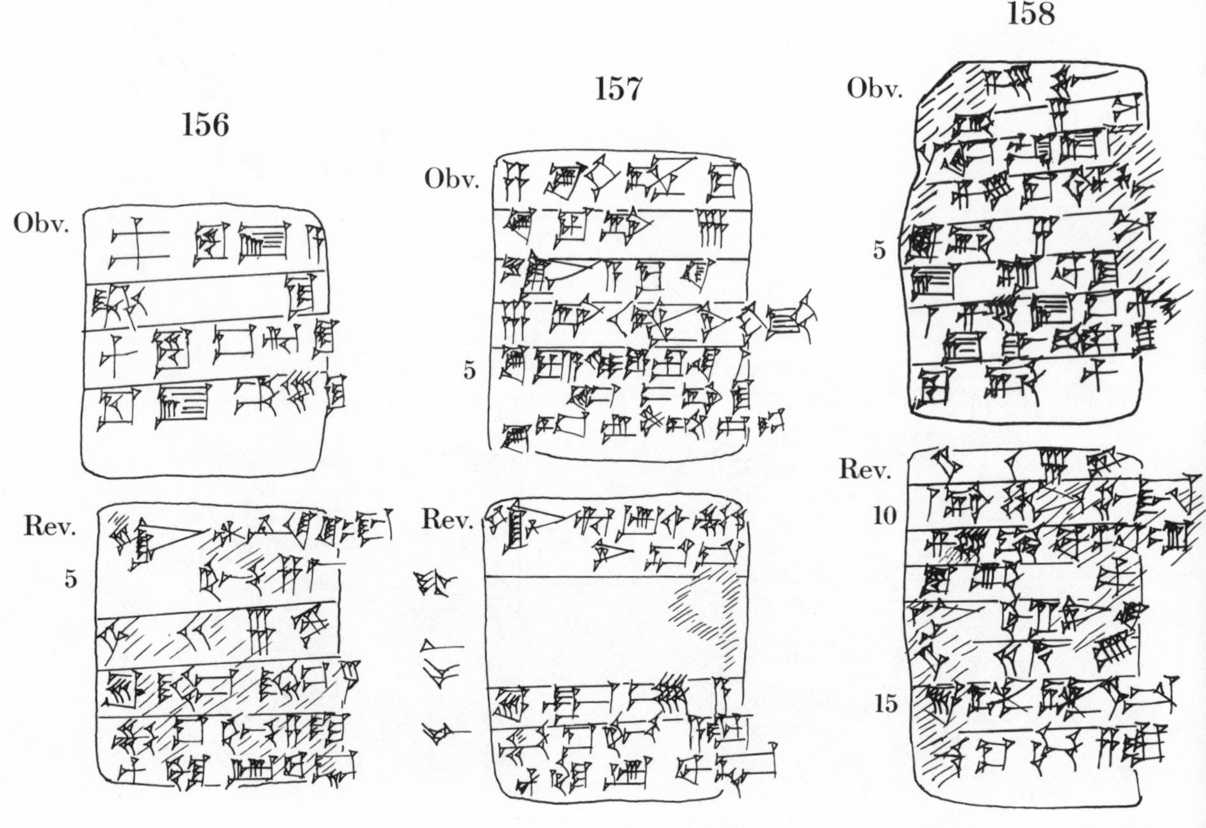

159

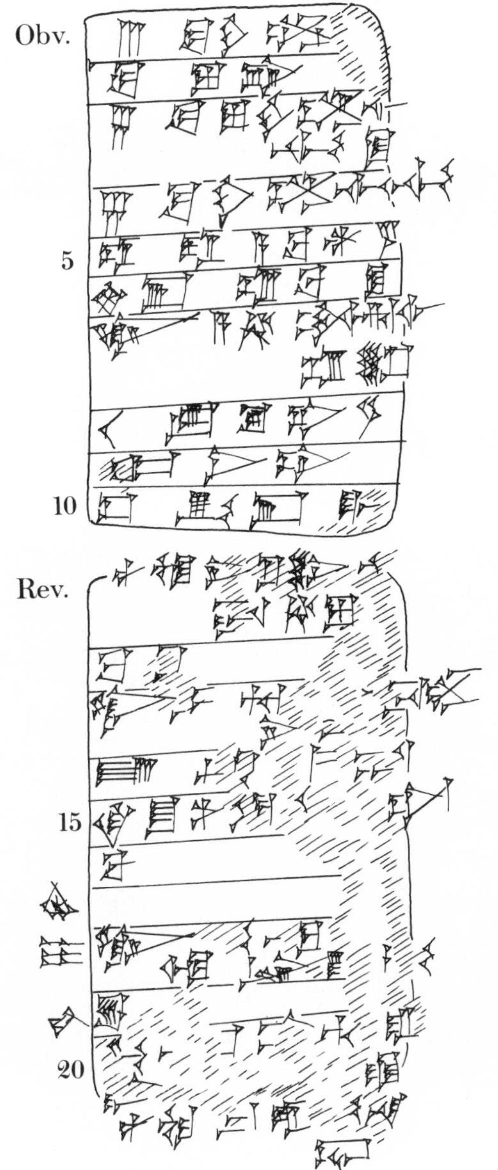

160

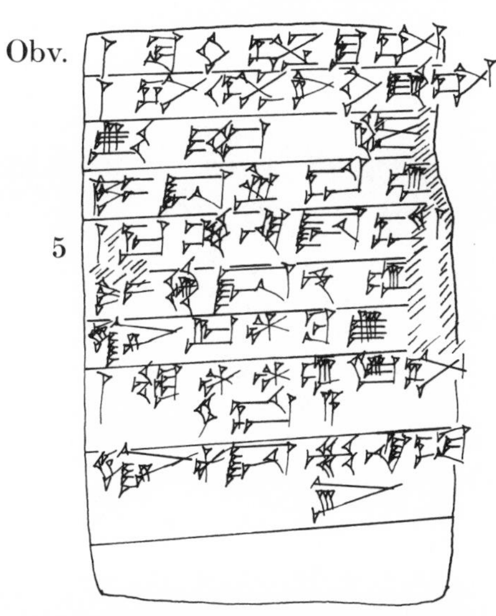

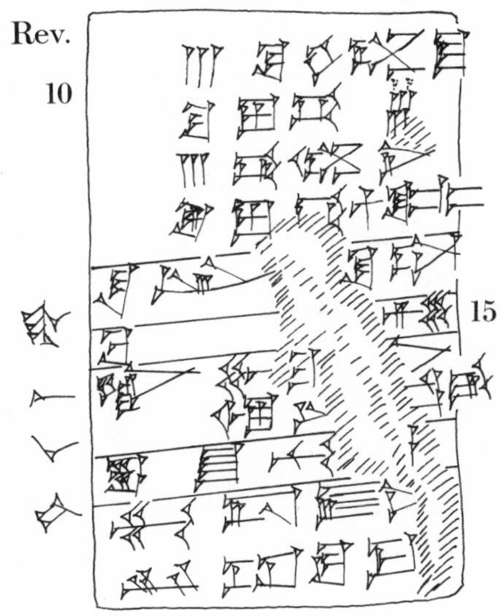

161

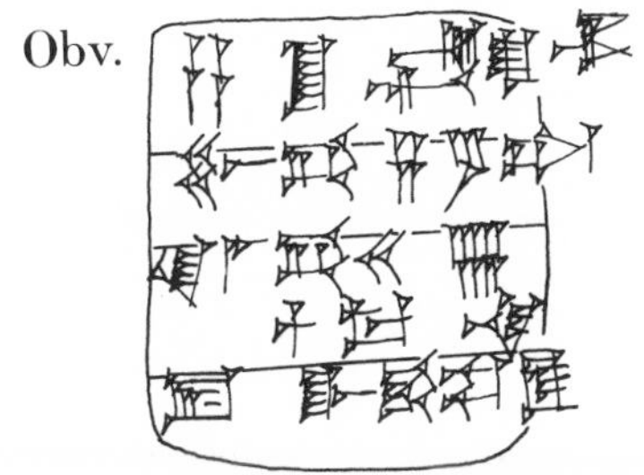

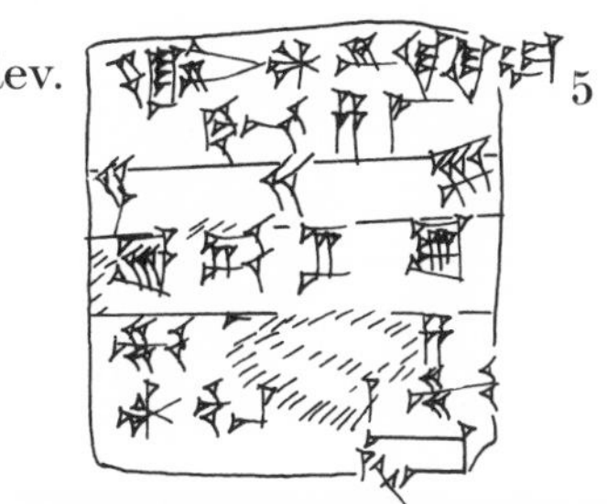

PLATE XXXII

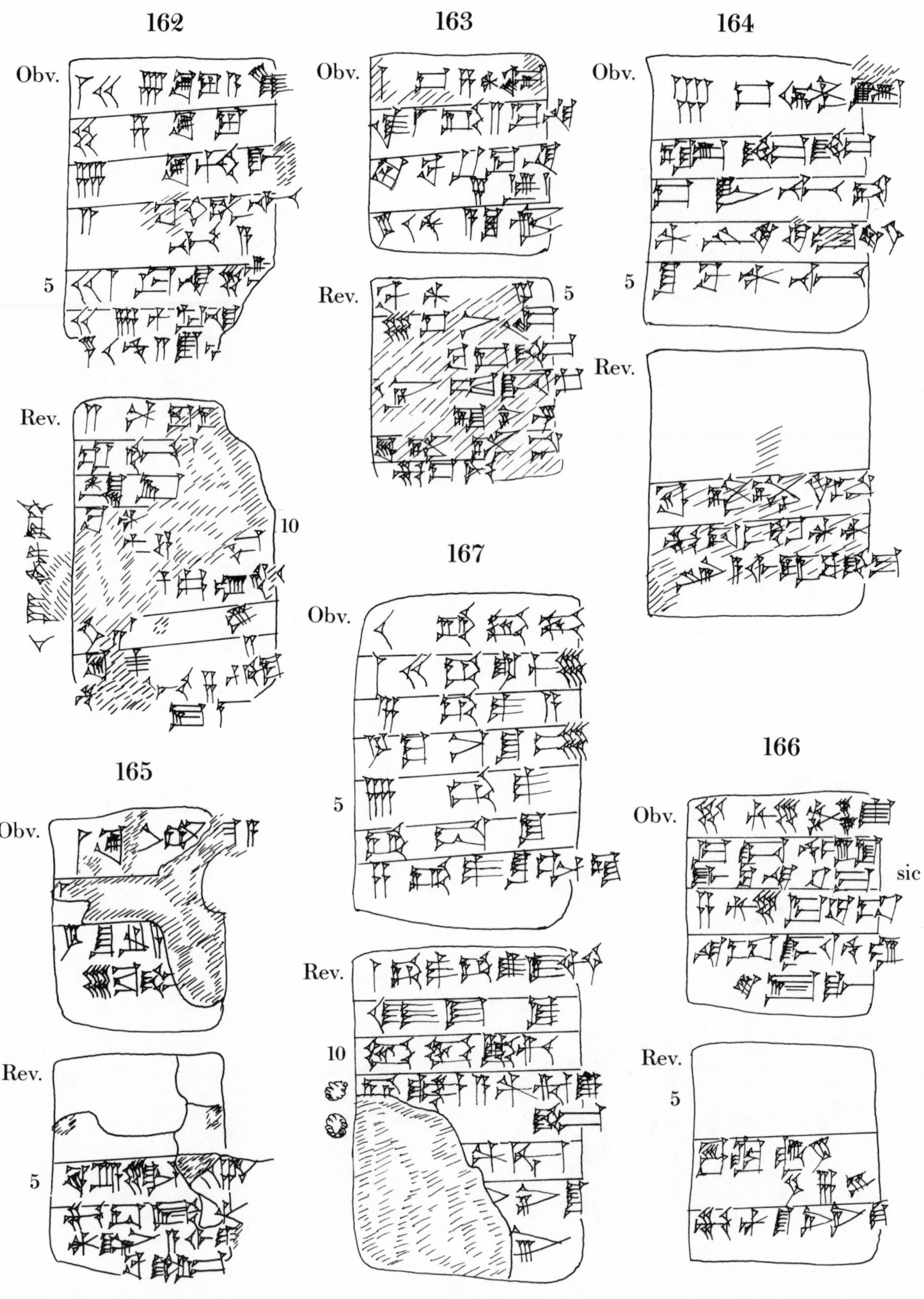
162
Obv.
Rev.
163
Obv.
Rev.
164
Obv.
Rev.
167
Obv.
Rev.
165
Obv.
Rev.
166
Obv.
sic
Rev.

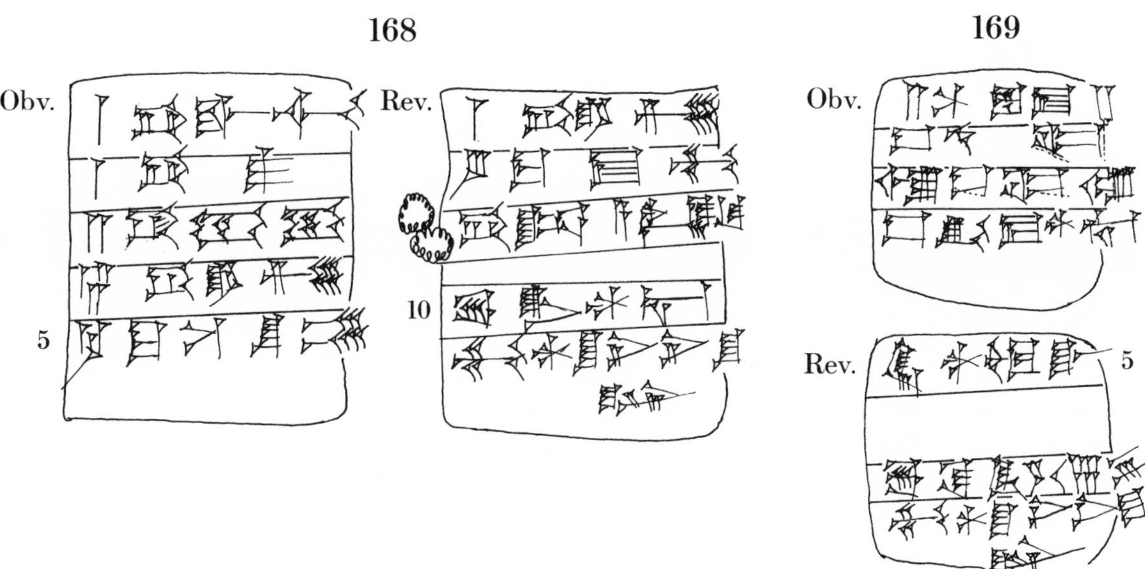

170

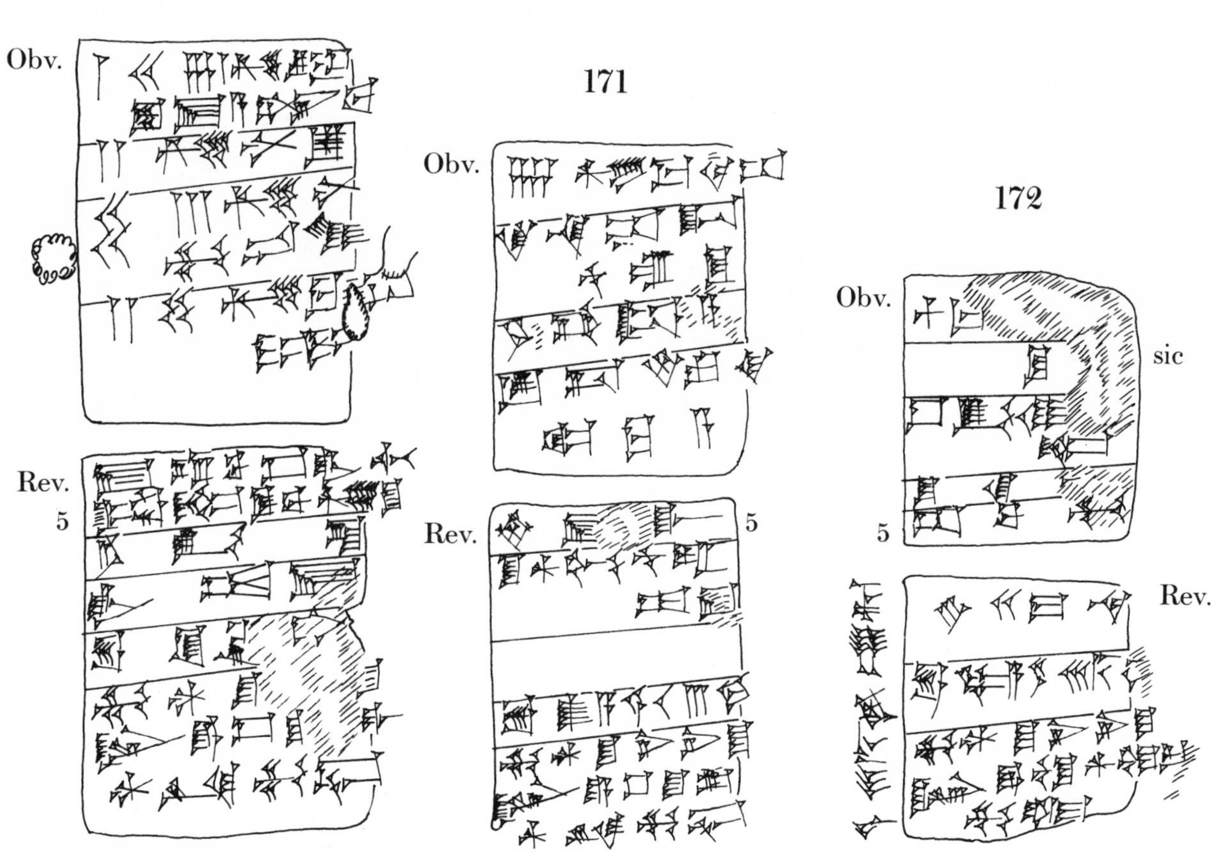

PLATE XXXIV

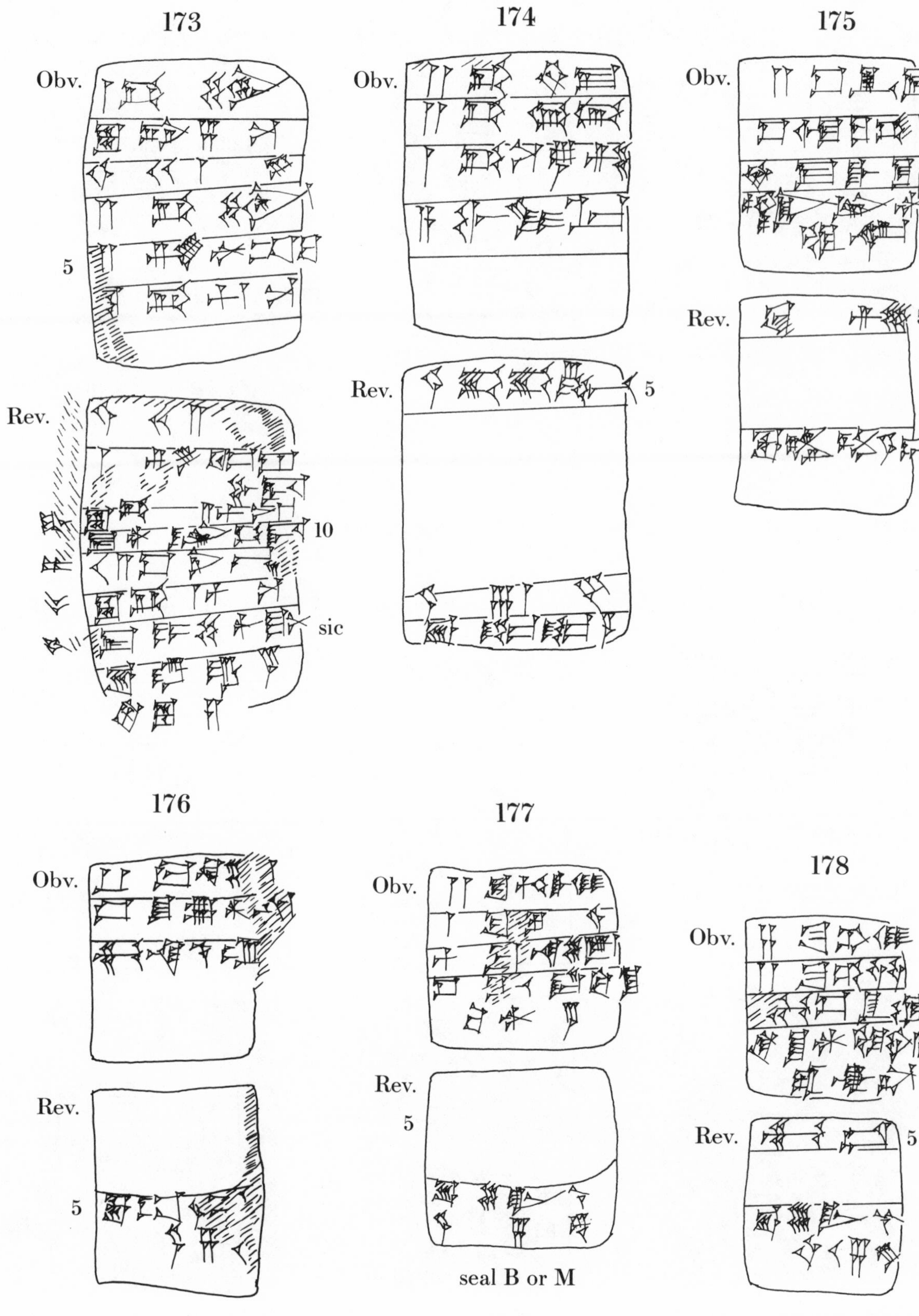
173
Obv.
Rev.
sic
174
Obv.
Rev.
175
Obv.
Rev.
176
Obv.
Rev.
177
Obv.
Rev.
seal B or M
178
Obv.
Rev.

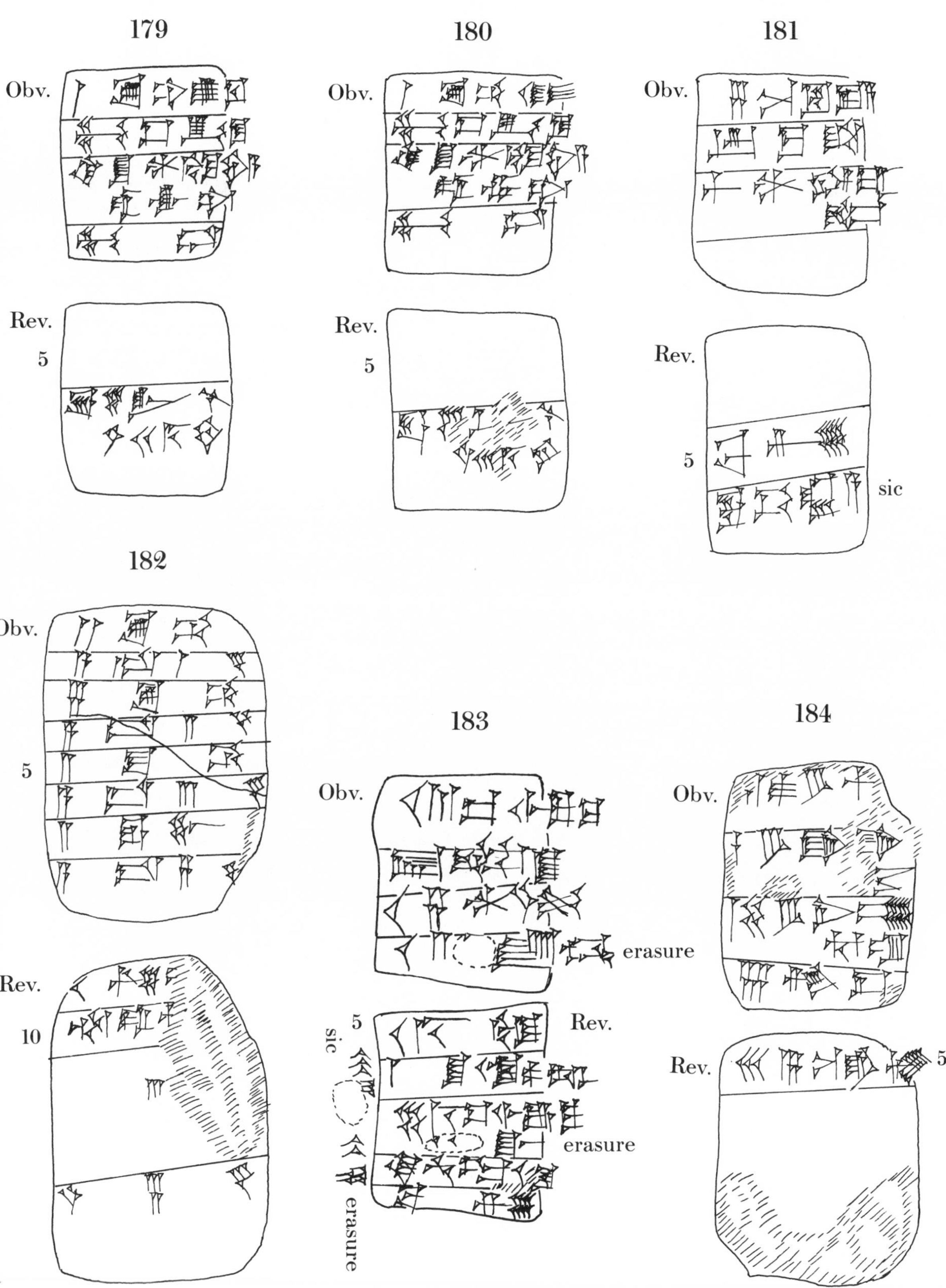
179
Obv.
Rev.
5
180
Obv.
Rev.
5
181
Obv.
Rev.
5
sic
182
Obv.
5
Rev.
10
183
Obv.
erasure
5
Rev.
sic
erasure
erasure
184
Obv.
Rev.
5

185

186

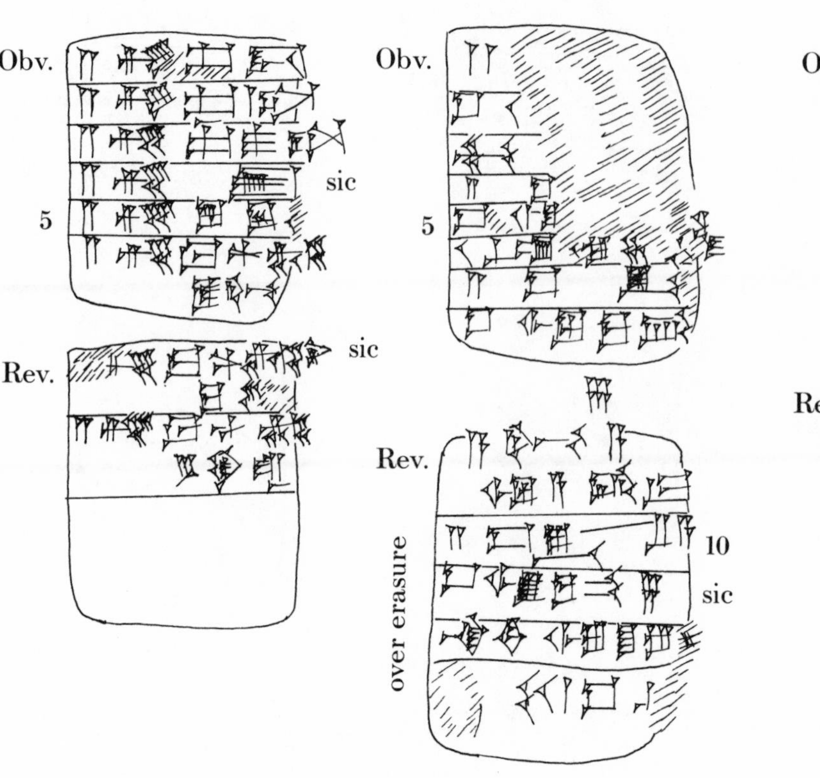

187

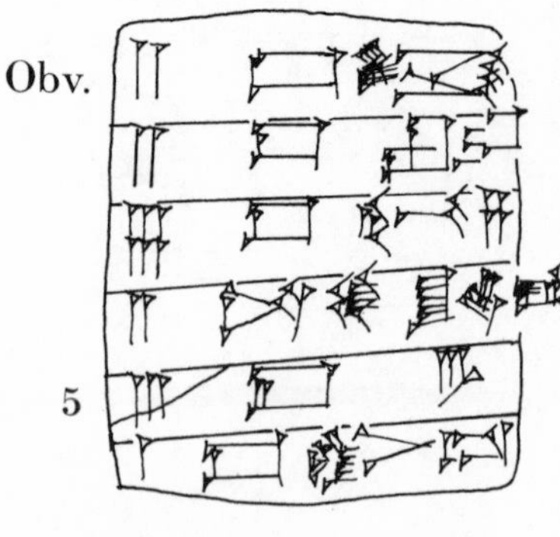

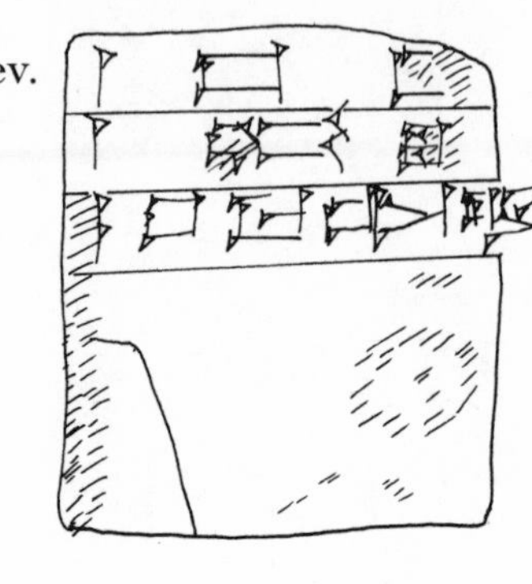

188

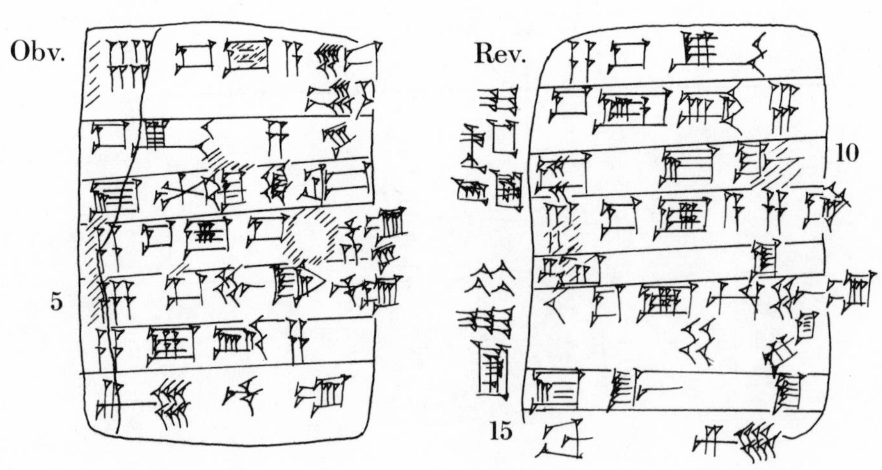

PLATE XXXVII

189

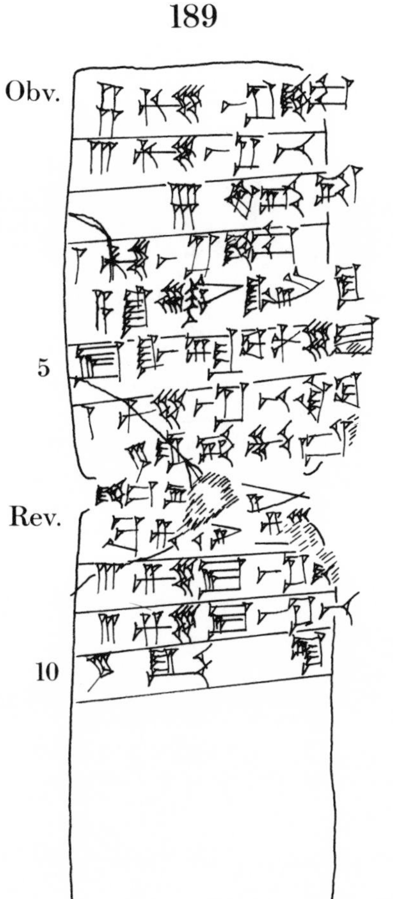

190

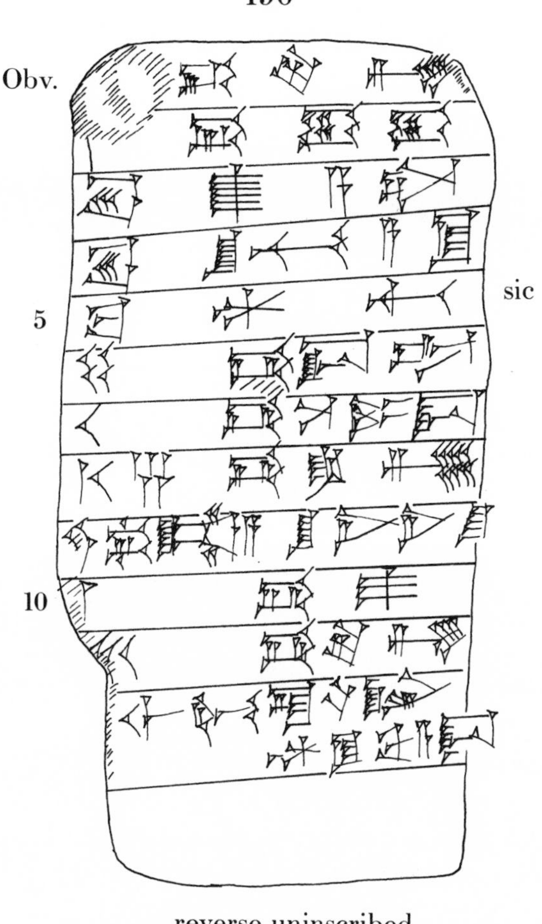

reverse uninscribed

191

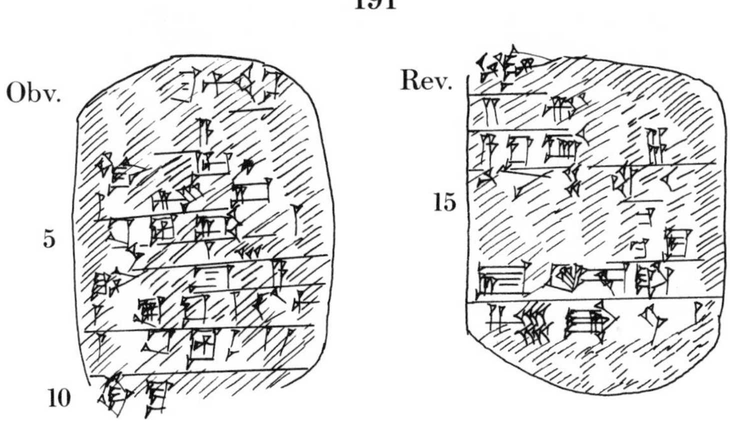

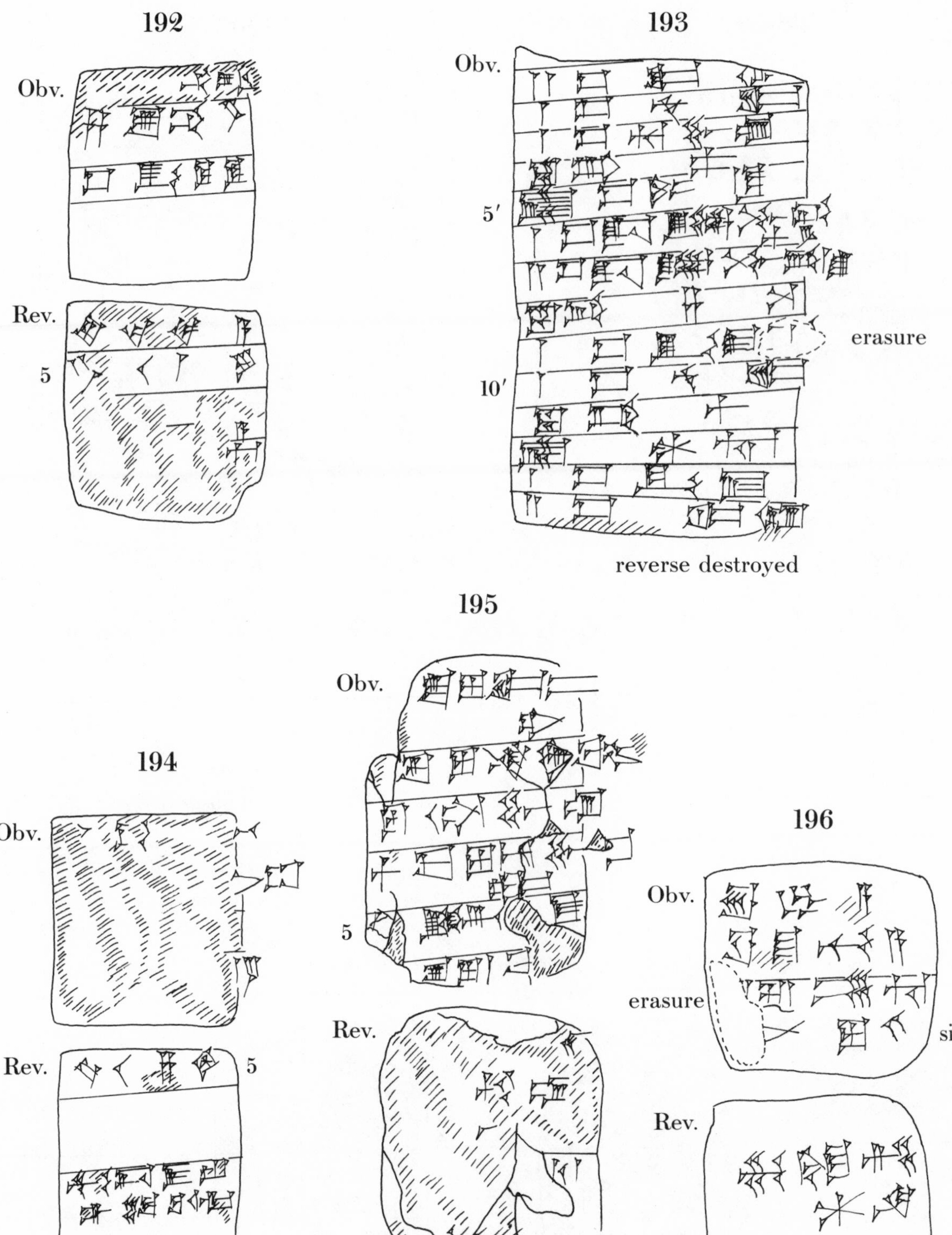
192
Obv.
Rev.
5
193
Obv.
5′
10′
erasure
reverse destroyed
195
Obv.
5
Rev.
194
Obv.
Rev.
5
196
Obv.
erasure
sic
Rev.

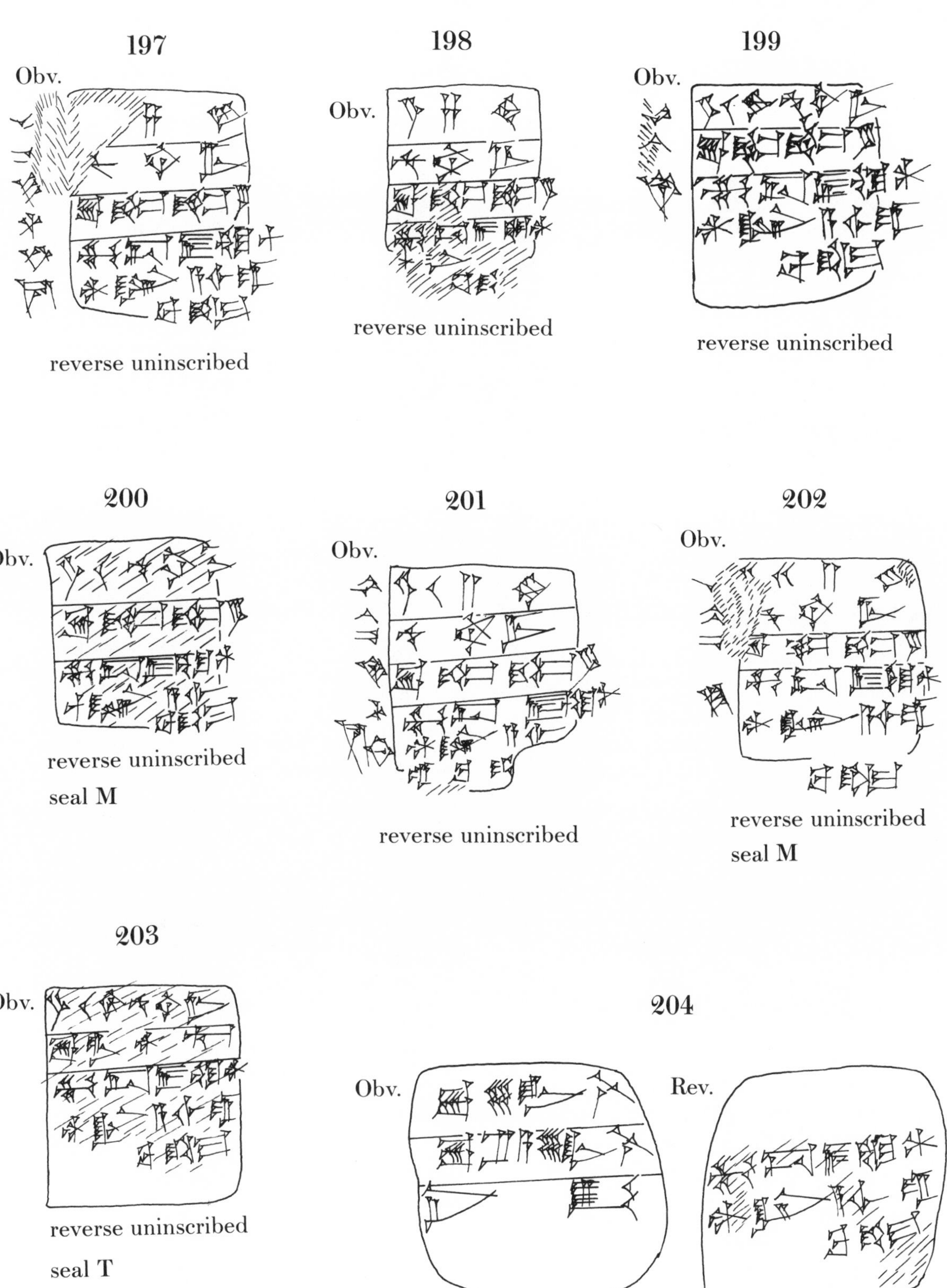
197
Obv.
reverse uninscribed
198
Obv.
reverse uninscribed
199
Obv.
reverse uninscribed
200
Obv.
reverse uninscribed
seal M
201
Obv.
reverse uninscribed
202
Obv.
reverse uninscribed
seal M
203
Obv.
reverse uninscribed
seal T
204
Obv.
Rev.

PLATE XL

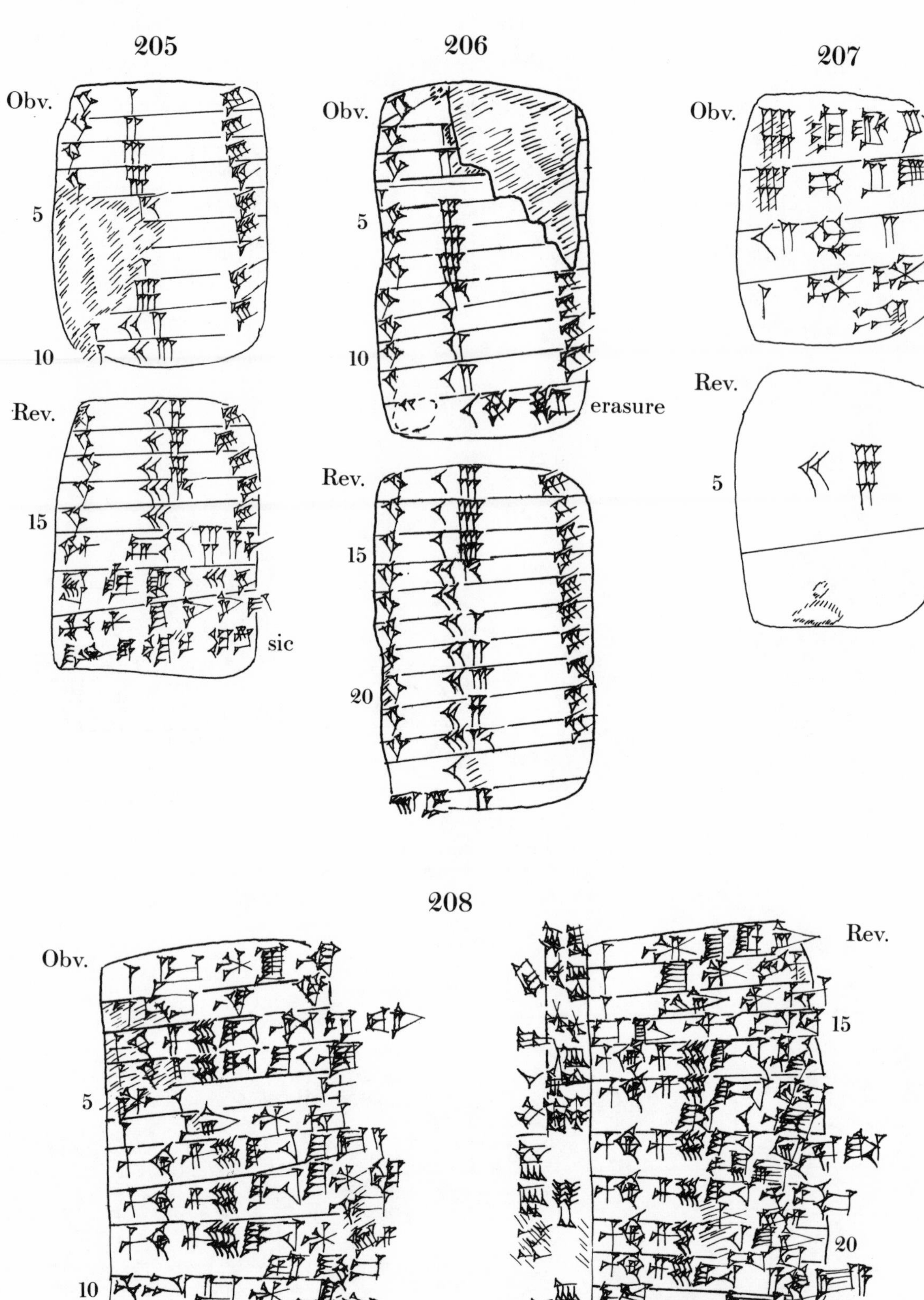
205
Obv.
5
10
Rev.
15
sic
206
Obv.
5
10
erasure
Rev.
15
20
207
Obv.
Rev.
5
208
Obv.
5
10
Rev.
15
20

209

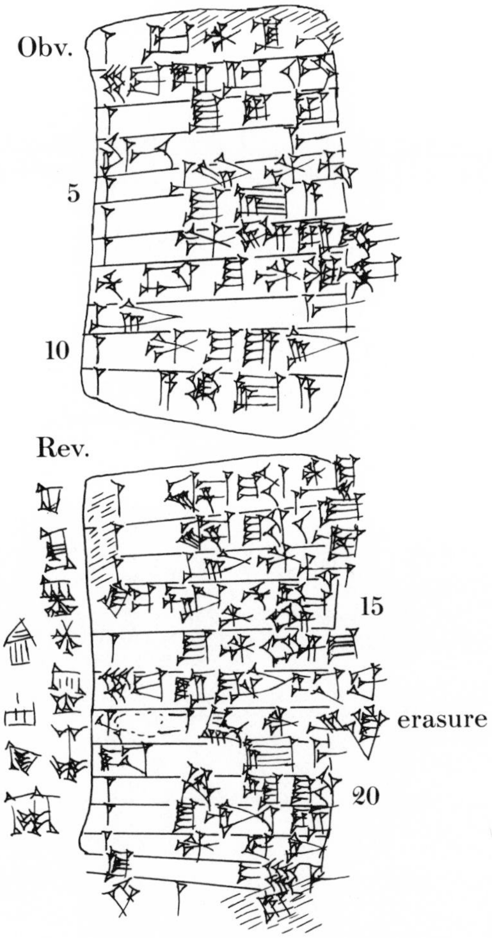

Obv.

Rev.

erasure

210

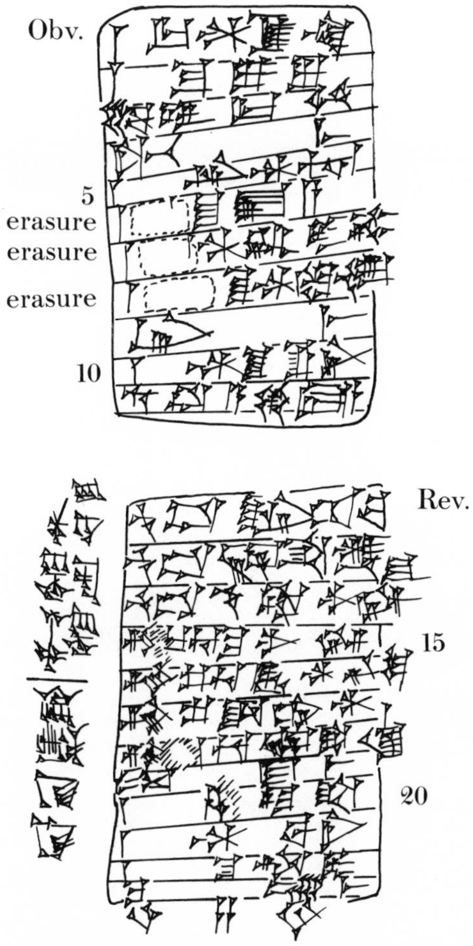

Obv.

erasure

erasure

erasure

Rev.

211

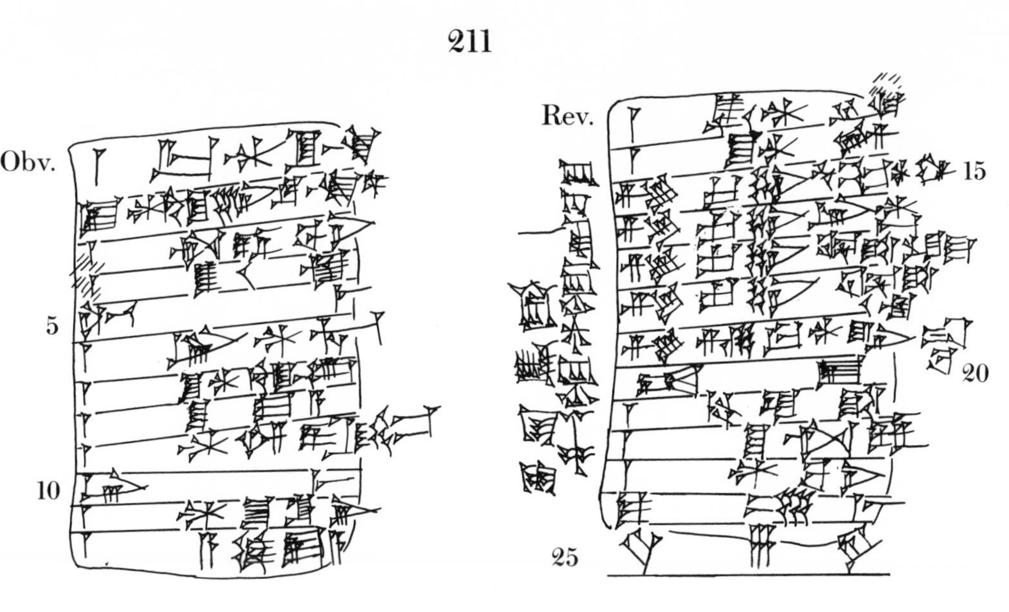

212

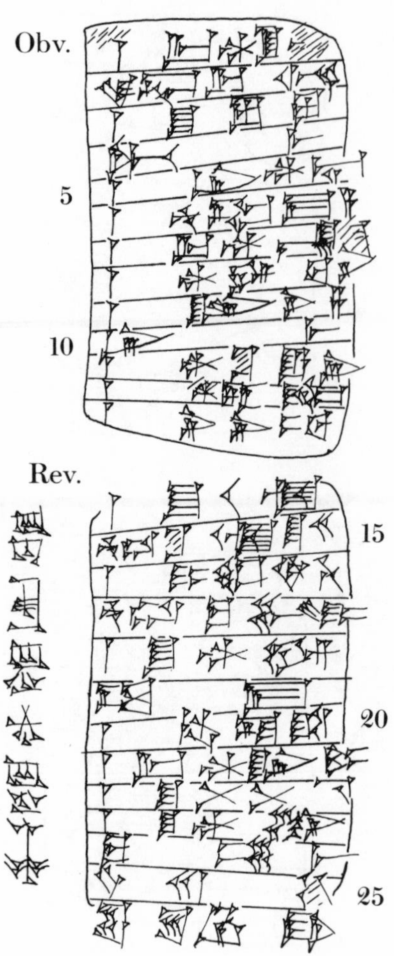

213

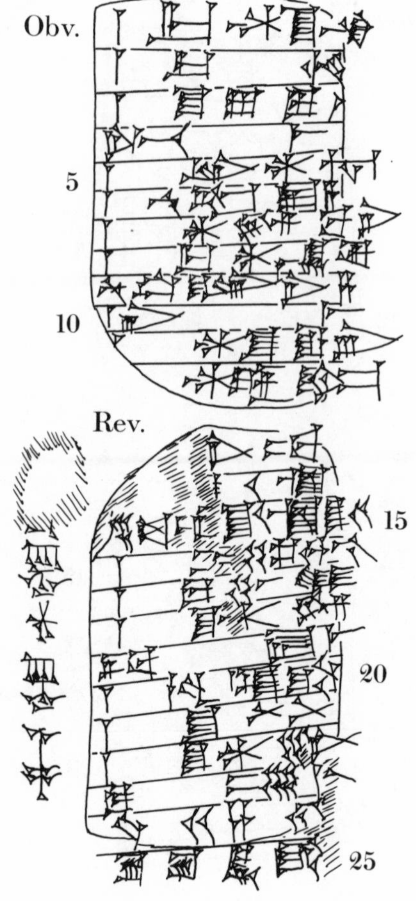

214

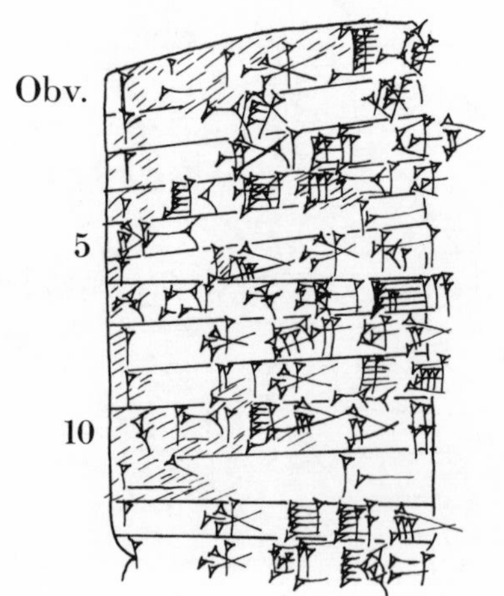

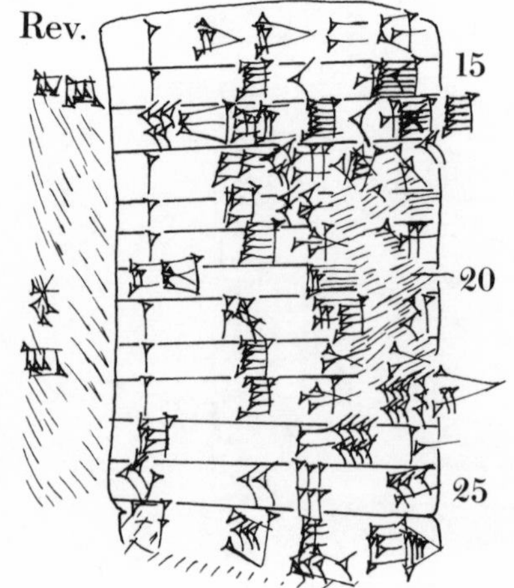

215

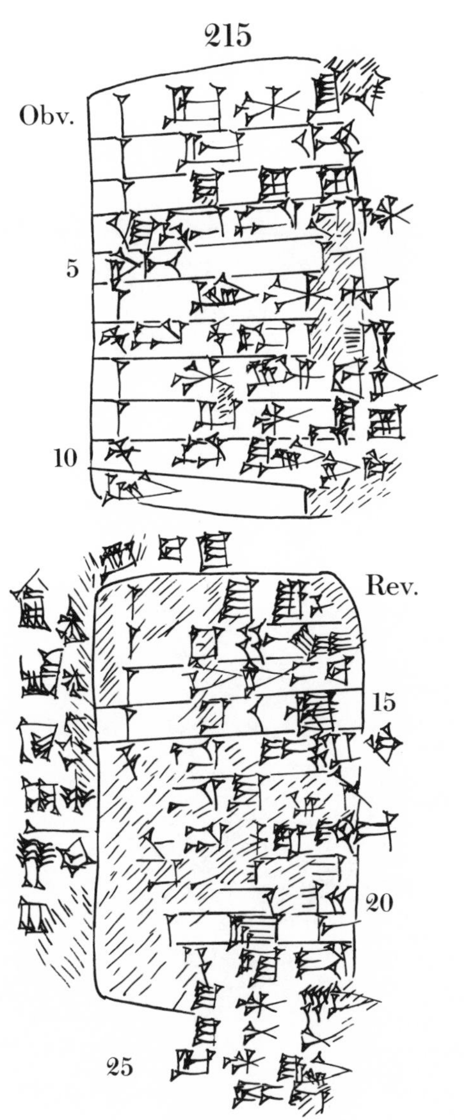

216

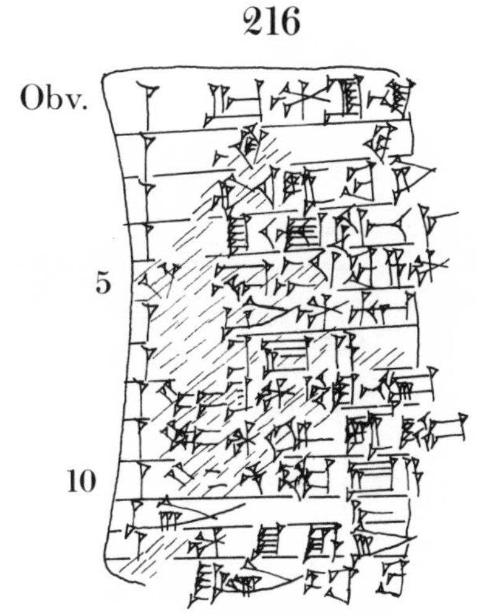

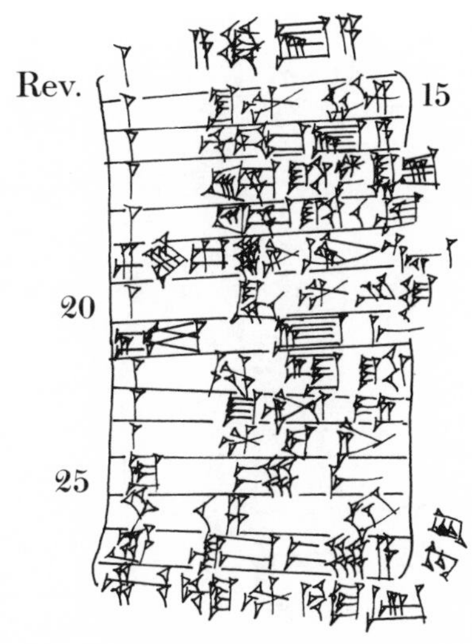

217

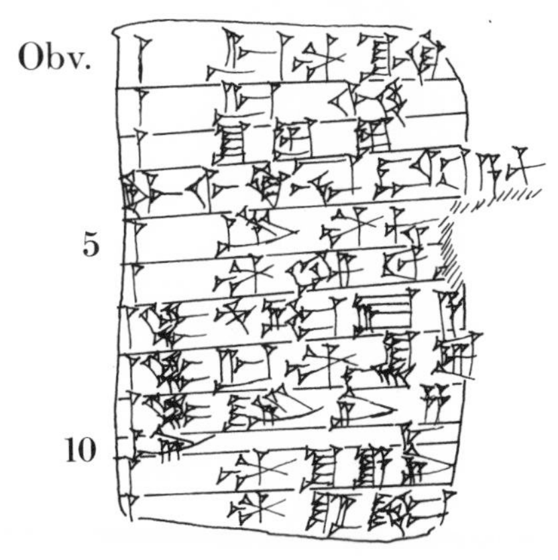

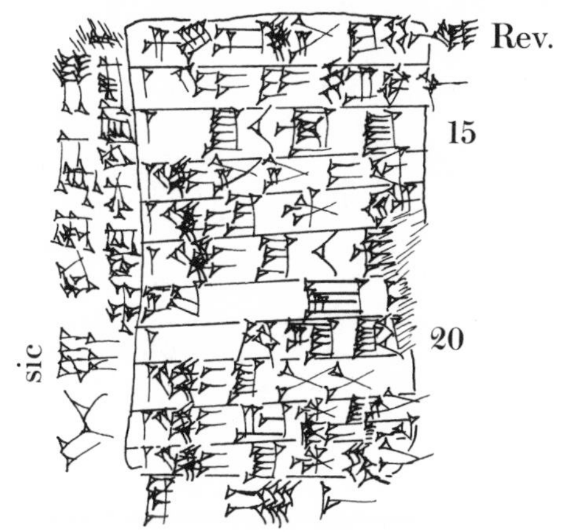

PLATE XLIV

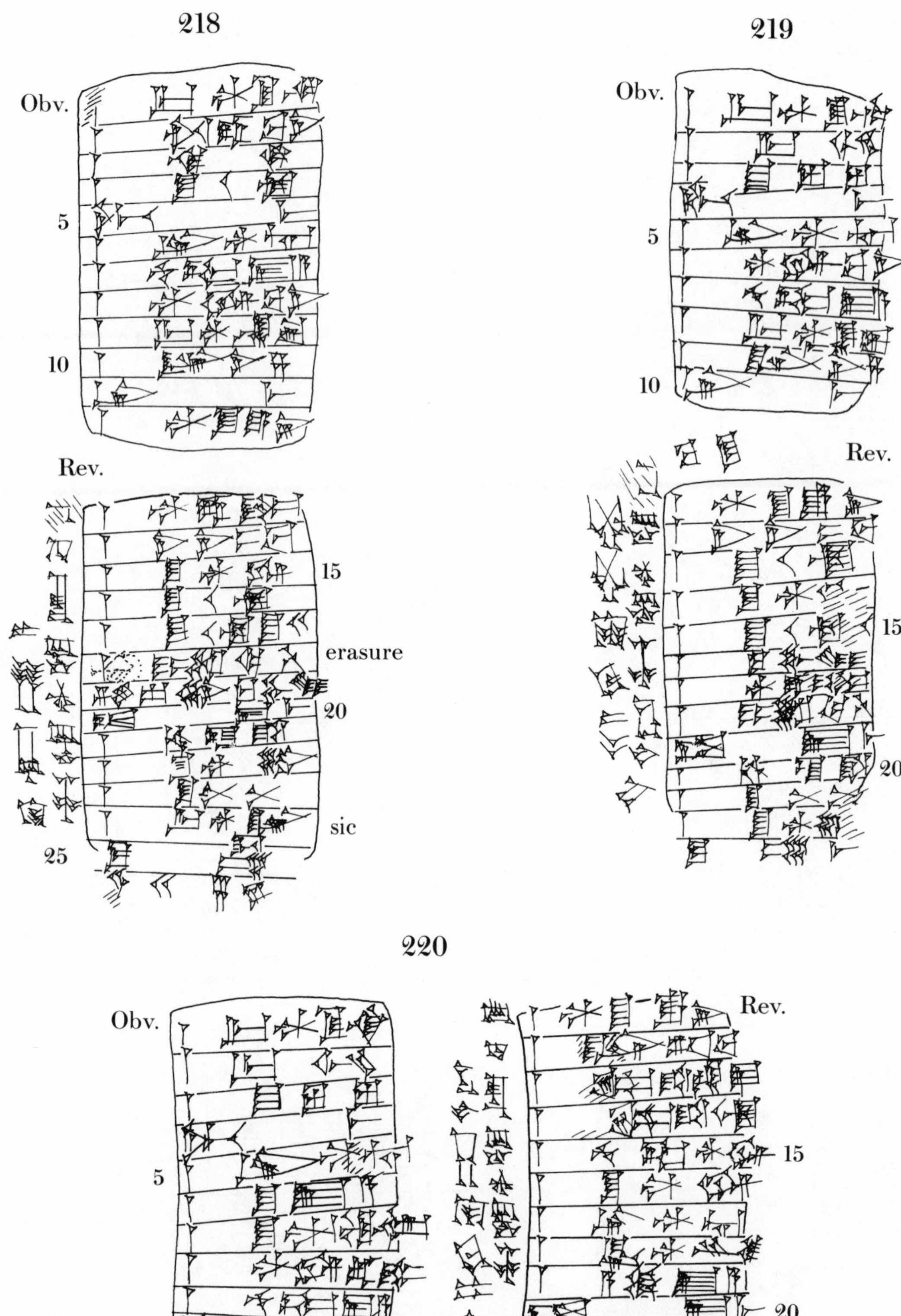

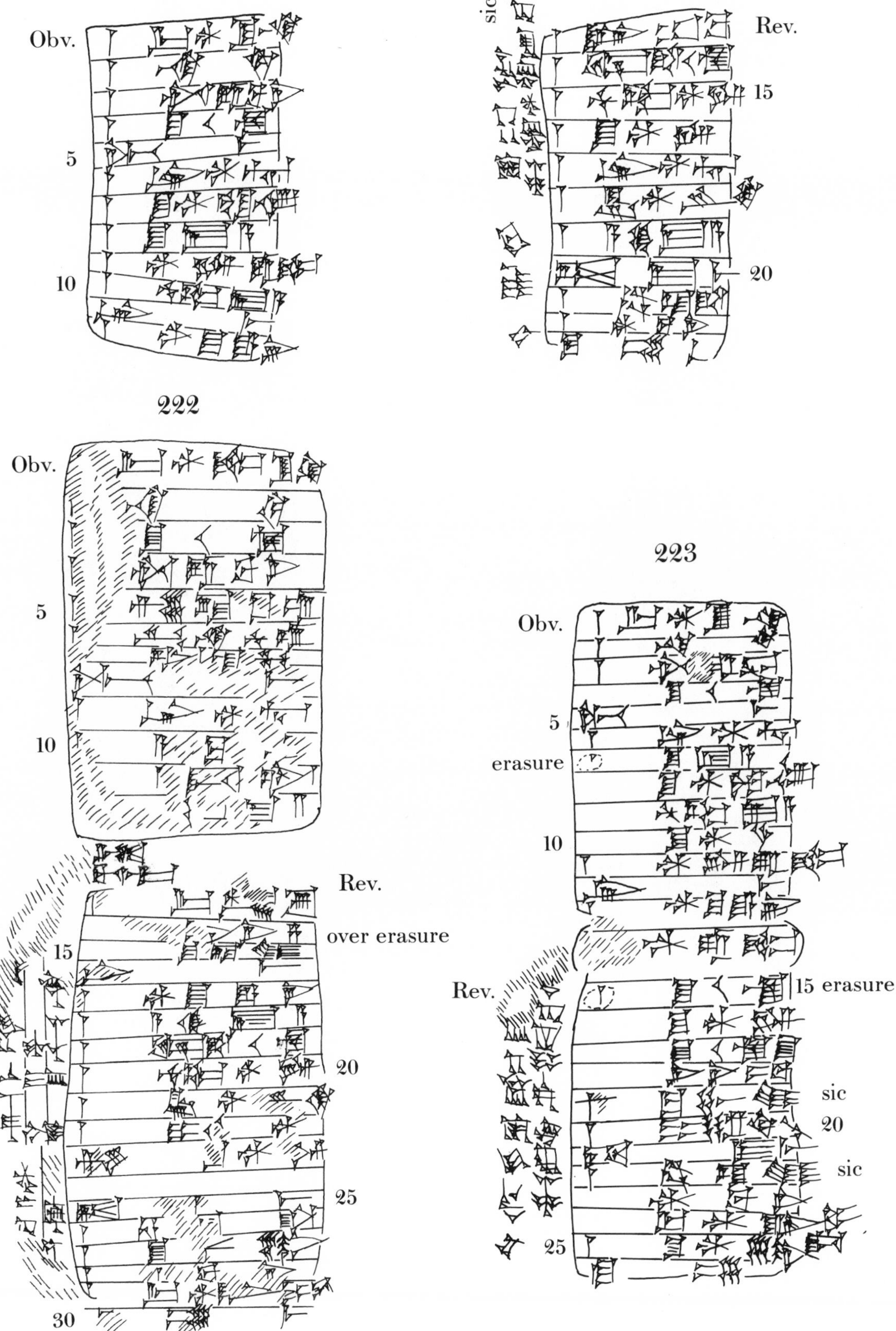
221
Obv.
5
10
sic
Rev.
15
20
222
Obv.
5
10
Rev.
over erasure
15
20
25
30
223
Obv.
5
erasure
10
Rev.
15 erasure
sic
20
sic
25

PLATE XLVI

224

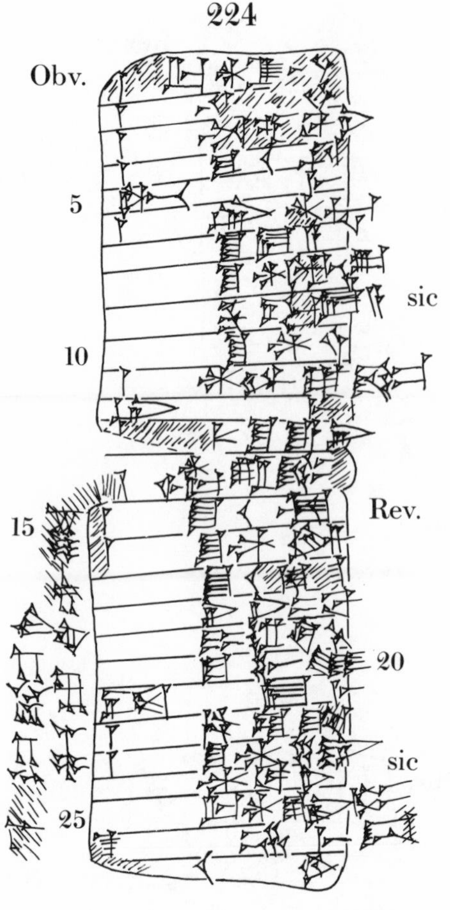

225

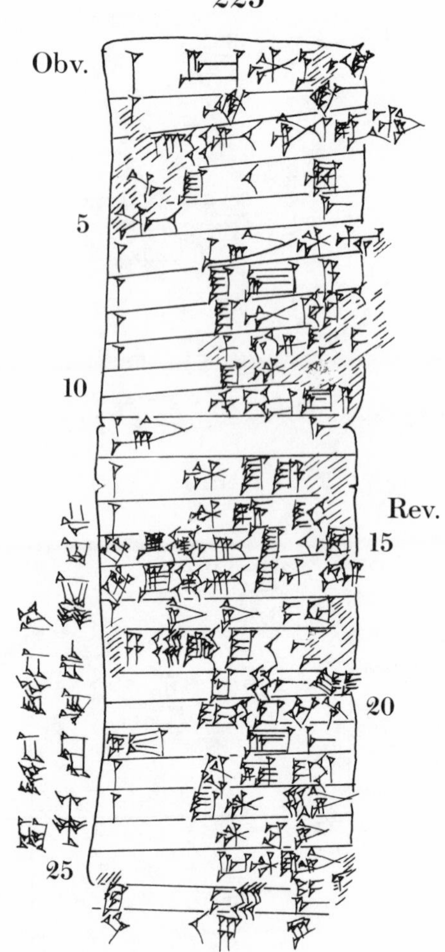

226

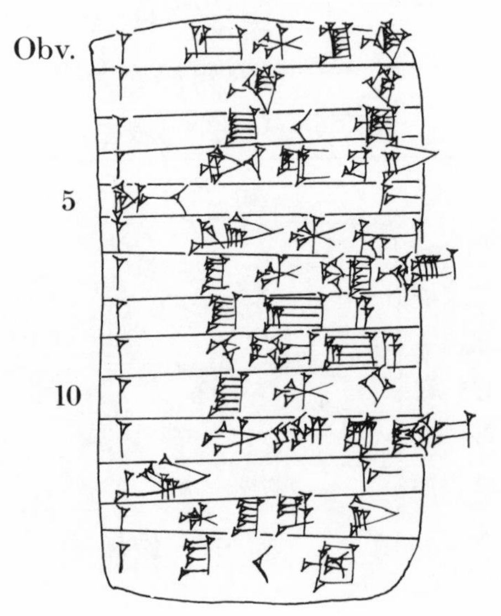

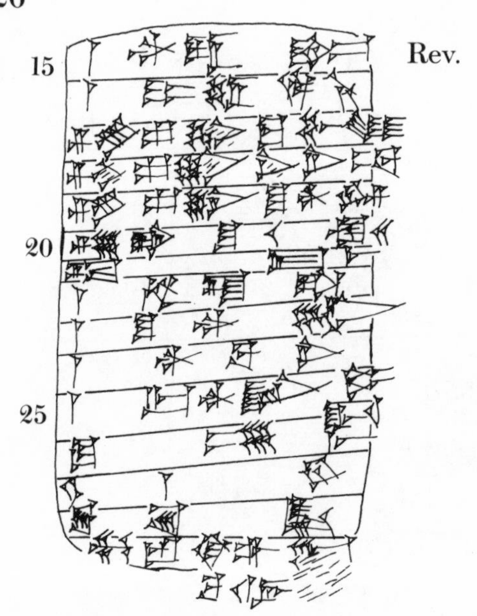

227

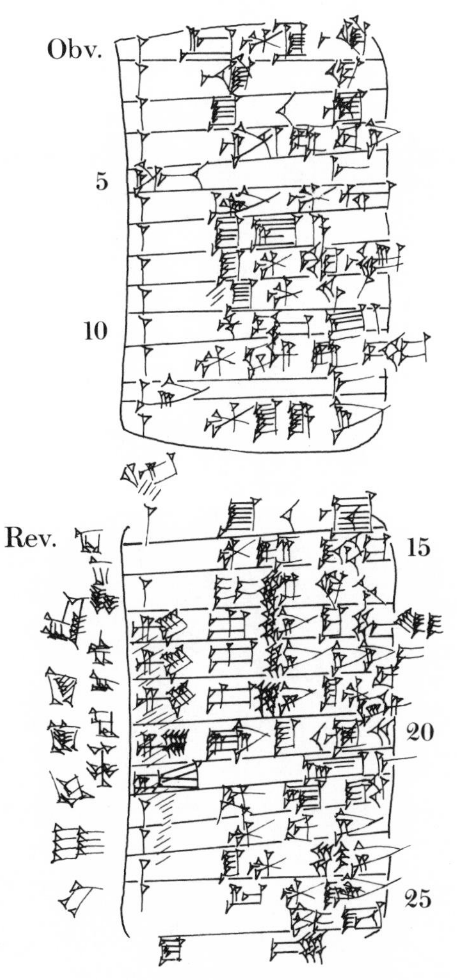

228

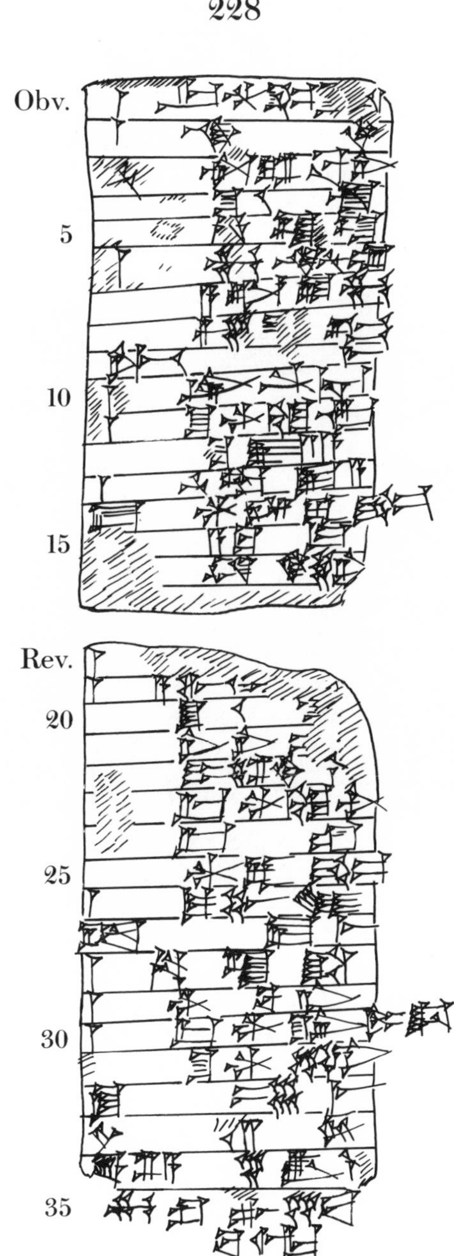

PLATE XLVIII

229

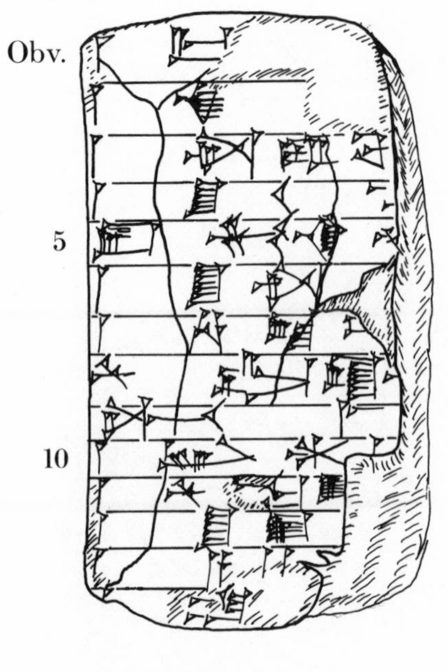

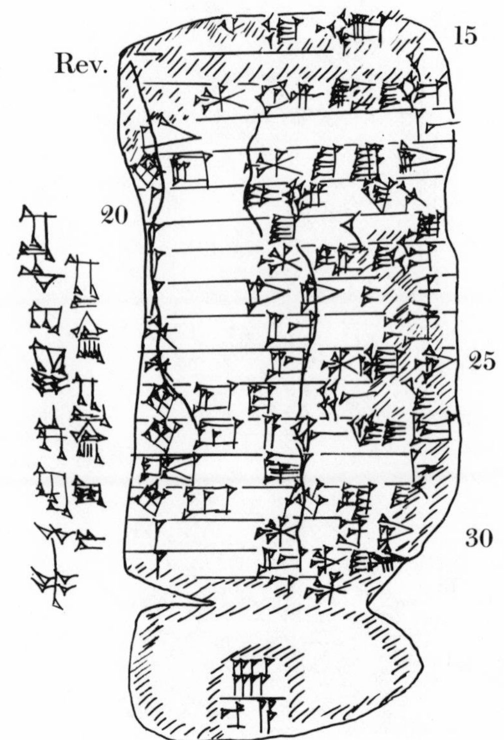

230

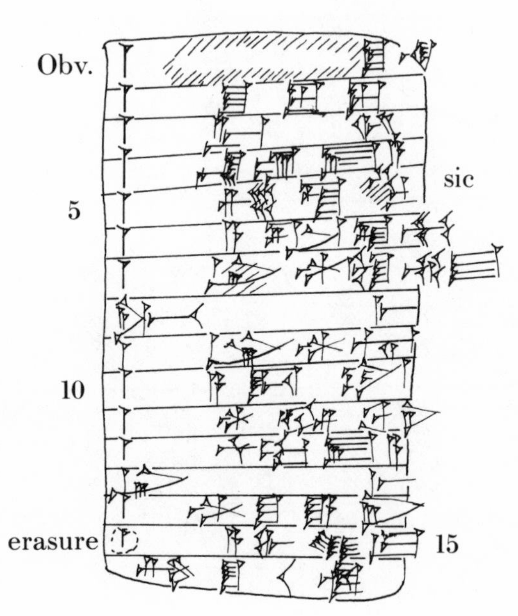

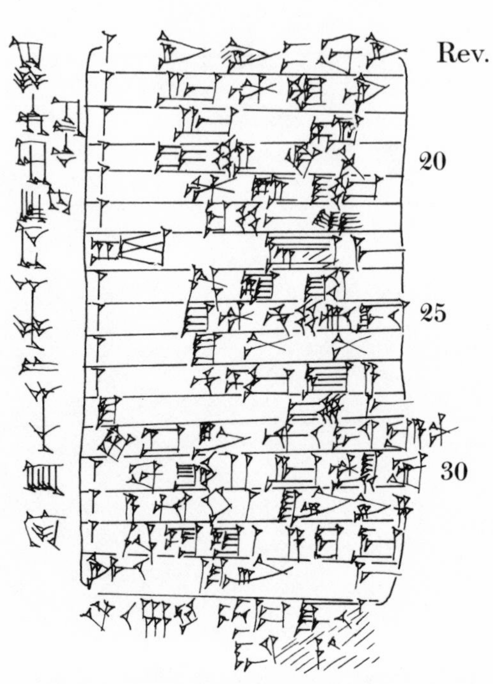

231

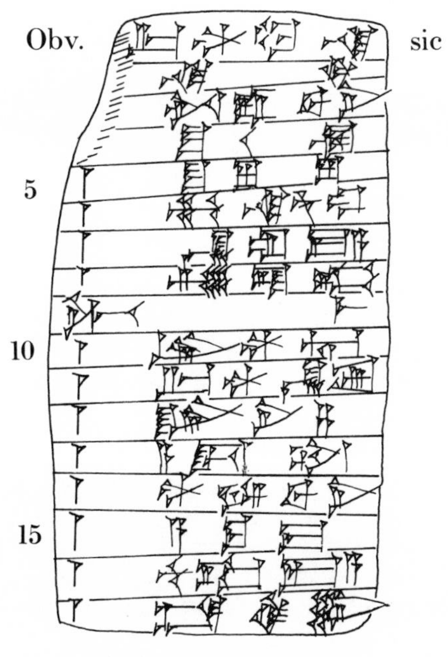

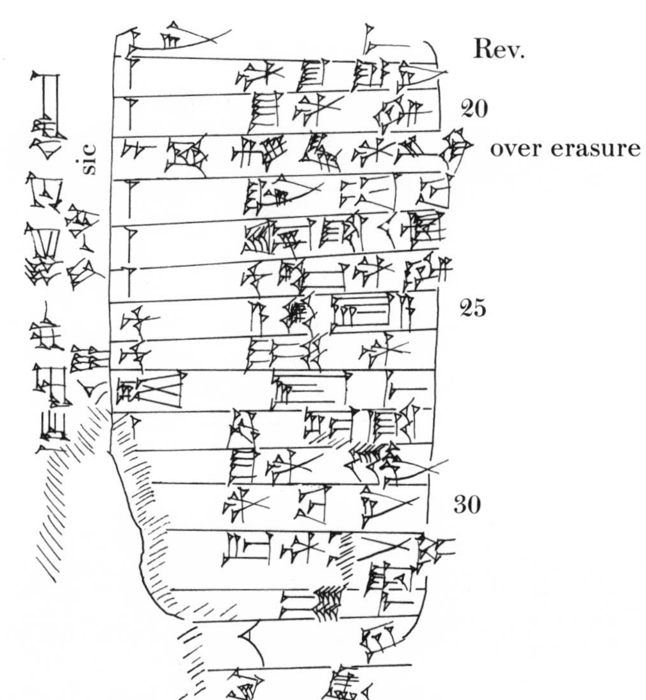

232

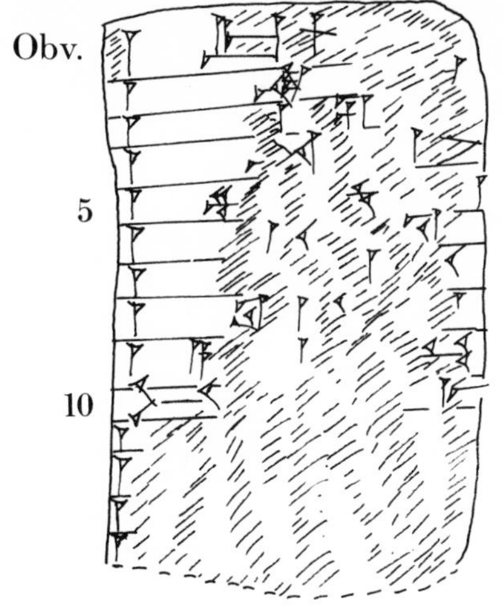

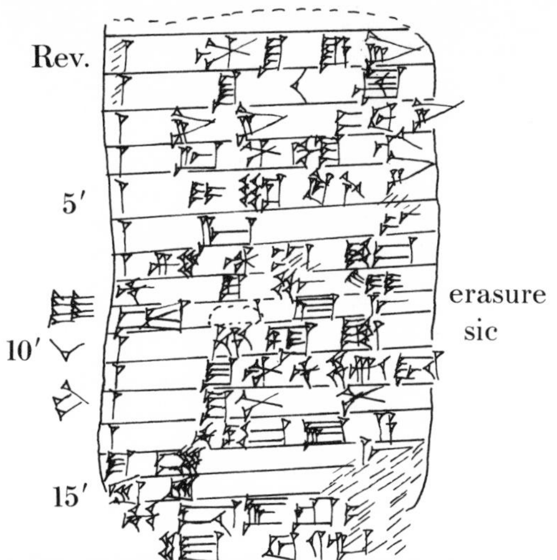

PLATE L

233

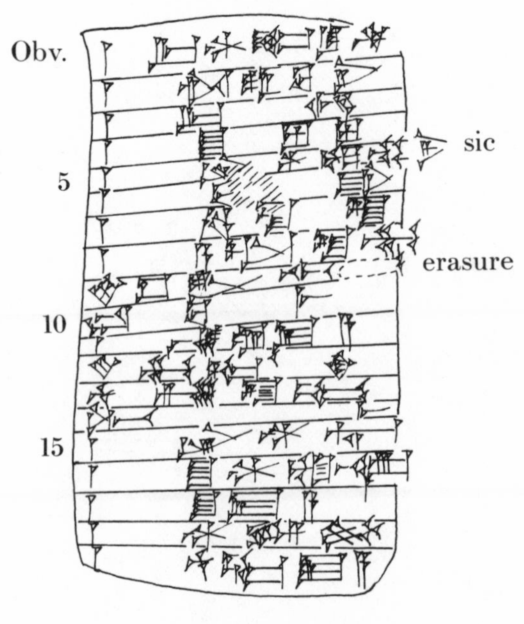

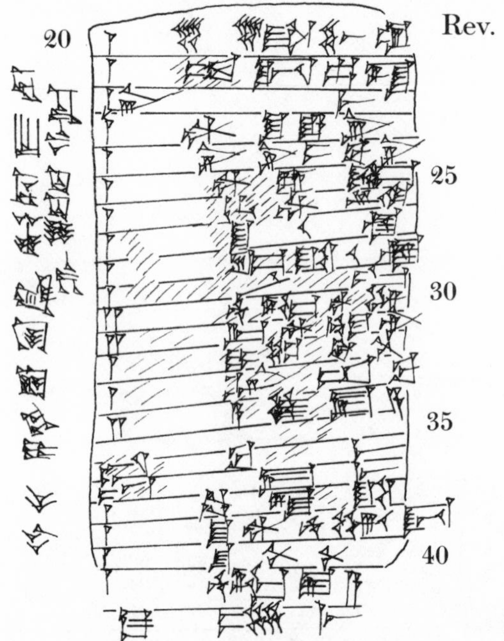

234

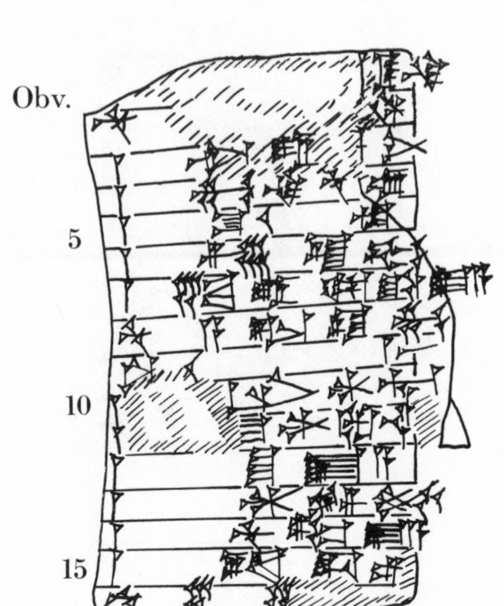

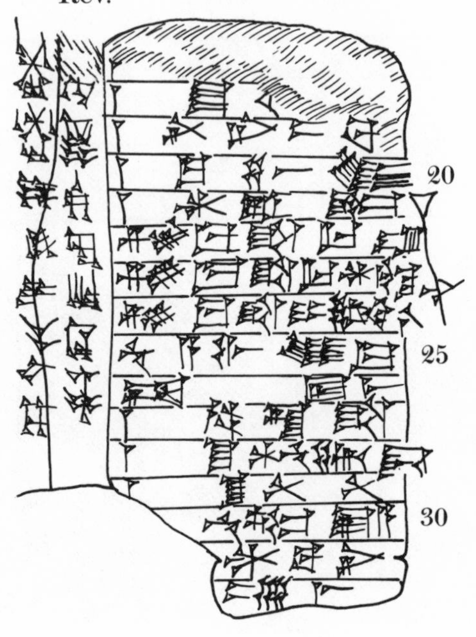

235

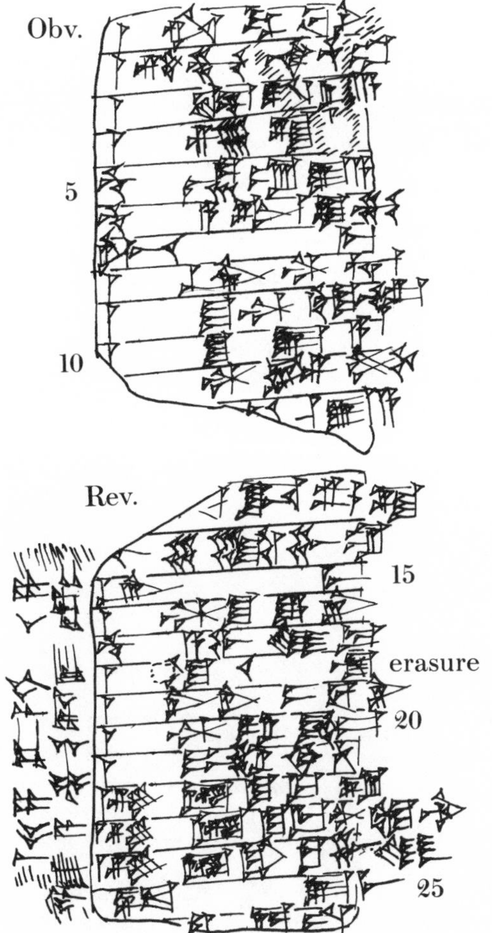

236

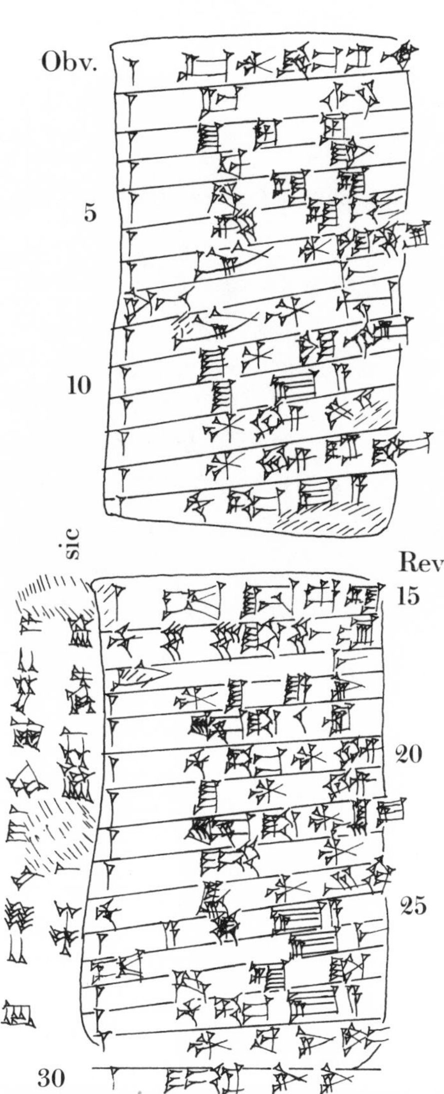

PLATE LII

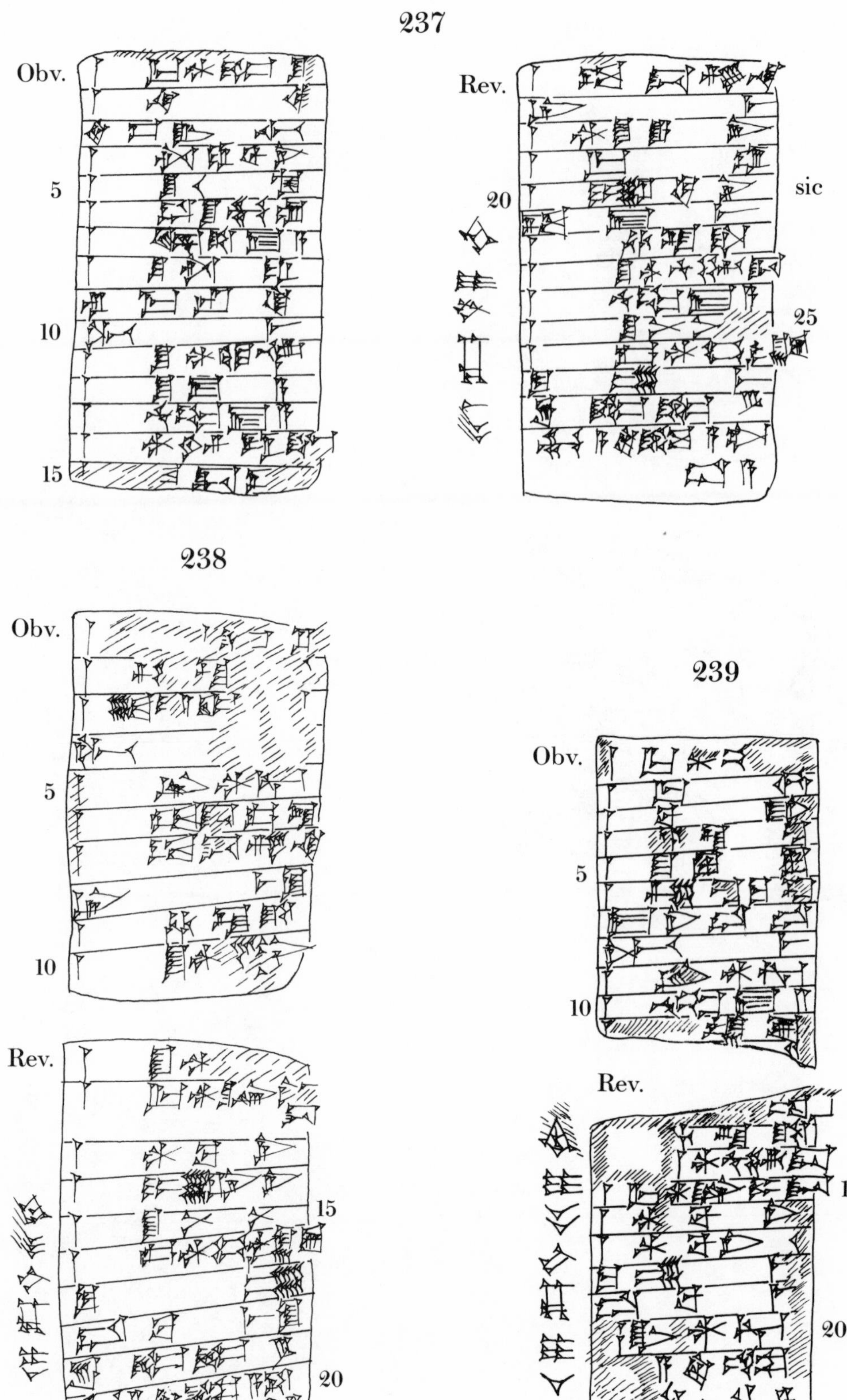

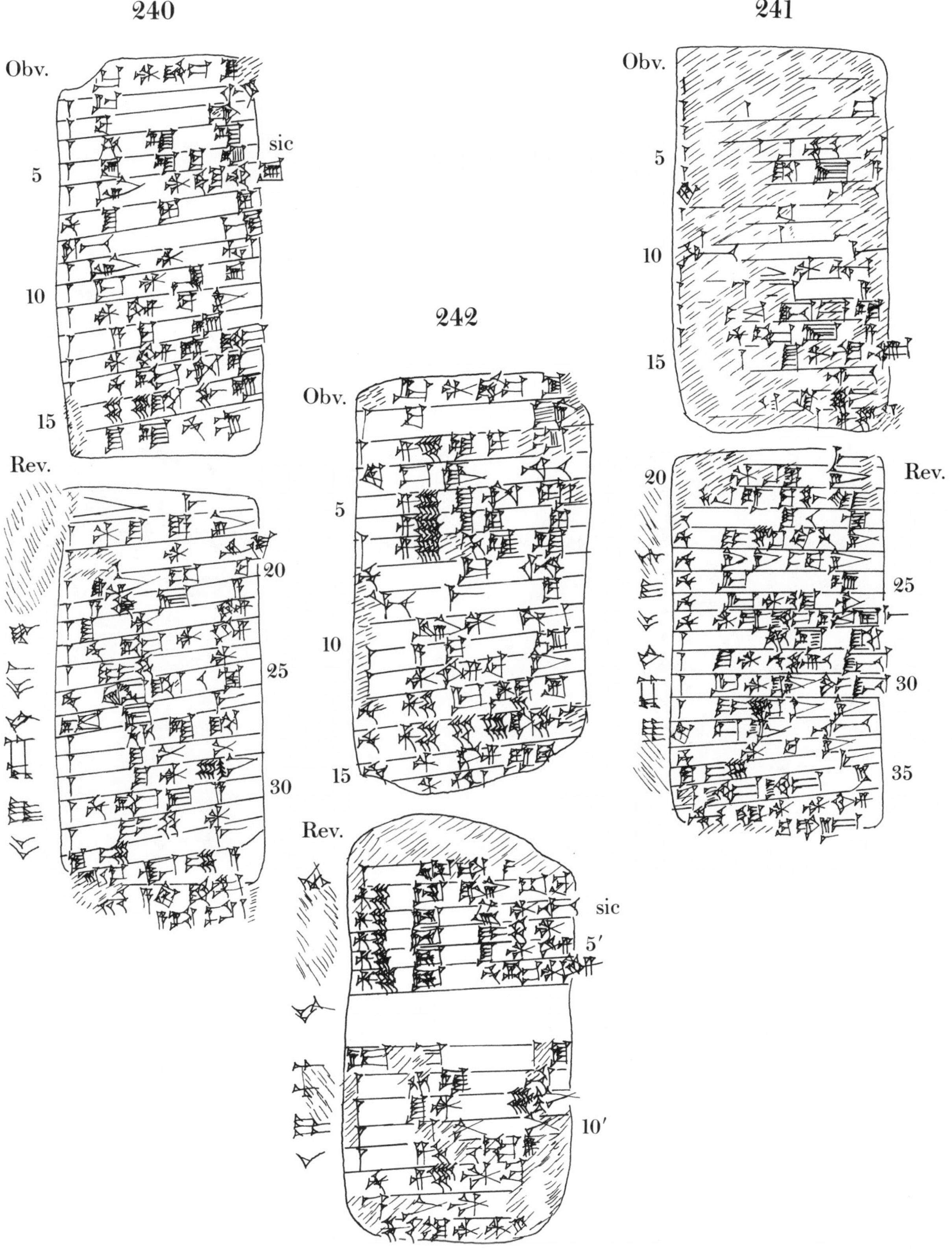
240
Obv.
sic
5
10
15
Rev.
20
25
30
241
Obv.
5
10
15
20
Rev.
25
30
35
242
Obv.
5
10
15
Rev.
sic
5′
10′

PLATE LIV

243

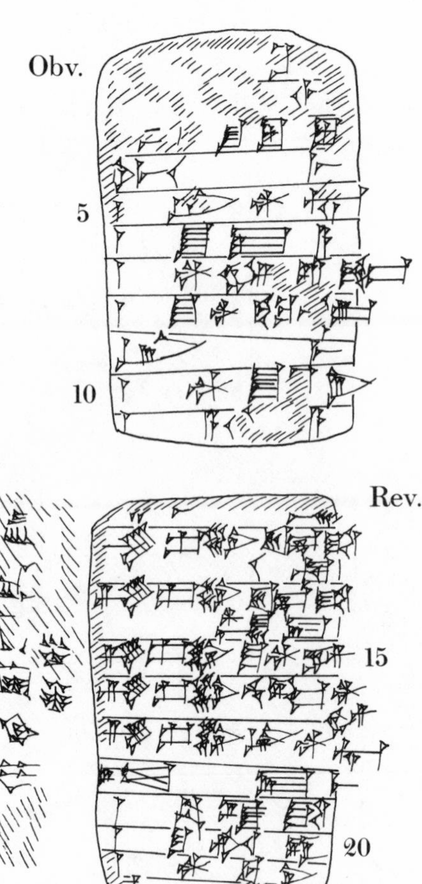

244

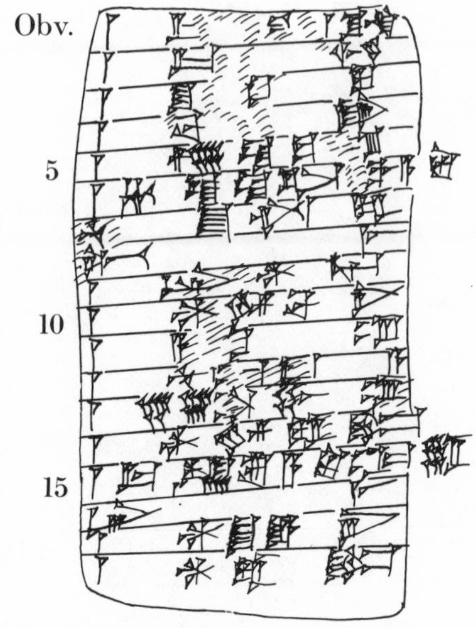

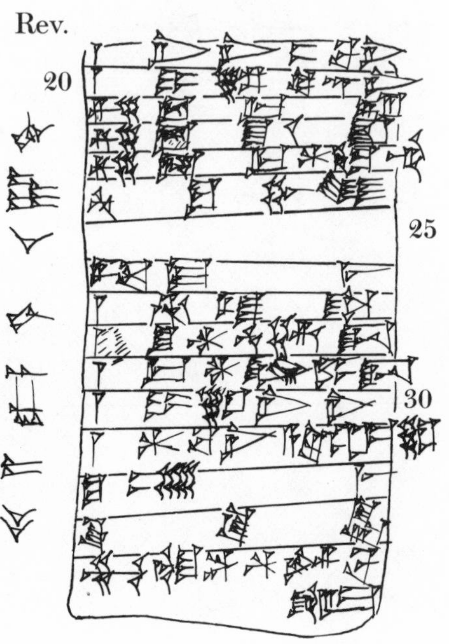

PLATE LV

245

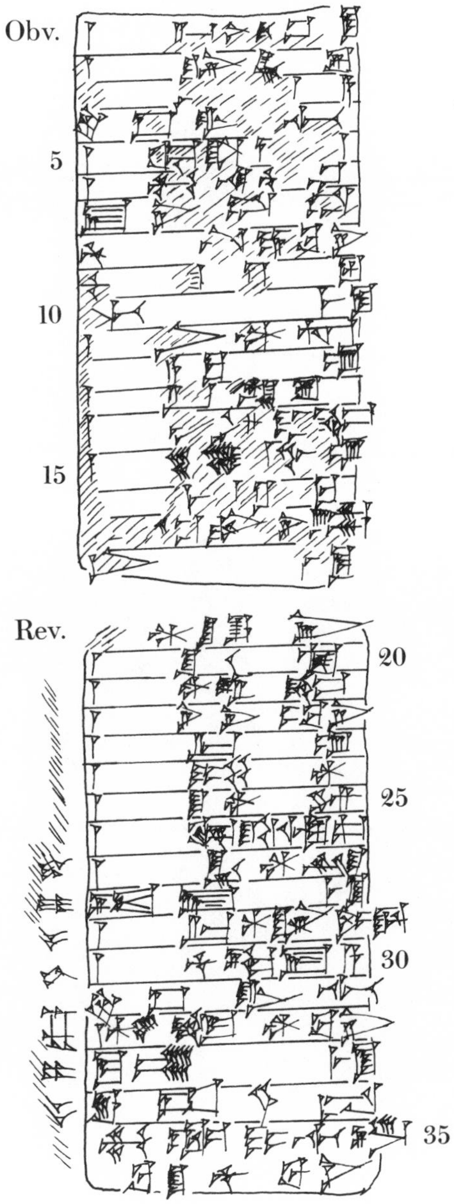

Obv.

Rev.

246

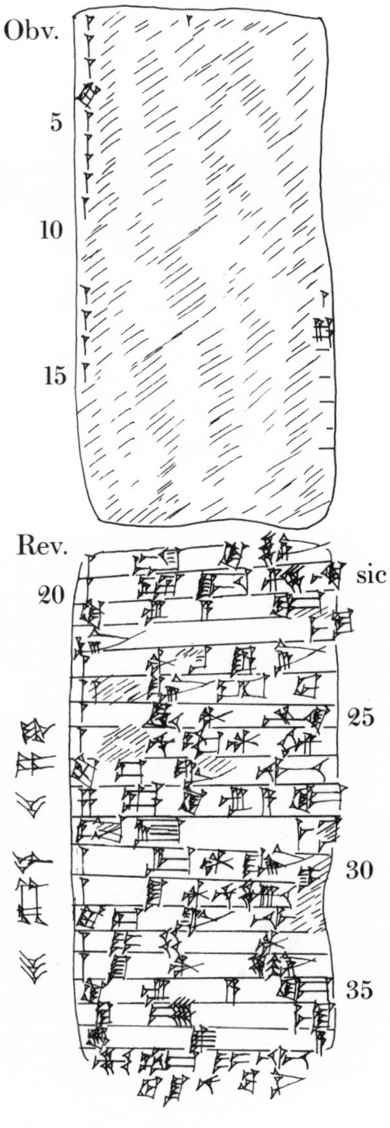

Obv.

Rev.

sic

247

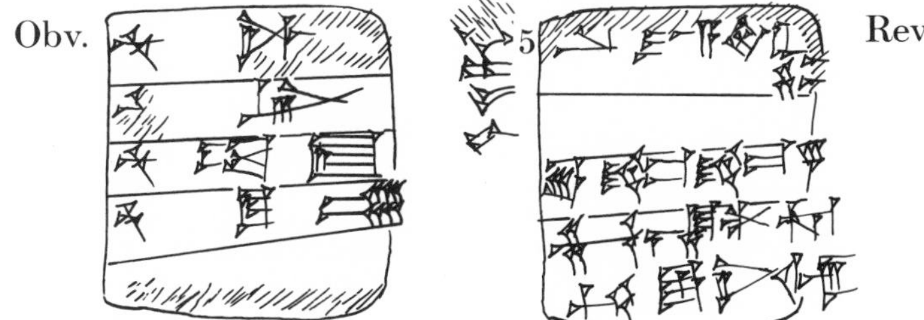

Obv.

Rev.

PLATE LVI

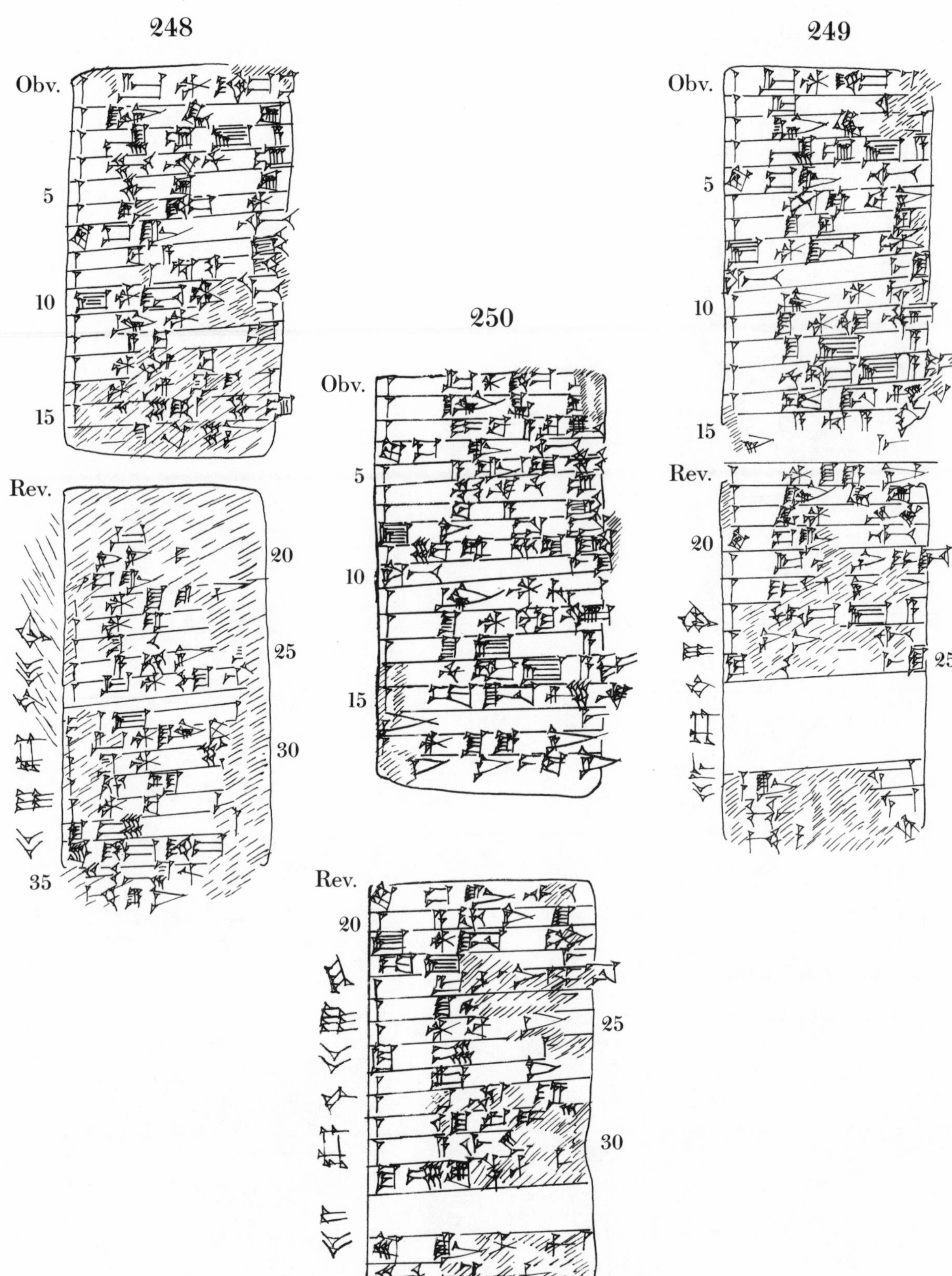

248
Obv.
5
10
15
Rev.
20
25
30
35
249
Obv.
5
10
15
Rev.
20
25
250
Obv.
5
10
15
Rev.
20
25
30

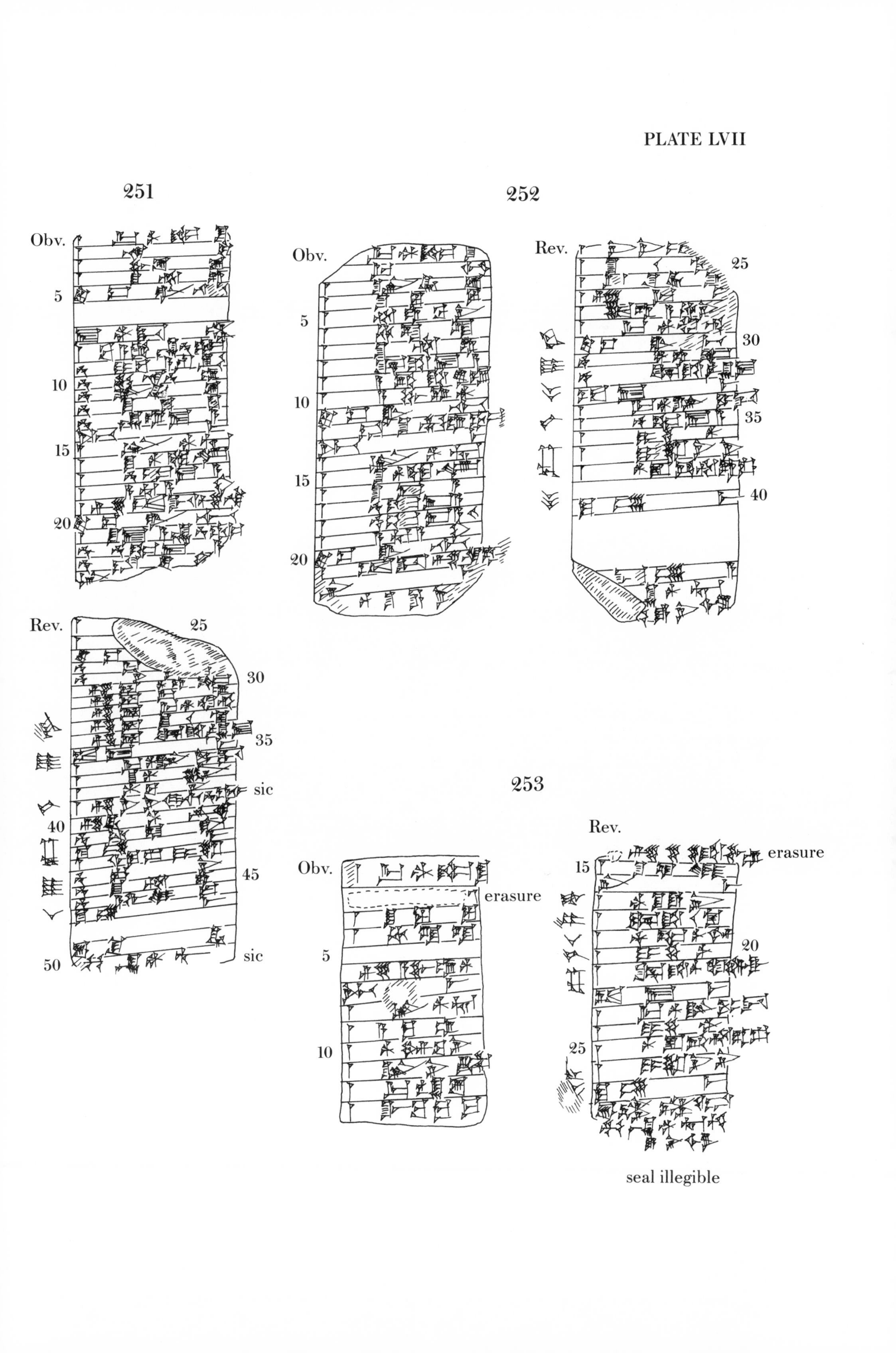

251

Obv.

Rev.

sic

sic

252

Obv.

Rev.

253

Obv.

erasure

Rev.

erasure

seal illegible

PLATE LVIII

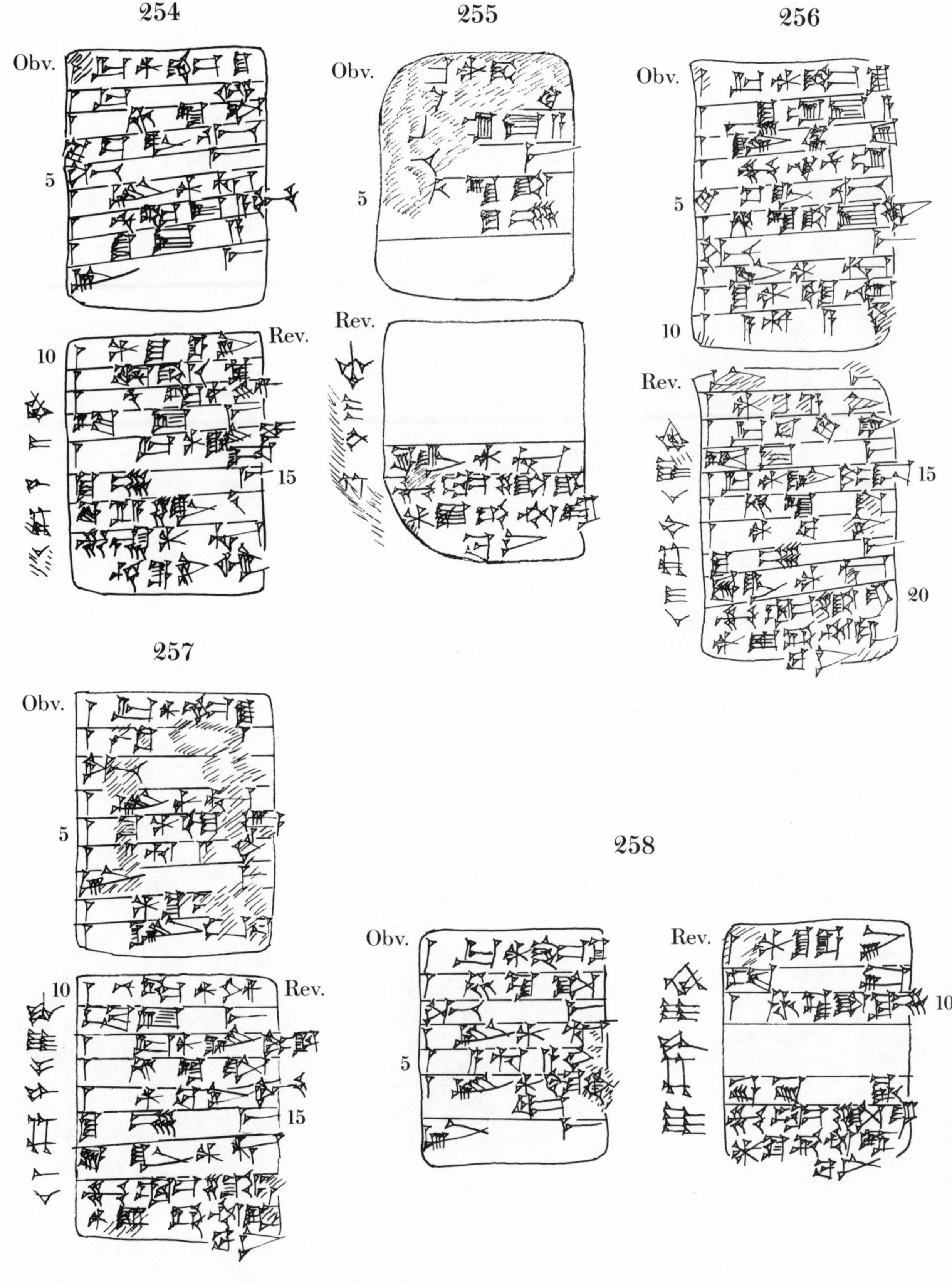

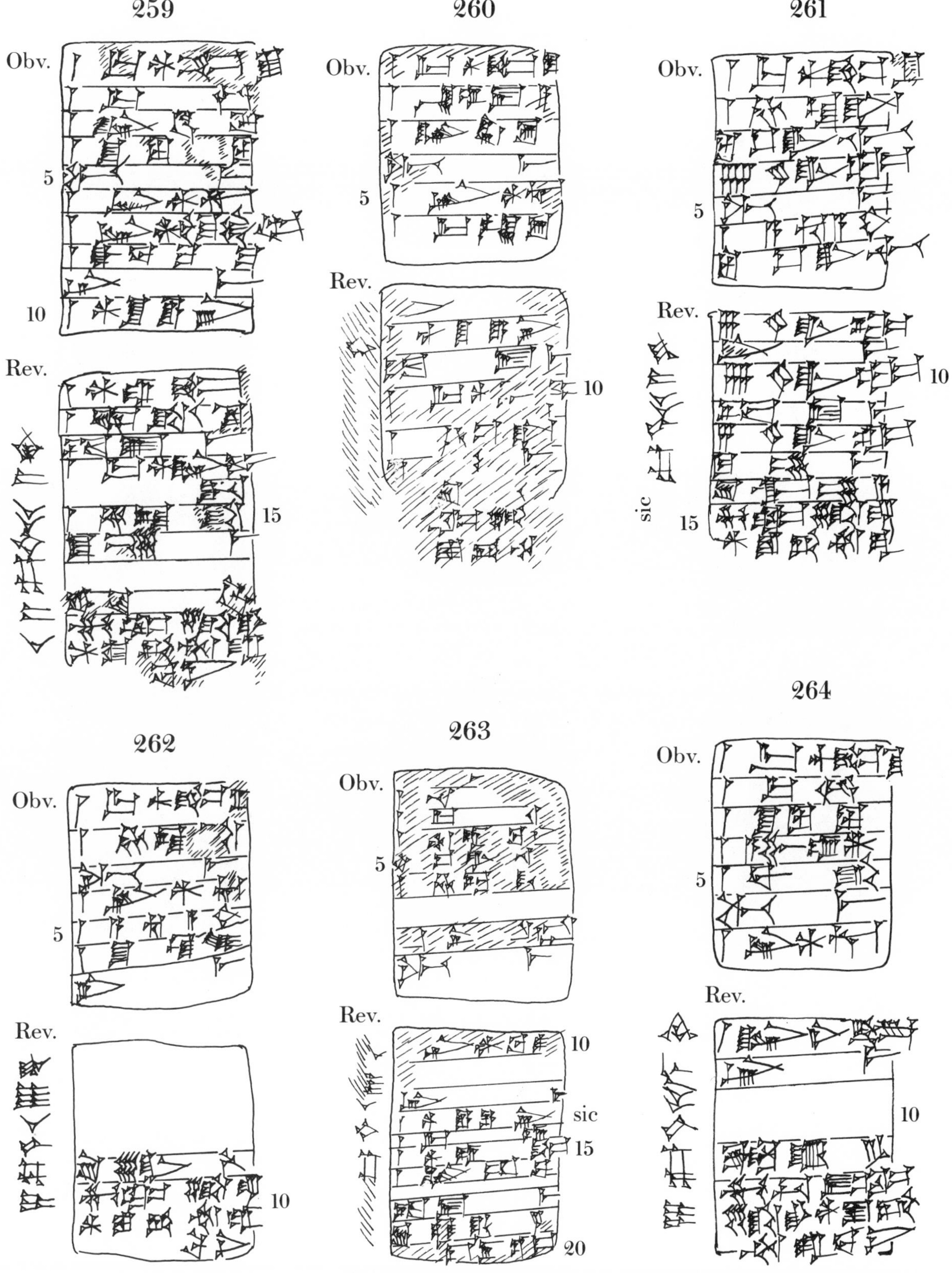
259
Obv.
Rev.
260
Obv.
Rev.
261
Obv.
Rev.
sic
262
Obv.
Rev.
263
Obv.
Rev.
sic
264
Obv.
Rev.

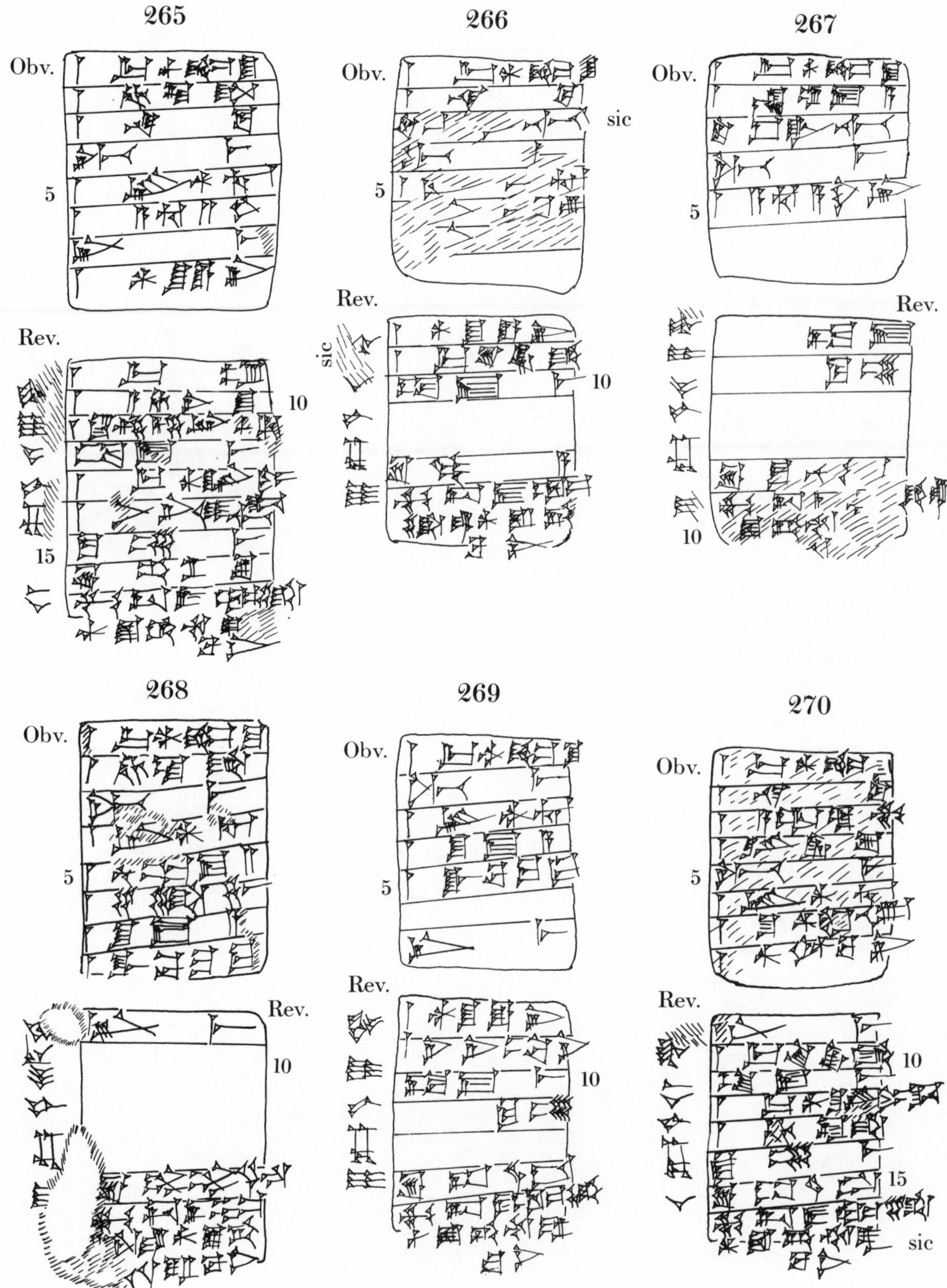
265
Obv.
5
Rev.
10
15
266
Obv.
sic
5
Rev.
sic
10
267
Obv.
5
Rev.
10
268
Obv.
5
Rev.
10
269
Obv.
5
Rev.
10
270
Obv.
5
Rev.
10
15
sic

271

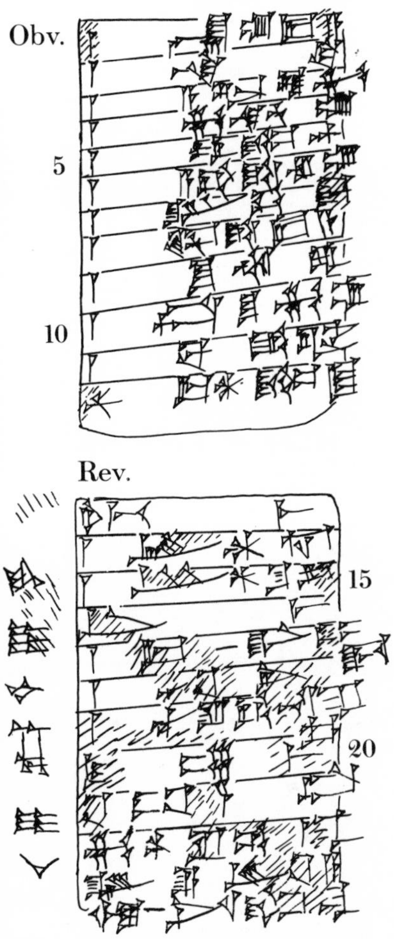

Obv.

Rev.

272

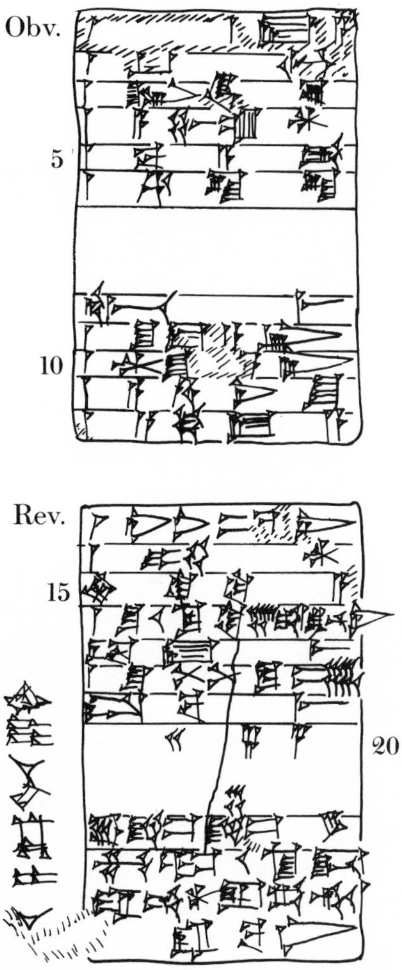

Obv.

Rev.

273

Obv.

erasure

Rev.

sic

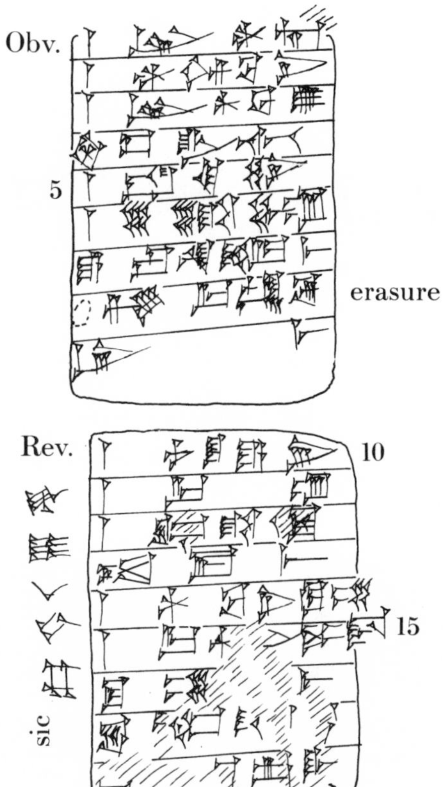

274

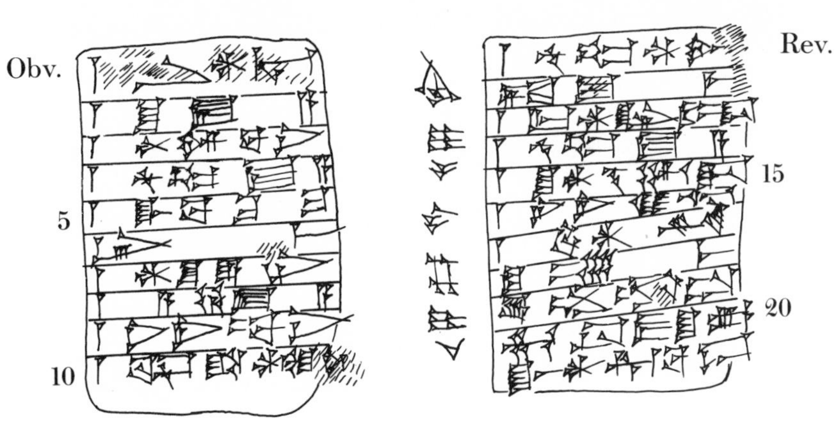

seal illegible

PLATE LXII

275

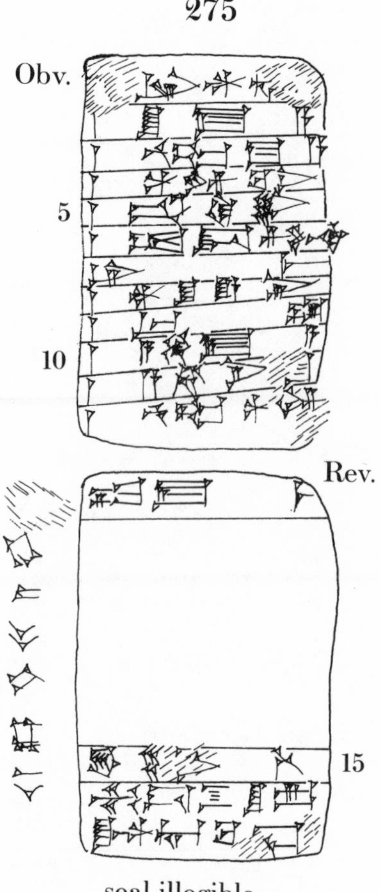

276

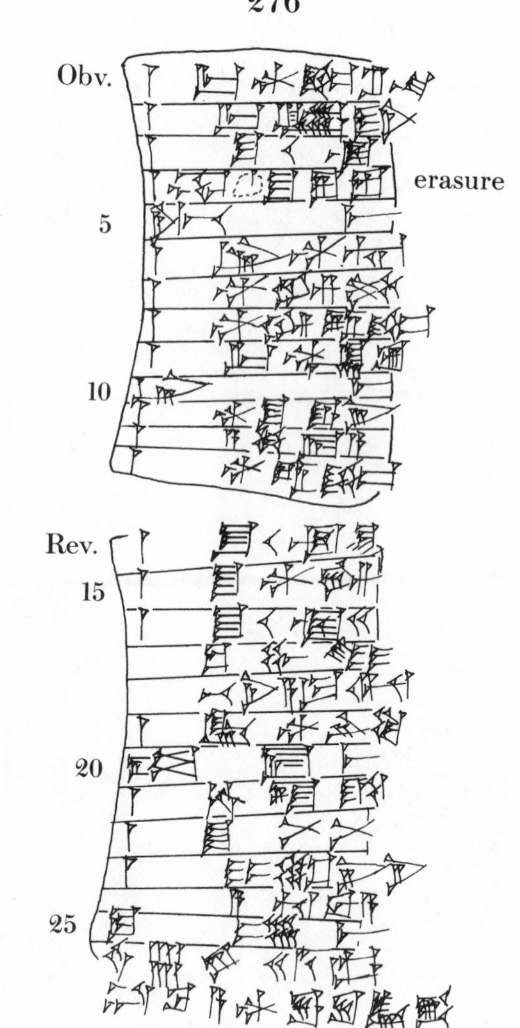

277

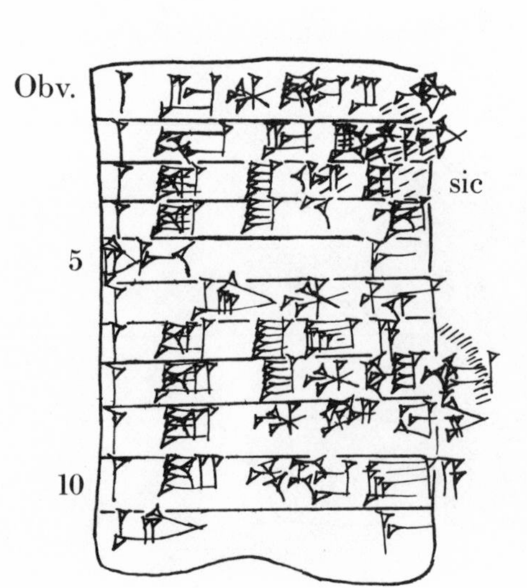

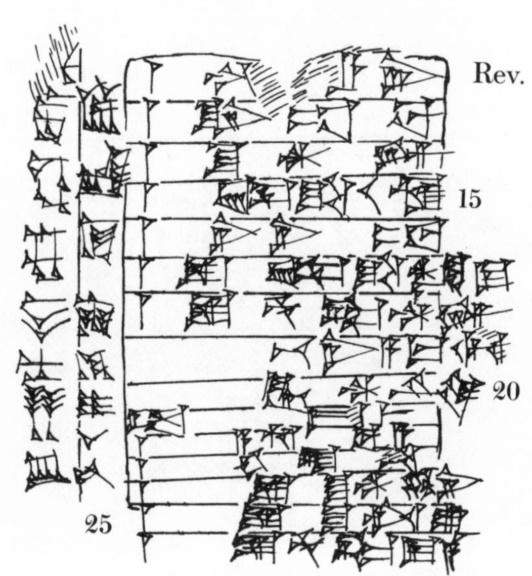

278

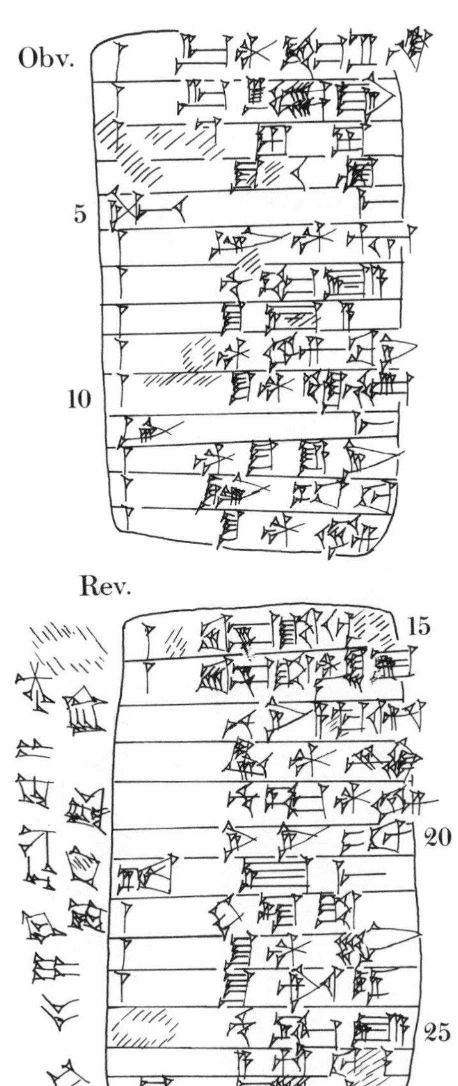

279

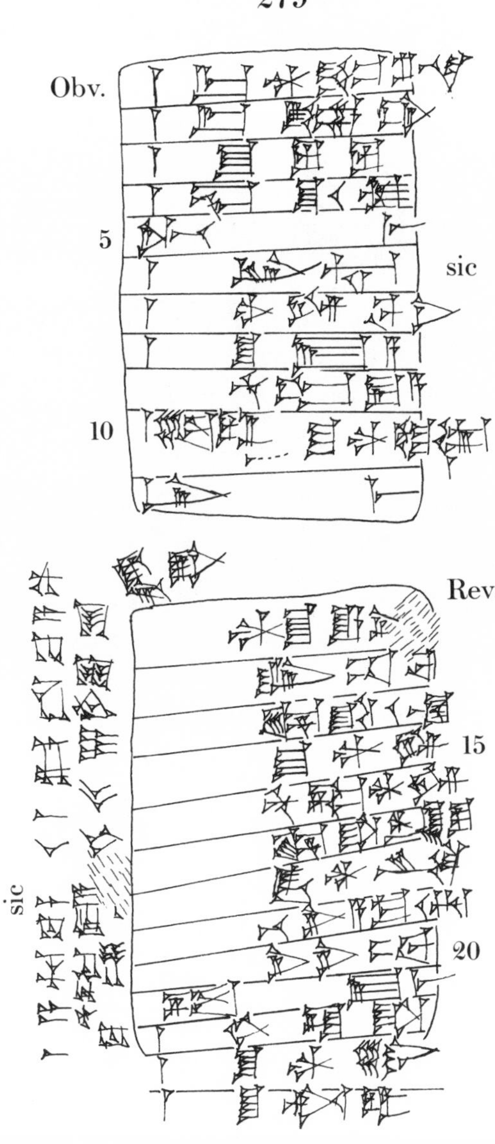

280

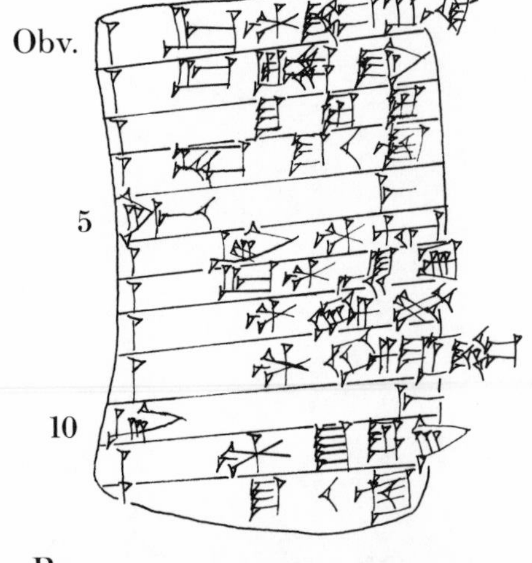

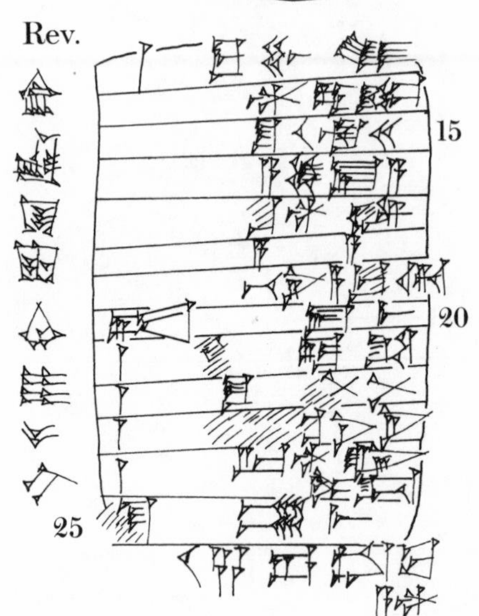

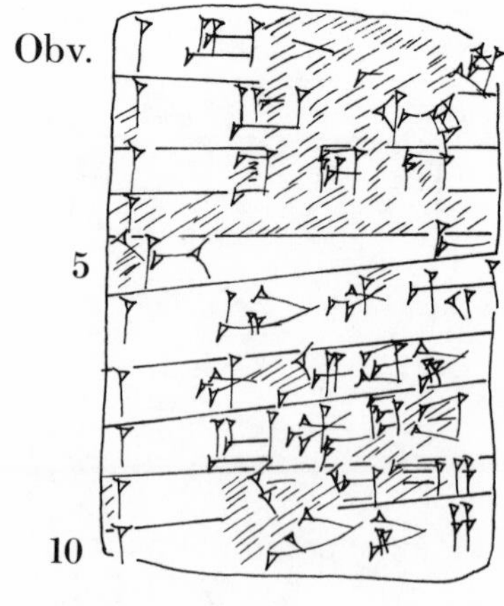

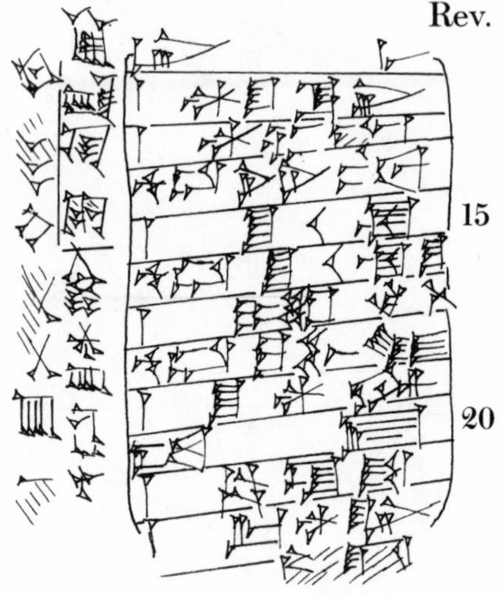

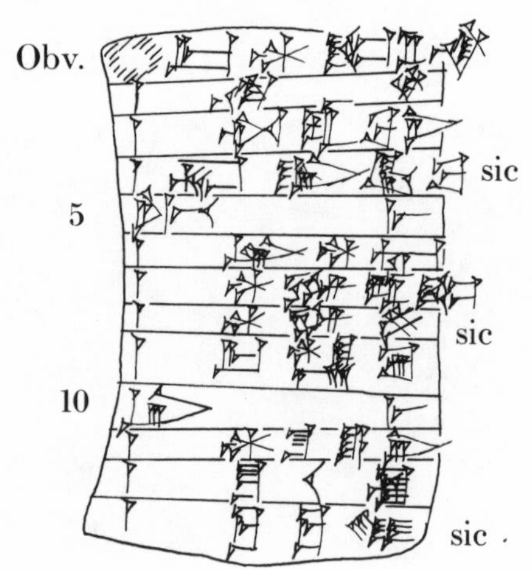

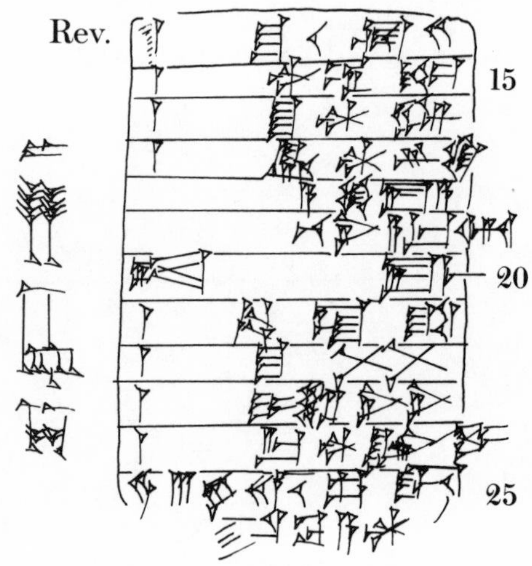

283

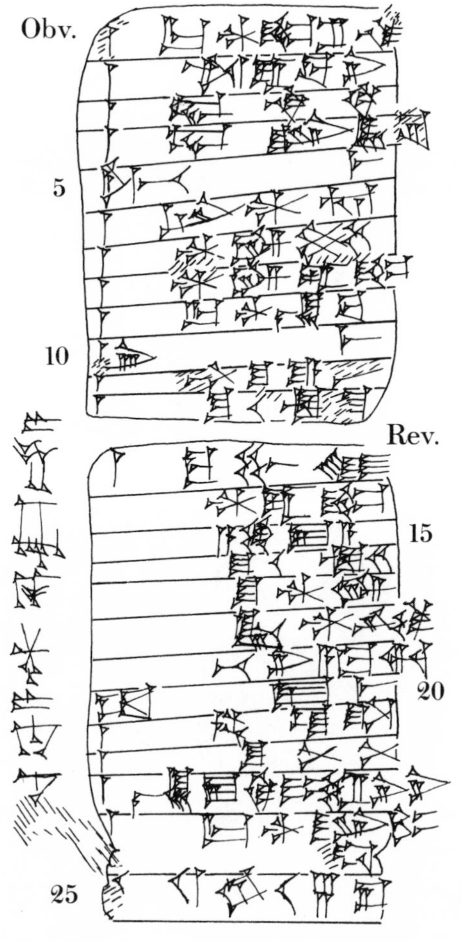

284

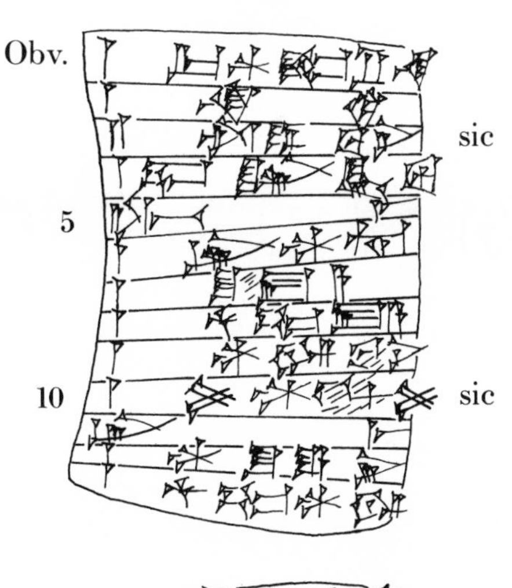

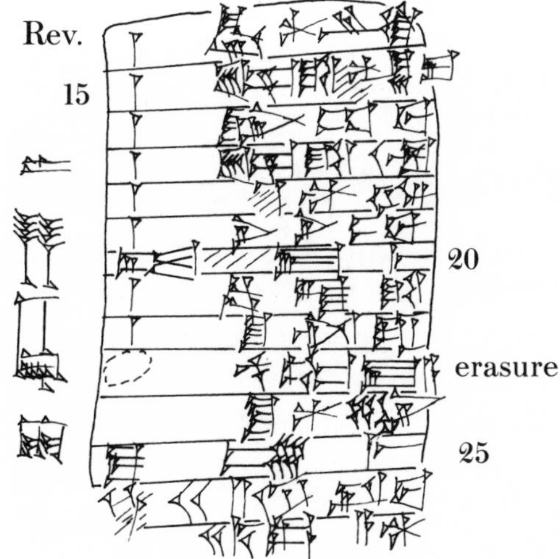

285

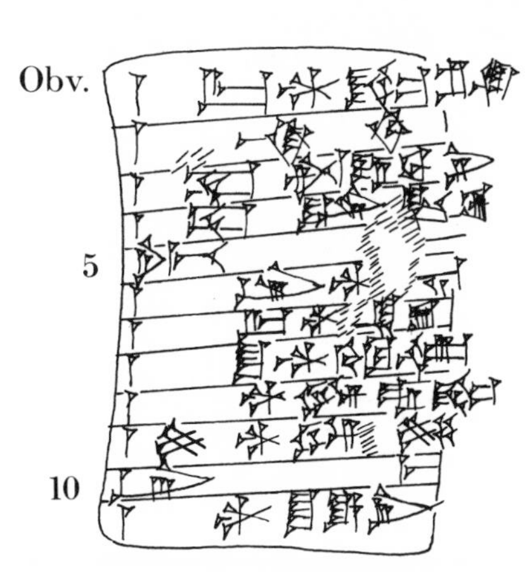

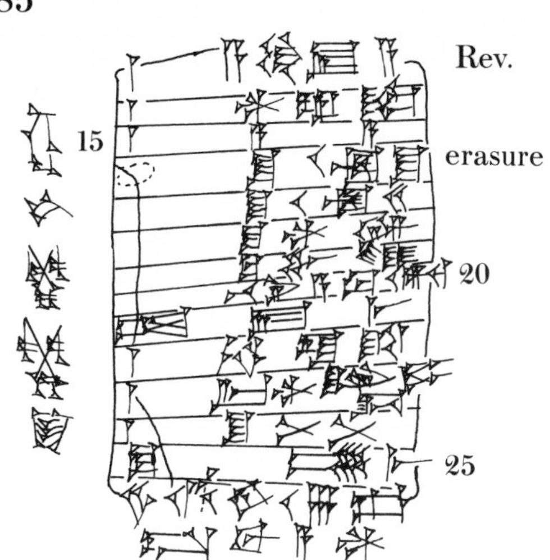

PLATE LXVI

286

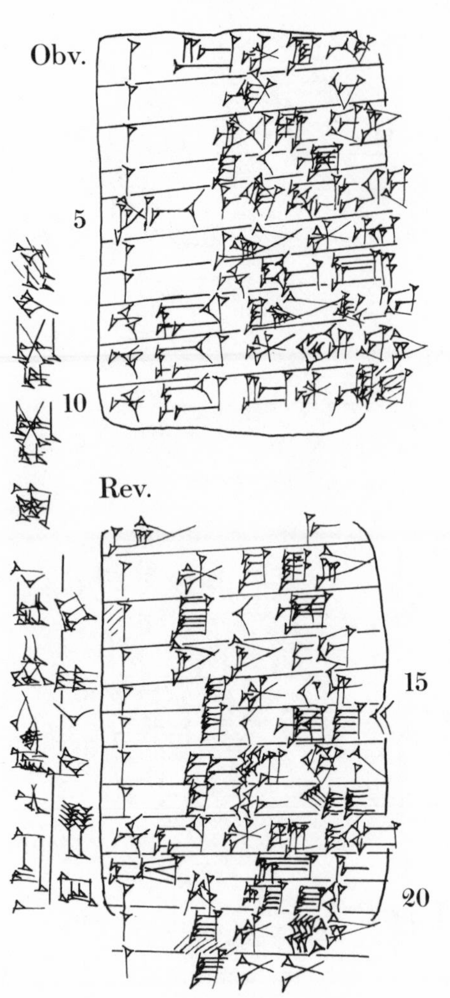

287

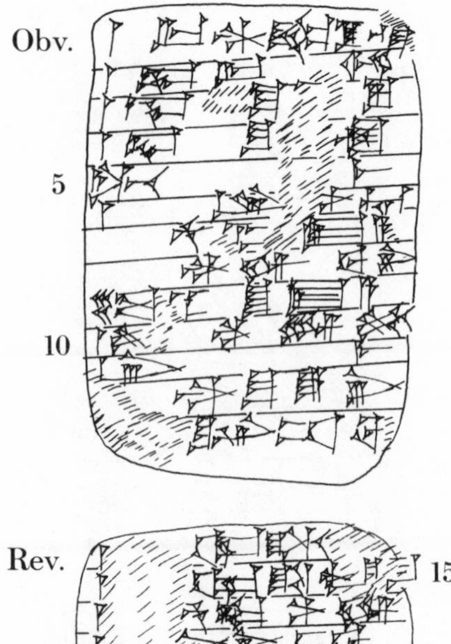

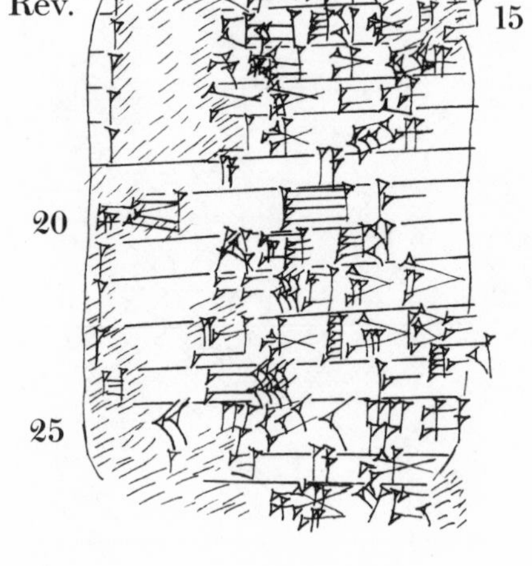

288

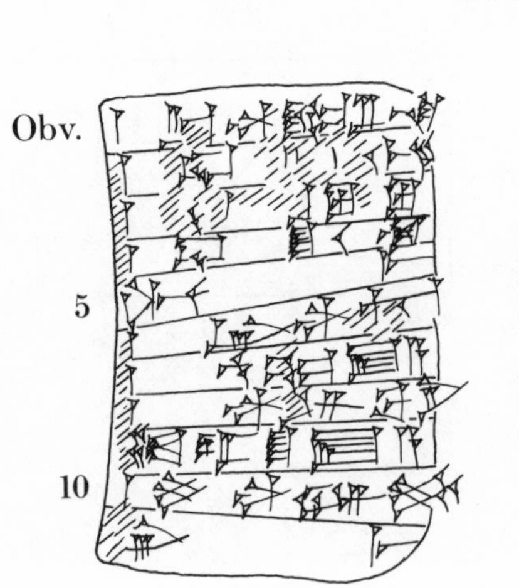

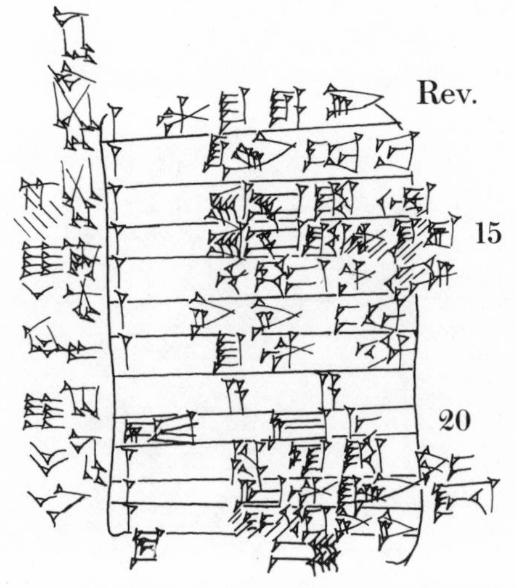

289

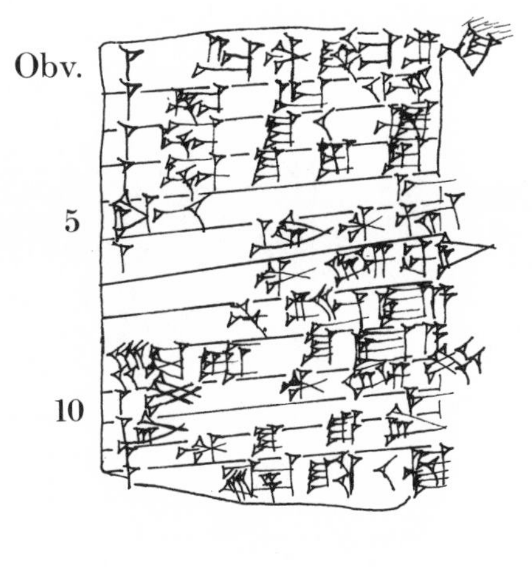

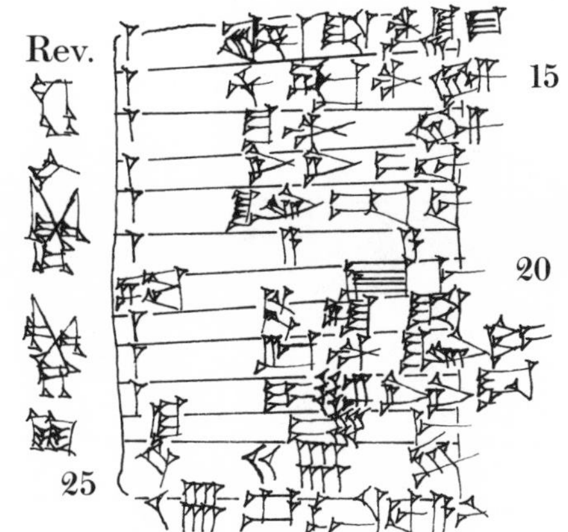

290

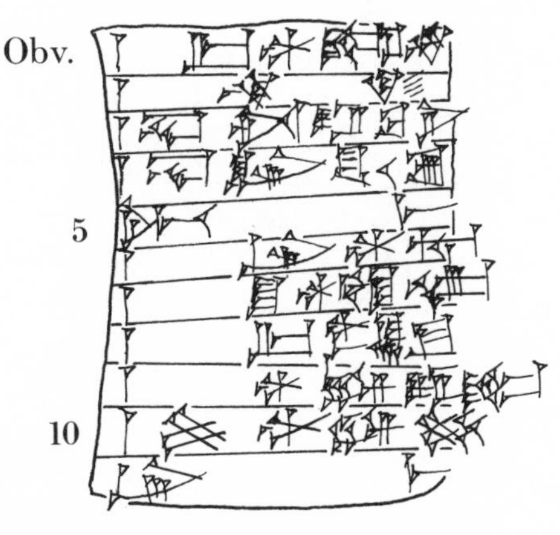

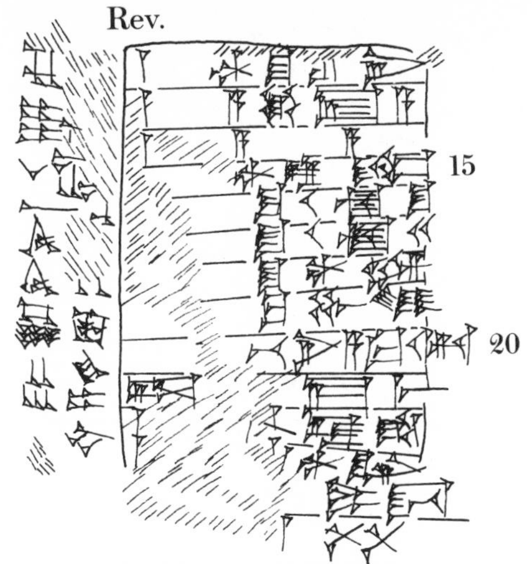

291

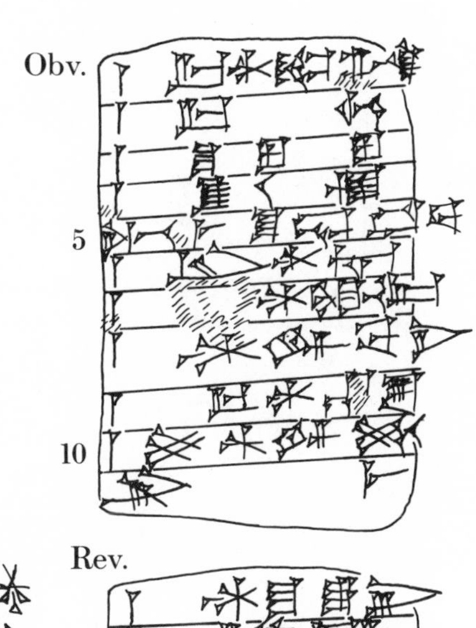

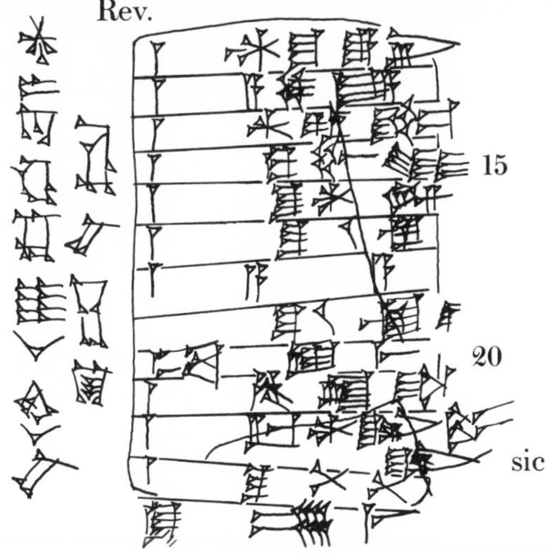

PLATE LXVIII

292

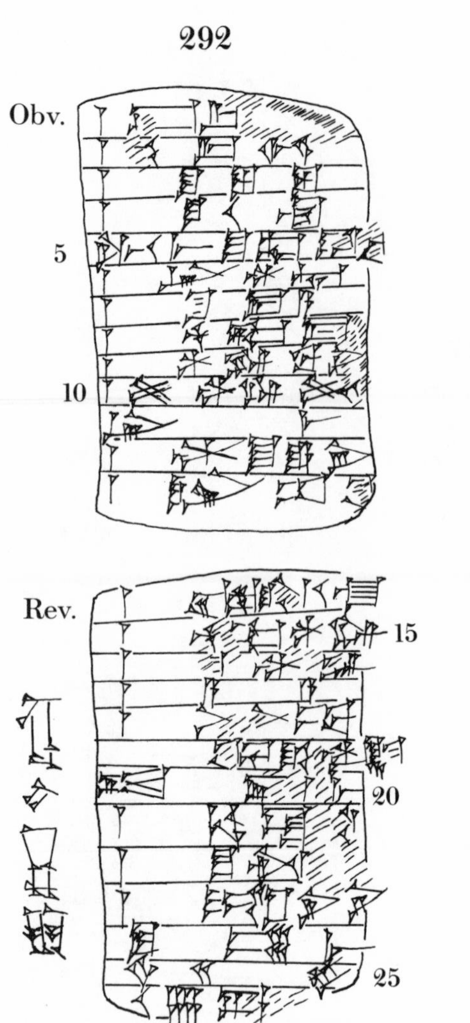

293

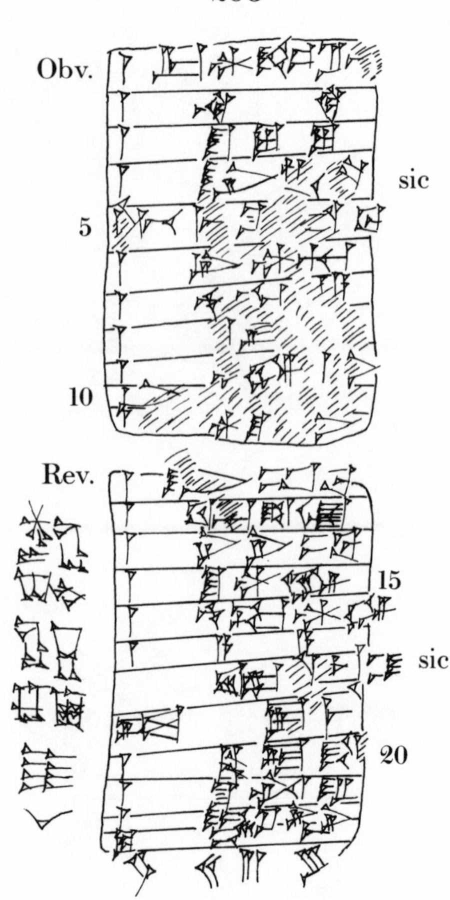

294

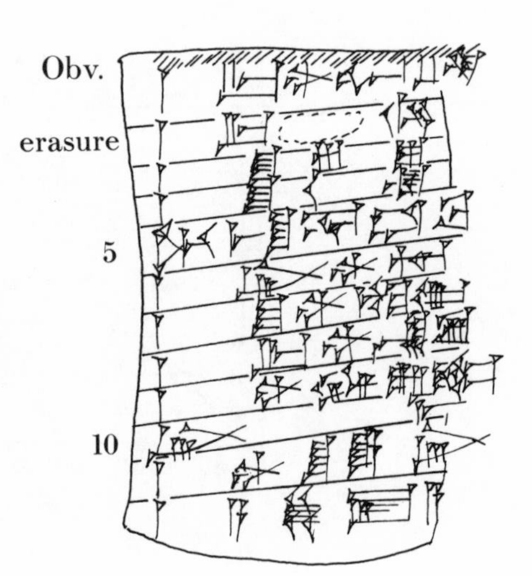

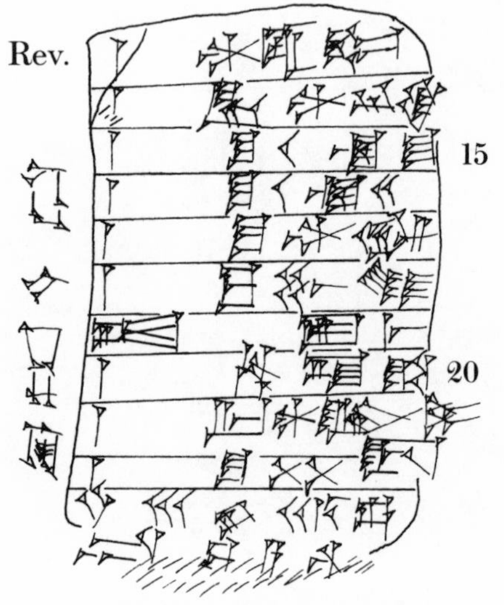

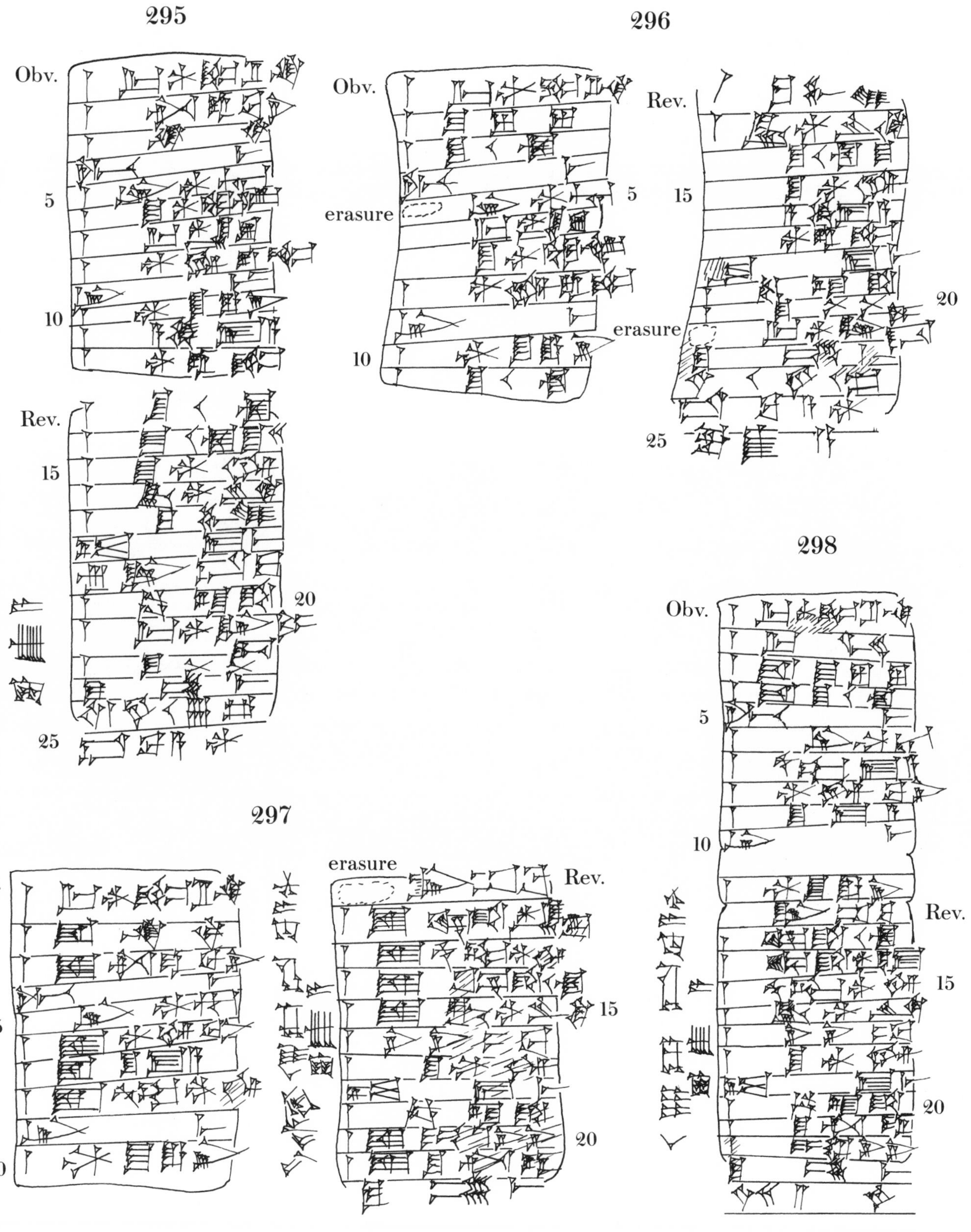
295
Obv.
Rev.
296
Obv.
erasure
Rev.
erasure
297
Rev.
erasure
298
Obv.
Rev.

299

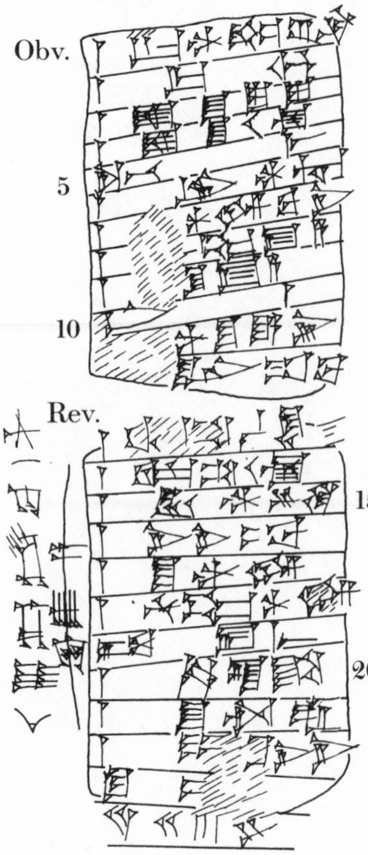

Obv.

Rev.

300

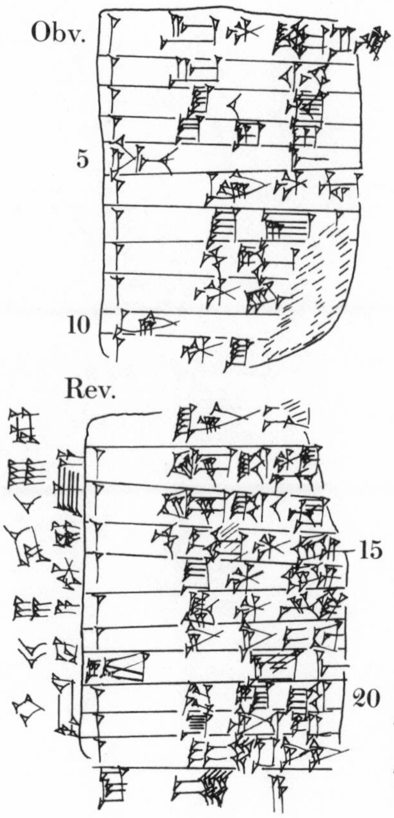

Obv.

Rev.

301

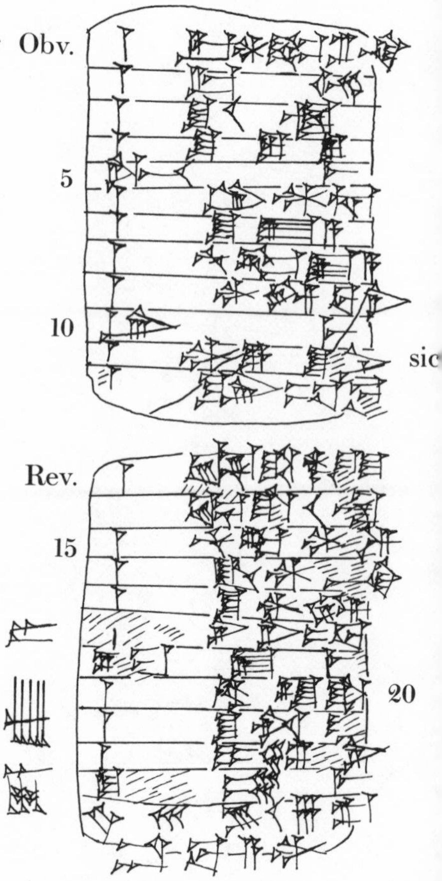

Obv.

sic

Rev.

302

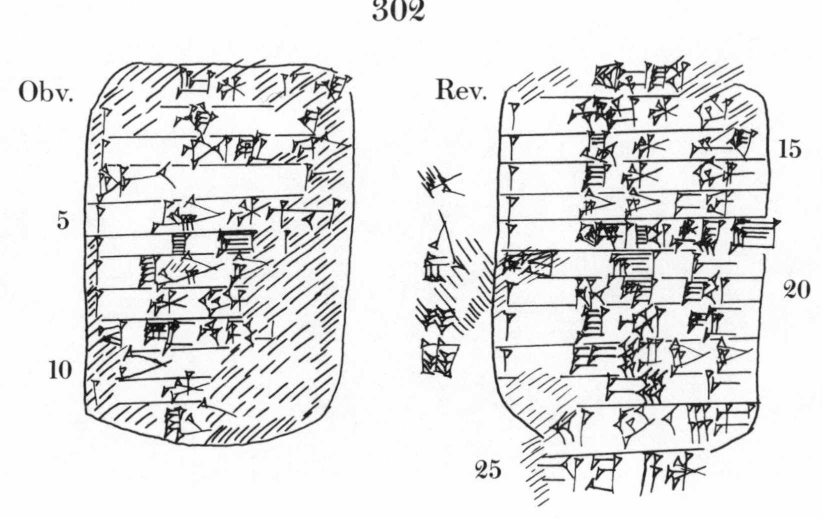

303

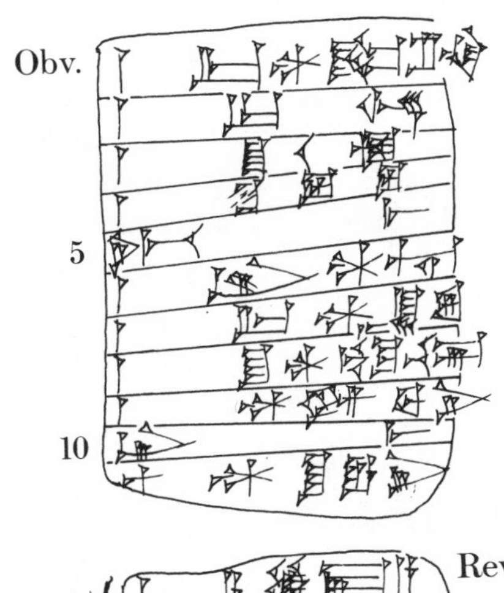

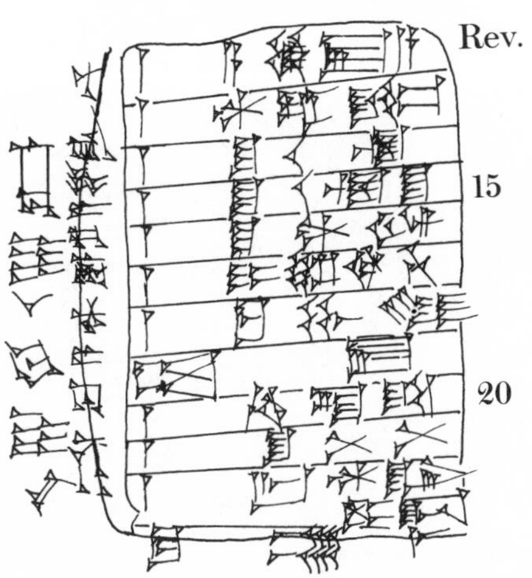

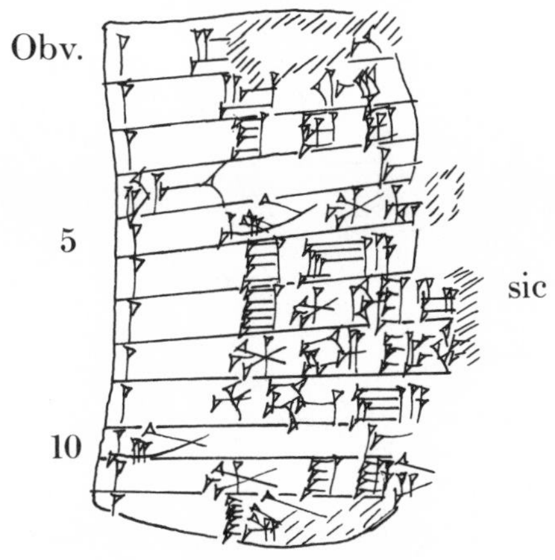

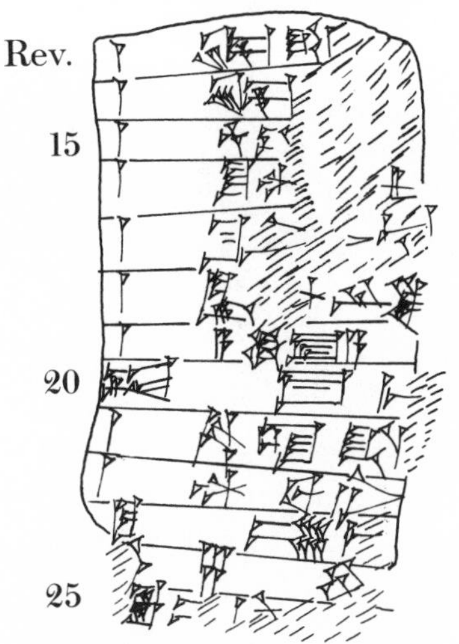

305

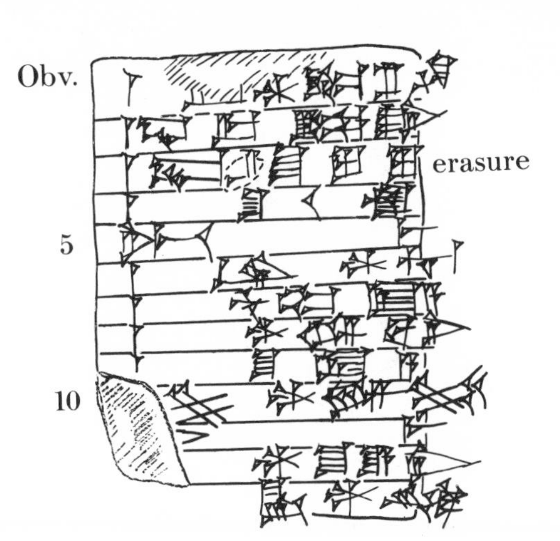

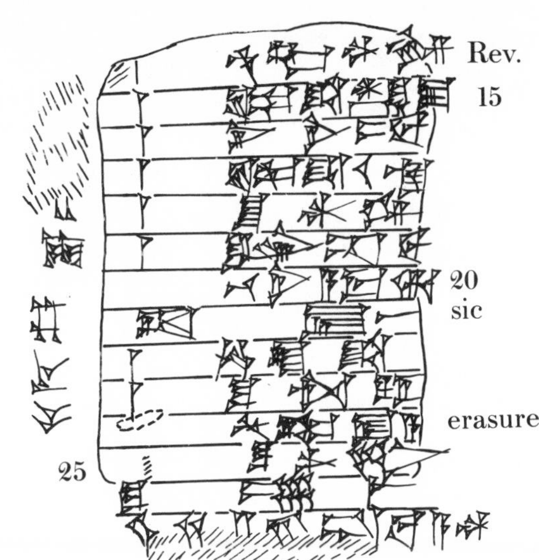

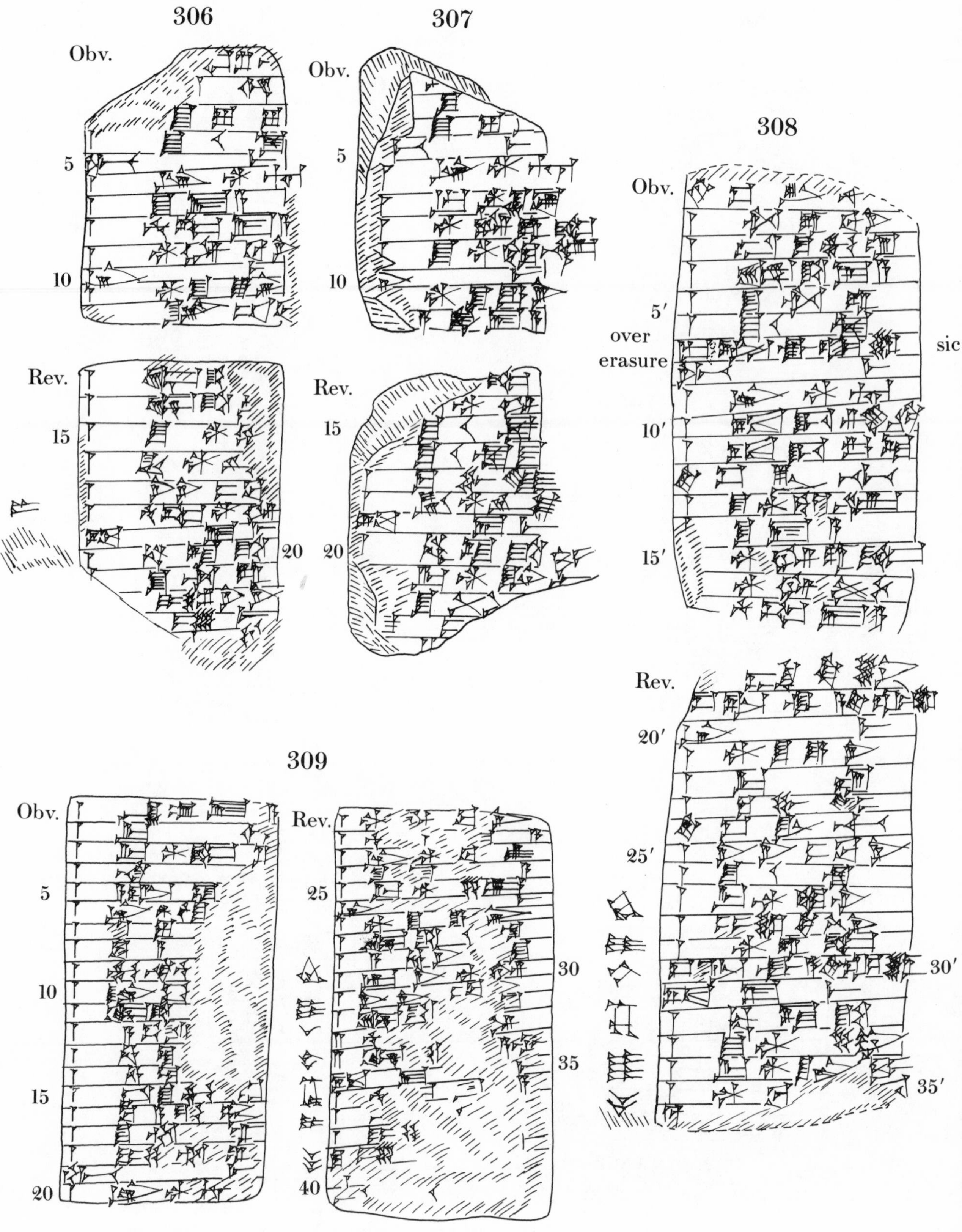
306
307
308
309
Obv.
Rev.
over erasure
sic

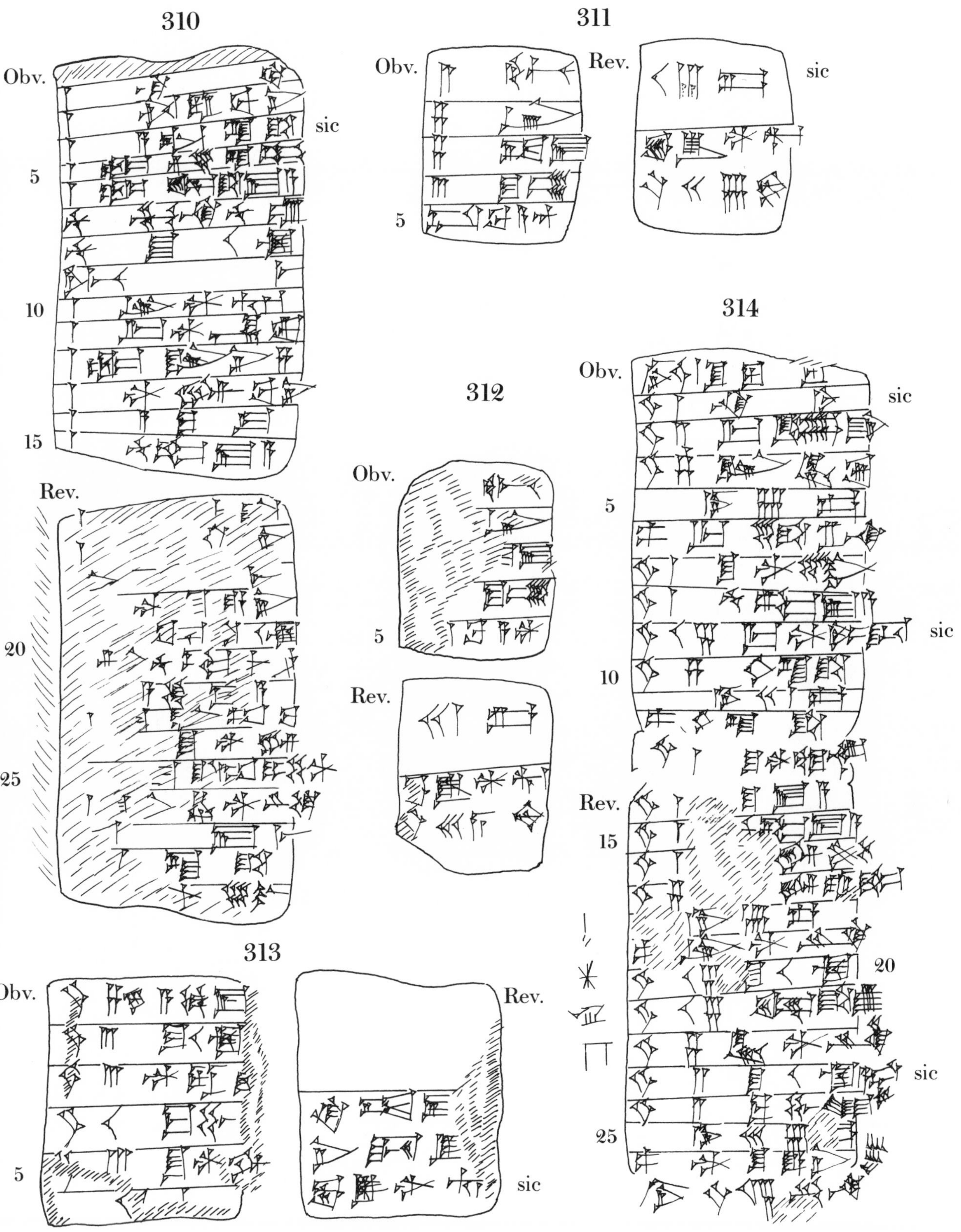
310
Obv.
sic
Rev.
311
Obv.
Rev.
sic
312
Obv.
Rev.
313
Obv.
Rev.
sic
314
Obv.
sic
sic
Rev.
sic

PLATE LXXIV

seal a

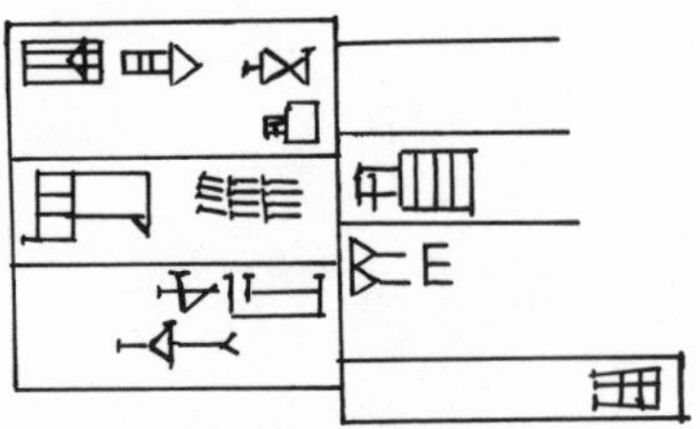

seal b

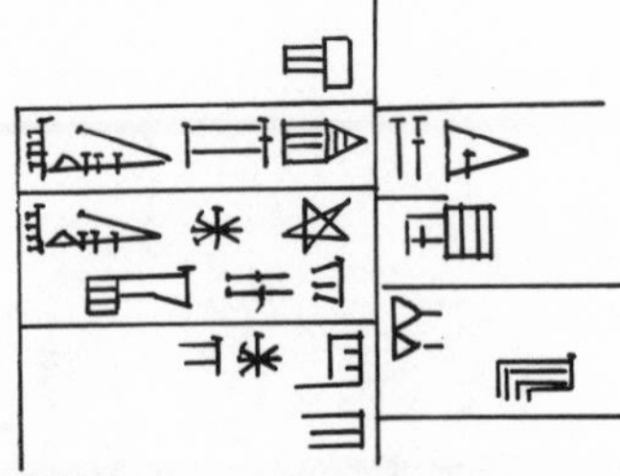

seal c

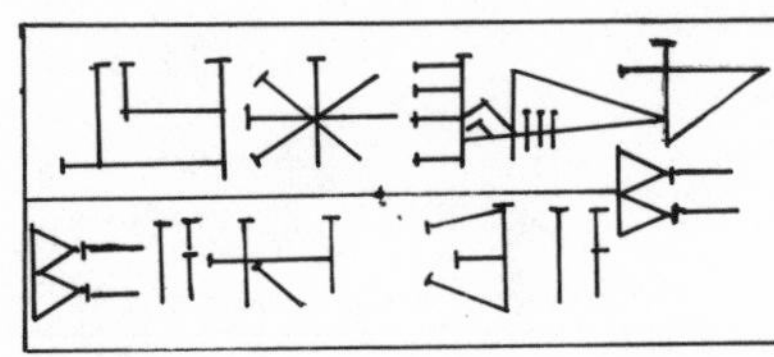

seal d

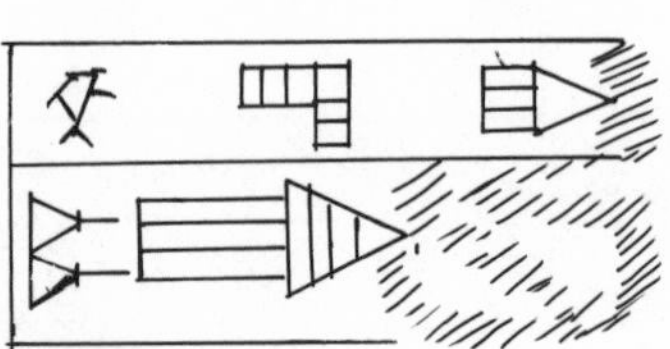

seal e

seal f

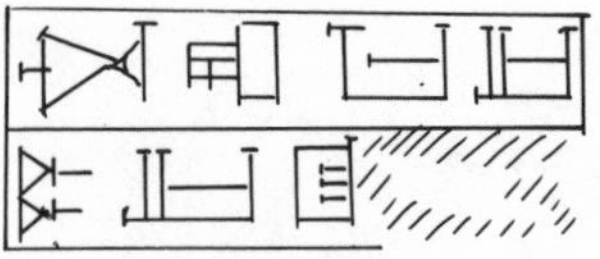

seal g

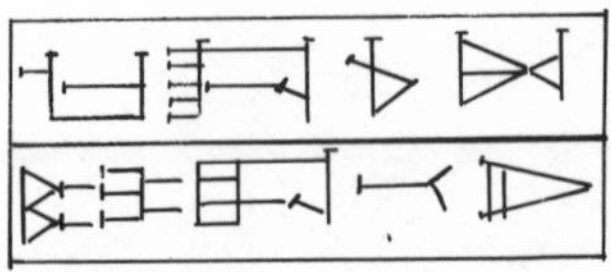

seal h

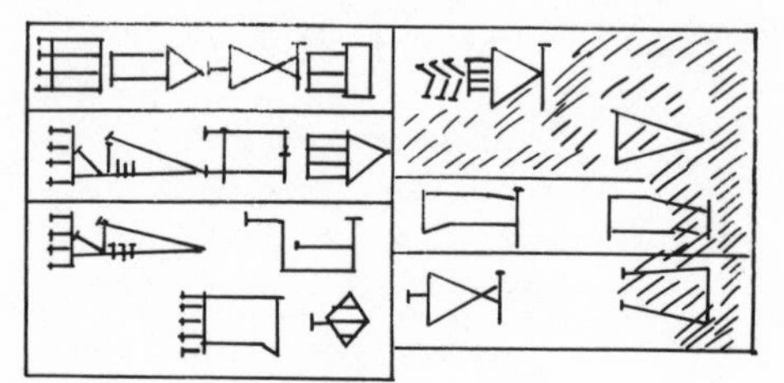

seal i

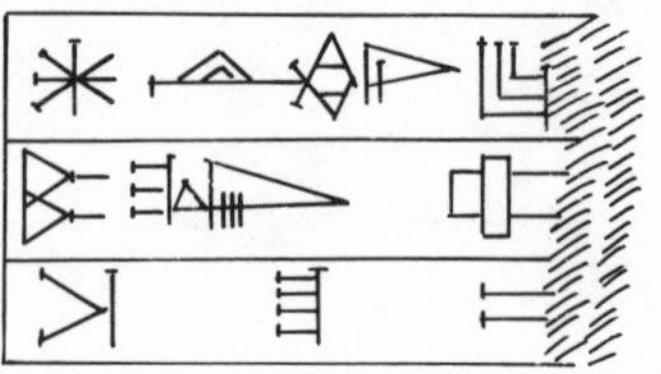

seal j

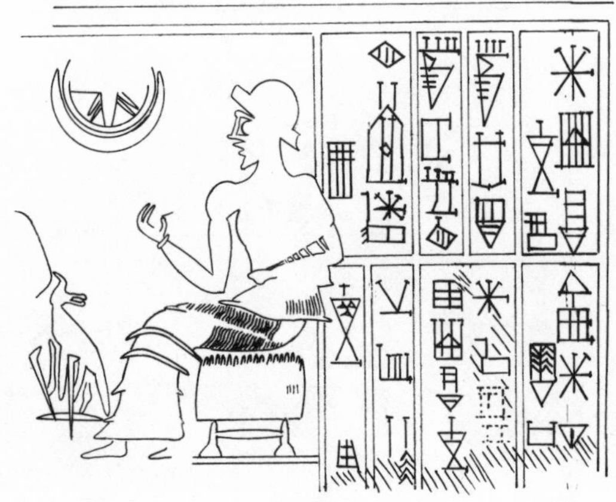

seal B

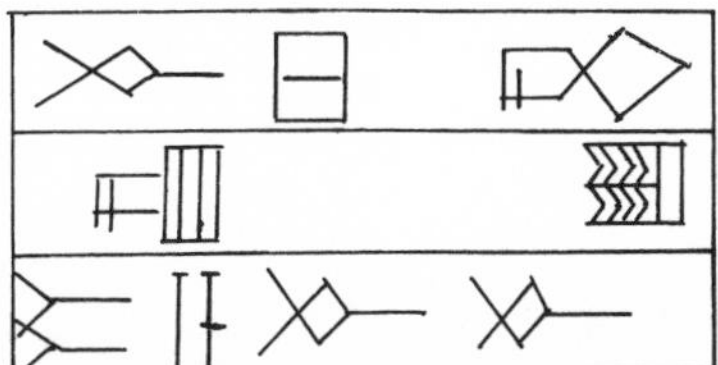

seal B or M

seal M

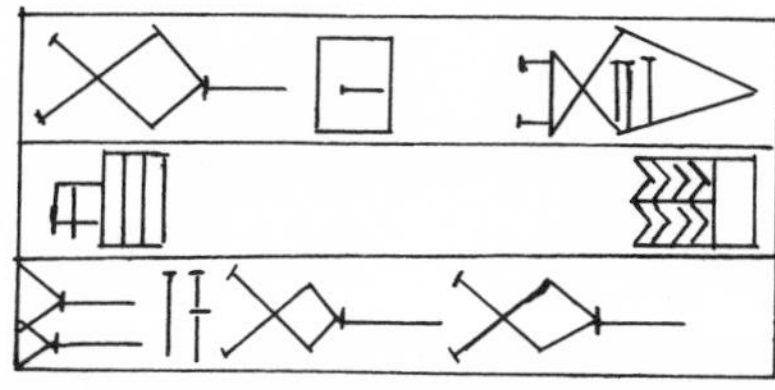

seal O

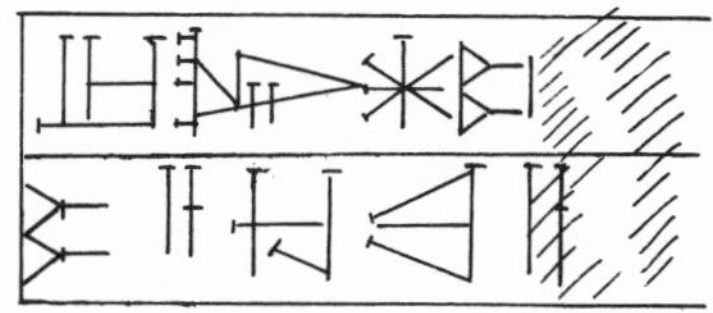

seal T

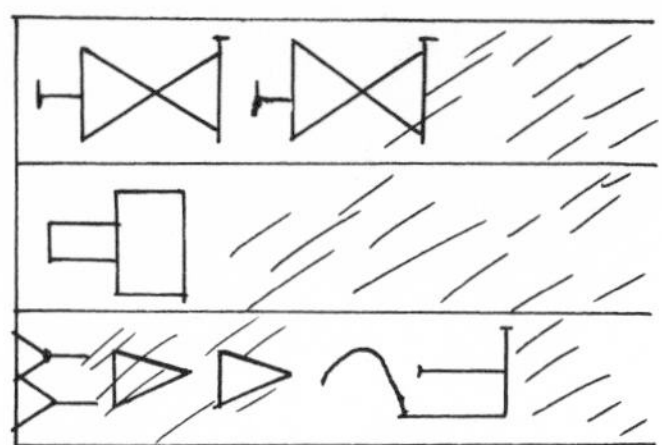